TRANSFORMATIVE STRATEGIES

Transformative Strategies is based around the idea that strategic thinking is critical for organizational success in today's environment. The financial crisis, continuing economic uncertainty, digitalization, environmental issues, and social issues involved in globalization present strategic problems for enterprises. Unlike other textbooks that take a standard solutions-based approach, *Transformative Strategies* provides readers with a way to develop strategies that fit their own complex situations and shows how models may be applied in different ways to different problems.

Each of the four key elements affecting the business environment (globalization, disruption, collaboration, and responsibility) are addressed as a set of tensions in eight areas: global competition, business model innovation, digital strategizing, business eco-systems, corporate social responsibility, top management teams, and trans-cultural leadership in a globalized world. This tension-based pedagogy enables readers to shift from dichotomized thinking (such as exploring or exploiting) to transformative thinking (such as exploring and exploiting; exploring through exploiting) and readers are challenged to solve real problems that companies face, encouraging them to acknowledge the broader context in which organizations operate and to analyze the problem from multiple perspectives. Each chapter is structured to aid engagement and discussion, including a discussion of the tension tied to the chapter's topic, learning objectives, theoretical frameworks, real-life case studies, exercises, and reflective questions.

A highly practical book that encourages readers to develop solutions that fit their own complex problems, it will be particularly suitable for those studying strategic management as part of an MBA, MA or MSc in Management, as well as those in executive education. It will also appeal to all those interested in learning how to lead and transform organizations towards impact, purpose and relevance. Online resources include discussions of the case studies, supplementary problems for class discussion, and an instructors' manual outlining the pedagogical approach.

Brian Tjemkes is an associate professor of Strategy and Organization at the Vrije Universiteit, Amsterdam, where he is head of the Strategy section and director of the International Business Administration program. Brian's research and education interests center on strategic alliances, business ecosystems, and corporate transformation.

Oli Mihalache is an associate professor of International Business at the Vrije Universiteit, Amsterdam, where he coordinates the International Business Master program. Oli's research aims to understand how organizations can innovate and transform themselves in today's increasingly digital and global environment.

TRANSFORMATIVE STRATEGIES

Strategic Thinking in the Age of Globalization, Disruption, Collaboration and Responsibility

Edited by Brian Tjemkes and Oli Mihalache

Routledge
Taylor & Francis Group
LONDON AND NEW YORK

First published 2021
by Routledge
2 Park Square, Milton Park, Abingdon, Oxon OX14 4RN

and by Routledge
52 Vanderbilt Avenue, New York, NY 10017

Routledge is an imprint of the Taylor & Francis Group, an informa business

British Library Cataloguing-in-Publication Data
A catalogue record for this book is available from the British Library

Library of Congress Cataloging-in-Publication Data
Names: Tjemkes, Brian, 1973- editor. | Mihalache, Oli, editor.
Title: Transformative strategies : strategic thinking in the age of globalization, disruption, collaboration and responsibility / edited by Brian Tjemkes and Oli Mihalache.
Description: 1 Edition. | New York : Routledge, 2021. | Includes bibliographical references and index.
Identifiers: LCCN 2020048180 (print) | LCCN 2020048181 (ebook)
Subjects: LCSH: Organizational change. | Strategic planning. | Competition. | Business enterprises-Technological innovations. | Social responsibility of business.
Classification: LCC HD58.8 .T6983 2021 (print) | LCC HD58.8 (ebook) | DDC 658.4/012-dc23
LC record available at https://lccn.loc.gov/2020048180
LC ebook record available at https://lccn.loc.gov/2020048181

ISBN: 978-0-367-22310-6 (hbk)
ISBN: 978-0-367-22311-3 (pbk)
ISBN: 978-0-429-27438-1 (ebk)

Typeset in Interstate
by KnowledgeWorks Global Ltd.

Access the Support Material: www.routledge.com/9780367223113

CONTENTS

FIGURES

TABLES

BOXES

CONTRIBUTORS

Brian Tjemkes holds a PhD from Radboud University, Nijmegen, and is currently employed as an associate professor of Strategy and Organization at the Vrije Universiteit, Amsterdam. He is head of the strategy section and director of the International Business Administration program. His research interests center on strategic alliances, business ecosystems, and corporate transformation. His work has been disseminated through various academic and professional conferences and publications in, among others, *Journal of Management Studies*, *Management Decision*, *Journal of International Management*, and *Journal of Cross-Cultural Psychology*. He is the co-author of the book *Strategic Alliance Management* (2nd edition). He devoted to sharing his insights with practice through executive education, workshops, presentations, and professional publications.

Christopher Wickert is an associate professor of Ethics and Sustainability in the Department of Management and Organization at the Vrije Universiteit, Amsterdam. His research examines corporate social responsibility (CSR) and corporate sustainability as well as the broader relationship between business and society by drawing on various strands of organization and management theory. Christopher obtained his PhD in Management from the University of Lausanne in Switzerland in 2013. During his doctoral studies, he has also conducted research and taught at the University of Zurich, the University of St. Gallen and at the IESE Business School in Barcelona. Prior to becoming a researcher, he worked as a consultant with the United Nations Global Compact Office in New York. He holds an MSc degree in business administration from WHU Otto Beisheim School of Management in Vallendar, Germany.

Enno Masurel is a professor in Sustainable Entrepreneurship at the Vrije Universiteit, Amsterdam. His educational background is in business economics; in the last decade he has moved more into the direction of business administration and entrepreneurship. He is the director-founder of the Center for Entrepreneurship at the Vrije Universiteit, Amsterdam (CfE@VU) and contributes towards bridging the gap between the academic world and the private sector by revealing the mutual benefits and helping to build long-term relationships between the two. He supervises PhDs from all over the world and trains university lecturers in Tanzania, Kenya, Ethiopia, and Zambia. Alongside his academic roles, he is the advisor/coach of entrepreneurs and SMEs, advisor to international publishers in the field of entrepreneurship, and speaker for various audiences.

Fons Trompenaars studied Economics at the Vrije Universiteit, Amsterdam, and later earned a PhD from Wharton School, University of Pennsylvania, with a dissertation on the differences in the conceptions of organizational structure in various cultures. He has spent over 25 years helping Fortune 500 leaders and professionals to manage and solve their business and cultural dilemmas to increase global effectiveness and performance, particularly in the areas of globalization, mergers and acquisition, HR, and leadership development. He is the author of the book *Riding the Waves of Culture: Understanding Cultural Diversity in Business*, which sold over 200,000 copies and was translated into 16 languages. He was also ranked in the bi-annual Thinkers50 ranking as one of the most influential management thinkers alive in 2011, 2013 and 2015, and shortlisted as making substantial strides in the contribution to the understanding of globalization and the new frontiers established by the emerging markets in 2011. He was inducted into the Thinkers50 Hall of Fame in November 2017.

Jingshu Du is associate professor of innovation and strategy at Lèonard de Vinci Pùle Universitaire Research Center, Paris, and "Qilu" youth scholar (with invited appointment) at the Business School of Shandong University, China. She was assistant professor of strategic management and innovation at the Vrije Universiteit Amsterdam, senior associate at Vlerick business school, KULeuven, and FWO research scholar at University of California, Berkeley. Jingshu's research focuses on open and collaborative innovation, strategic management, and is conducted in close collaboration with leading European firms in the manufacturing and pharmaceutical industry. Her research output has appeared on leading international academic journals, such as *Industrial Marketing Management* (single-author), *Research Policy, Journal of Product Innovation Management*, and *R&D Management*. She has received several awards, among which, the prestigious "National outstanding student" 1st in province (2006, Beijing); "Best doctoral dissertation" of the 25th international society for professional innovation management (2014, Dublin); Top 1% "highly-cited paper" on Web of Science (2017-); "Best paper" notification of the Strategy division at the 80th Academy of Management (2020, Vancouver).

Martijn van der Kamp is a scholarly teaching fellow at the Monash Business School, where he teaches Leadership in the MBA program, heads the MBA integrated team program, and engages in executive education. He holds degrees from the Rotterdam School of Management (BA), the Erasmus University Rotterdam (MBA), and the University of Melbourne (PhD). Driven by the firm belief that only through collaboration can we face our biggest challenges, Martijn aims to educate, inspire and equip those who are tackling these challenges through the topics of teamwork, strategy, and leadership. As a researcher, teacher, and consultant, he has worked with teams in business, government, and elsewhere on the design and implementation of teamwork and partnership strategies. In his research, he links strategy, organizational design, and organizational behavior, with a focus on teamwork in strategic alliances. His current studies mainly focus on how diversity and team composition affect team effectiveness and outcomes, especially in networks of teams across organizations.

Oli Mihalache is an associate professor of International Business at the Vrije Universiteit, Amsterdam. He obtained a bachelor's degree in Commerce and Finance from University of Toronto (2006), and MPhil and PhD degrees in Strategic Management from Erasmus University Rotterdam (2009 and 2012). His research focuses on trying to understand how companies can transform themselves. To this end, his research considers particularly the role of the international context and top management team processes. His research is published in top academic outlets such as *Decision Sciences*, *Journal of Management Studies*, *Organization Studies*, *Strategic Entrepreneurship Journal*, and *Strategic Management Journal*. Oli acted as an associate editor for the *European Management Review* journal and was a guest editor for *Organization Studies*, *Long Range Planning*, and *Management and Organization Review*.

Saeed Khanagha is Associate Professor of Strategy at the department of Management and Organization of Vrije Universiteit, Amsterdam. He obtained his PhD in 2015 at the Erasmus University Rotterdam. His research is broadly focused on understanding the factors that determine the success of an organization in the adoption of emerging digital technologies at the individual, team, organization, and ecosystem levels, using a variety of qualitative and quantitative data methods, including single-case studies, multiple-cases studies, surveys, and experimental designs. His ongoing research mostly explores the different dimensions of strategizing for digital technologies, particularly in regard to digital platforms and ecosystems. His research has been published in outlets such as *Strategic Management Journal*, *Journal of Management Studies*, *Long Range Planning*, and *R&D Management*. He currently serves as organizer and guest editor of a *Long Range Planning* special issue entitled Strategizing in a digital era.

PREFACE

This is not a book about strategic management theory. It is not about assumptions, core tenets, concepts, and normative managerial recommendations. Instead, this book is about real-life business challenges and how to deal with them. Business leaders operate in environments that are changing quickly, drastically, and in ways that are difficult to predict. They are confronted with pressures to globalize their business and collaborate with others to build and sustain a competitive advantage, while dealing with disruptive forces and sustainability challenges.

Future-proof organizations that are healthy, resilient, and socially impactful need business leaders who stand out from the crowd. Not leaders who are equipped with linear thinking solely in pursuit of corporate interests, but change-makers, purpose-driven pioneers who are equipped with the tools to engage in transformative strategizing and who can formulate and implement transformative strategies. Such leaders need to:

- Understand that the best way to predict the future is to create it
- Understand that seemingly contradictory pressures can be reconciled through creativity and imagination
- Embrace diversity and inclusivity, rather than sustaining the old institutionalized practices
- Be able to recognize and shift between perspectives
- Become part of the solution, rather than part of the problem
- Develop meaningful solutions and implement them in a responsible manner
- Recognize the need for and have the ability to engage in transformative strategizing.

Such business leaders embrace the variety of views, opinions, and interests held by majority and minority stakeholders. They broaden their horizons, enlarge their repertoire of skills, reflect continuously upon their own actions, and have a profound ability to engage in constructive dialogues. These leaders will inspire and lead their people, teams, and organizations to success in a rapidly changing world. It is our hope that this book will inspire (future) business leaders.

The book does not provide a comprehensive overview of strategic management practices, but rather details on a (arbitrary) selection of contemporary themes relevant to business leaders. Admittedly, other themes could have been included, and any mistakes are our responsibility. Nonetheless, the book provides insights into how business leaders can cope with contemporary strategic challenges and offers insights into how they can adopt transformative strategizing. This practice is applicable well beyond the scope of the book and is one we are working on every day.

Enjoy reading.

Brian Tjemkes & Oli Mihalache

1 Strategizing the unknown and transformative strategizing

Strategizing the unknown

Traditional (linear) strategic thinking and execution has become ineffective. Companies must move away from repetitive-function hierarchies with rules, enforcement and silo-thinking. Instead, companies need to formulate and effectuate transformative strategies that allow them the flexibility to deal with unexpected and unpredictable changes in their environments. This requires strategists to rethink, reconsider, and redevelop their organizational practices of formulating strategies as well as the content of their strategies. In today's competitive environment, success lies in organizations' ability to develop and execute strategies, allowing companies to navigate the unknown.

We are living in a world characterized by high levels of volatility, uncertainty, complexity, and ambiguity (VUCA, see Box 1.1). That is, organizations operate in environments that are, for a number of reasons, changing quickly, drastically, and in ways that are difficult to predict. Although the term VUCA is not new - Bennis and Nanus (1985) coined it over three decades ago - VUCA levels have now reached unprecedented heights. As a consequence, decision-makers are continuously confronted with emerging, unexpected, and high-impact challenges that require new decision-making approaches (consistent with our view that strategizing represents a company-wide endeavor, we purposively use the term 'decision-makers' and not 'strategist' or 'leaders'). In today's world, four overarching developments are reshaping the business environment and continuously changing the rules of the game: globalization, disruption, collaboration, and social responsibility.

Globalization. Decision-makers are confronted with the diffusion of products, technology, information, and jobs across countries and cultures (Tallman, Luo & Buckley 2018). In economic terms, globalization describes an interdependence between companies around the world, fostered through free trade. On one hand, globalization has created extant business opportunities through the cross-border flow of knowledge, resources, and labor. On the other hand, globalization also brings risks, as local and global contingencies (such as trade wars, (de)regulation, and crises) may jeopardize the viability of globally interconnected supply chains. To operate successfully in this global economy, decision-makers must embrace the unknown and formulate strategies while accounting for change.

Disruption. Decision-makers are challenged to disrupt or to respond to disruptors. Although there are multiple views on disruption, the term essentially describes a process

Box 1.1 A VUCA world

Coined by Warren Bennis and Burt Nanus, VUCA (volatility, uncertainty, complexity, ambiguity) is an acronym to describe the general condition of a business environment.

V - Volatility:	The nature and dynamics of change, and the nature and speed of change forces and change catalysts.
U - Uncertainty:	The lack of predictability, the prospects for surprise, and the sense of awareness and understanding of issues and events.
C - Complexity:	The multiplicity of forces, the confounding of issues, no cause-and-effect chain and confusion that surrounds organization.
A - Ambiguity:	The haziness of reality, the potential for misreads, and the mixed meanings of conditions; cause-and-effect confusion.

VUCA relates to how decision-makers view the circumstances under which they initiate change and cope with challenges. In general, the premises of VUCA tend to shape an organization's ability to: (1) anticipate challenges; (2) understand the repercussions of issues and actions; (3) appreciate the interdependence between drivers; (4) prepare for alternative futures; and (5) interpret and deal with relevant opportunities. VUCA is a way to enact preparedness, anticipation, evolution, and intervention.

Source: Bennis and Nanus (1985)

whereby new market entrants, often smaller firms with fewer resources, successfully challenge established incumbent businesses by taking advantage of new technologies (Christensen et al. 2018). Whereas incumbents focus on improving their products and services for their existing customers, entrants seek to gain a foothold by delivering more-suitable functionality, frequently at a lower price, to serve overlooked market segments. Decision-makers need to understand whether they are the disruptor or disruptee, and formulate strategies while accounting for emerging, yet unknown, competitive dynamics.

Collaboration. Decision-makers are challenged to pro-actively seek collaboration with a wide range of partners. Collaboration has become a cornerstone for the competitive strategy of many firms and (non-profit) organizations, enabling them to achieve objectives that would be difficult to realize individually. Although collaboration could result in financial gains, increased market share, and continued innovation, forging collaborative arrangements also comes with (financial and reputational) risks, adverse dependencies, and possible loss of core competences. Decision-makers must build and deploy collaborative competences and formulate strategies to reconcile cooperative and competitive forces that are inherently tied to collaboration.

Social Responsibility. Social responsibility entails that companies, in addition to maximizing shareholder value, must act in a manner that contributes to the welfare of society. Acting responsibly has become increasingly important to investors, employees, customers, and other stakeholders. Whereas some companies enact responsibility via 'green-washing' – a marketing practice to persuade customers that a company is environmentally friendly, even though investments suggest otherwise – other companies are intrinsically motivated to reconcile a corporate profit–logic with social responsibility practices. Decision-makers need to understand the dynamics (changes) that underpin stakeholders' interests, and formulate strategies to effectively navigate and accommodate corporate and societal interests.

Taken together, globalization, disruption, collaboration, and social responsibility increase the level of uncertainty and complexity that firms need to consider when developing and executing their strategies. The ***unknown*** is now the defining characteristic of the business environment. The particular meaning and relevance of unknown relates to how people view the conditions under which they make decisions, plan, manage risks, foster change, and solve problems. In short, in a world with 'knowns', strategic decision-making centers on planning, prediction, providing answers, and articulating and implementing strategies pushing 'blueprint' solutions. As the quotes at the beginning of this chapter illustrate, strategic decision-making in a world with 'unknowns' centers on preparation, anticipation, asking questions, and articulating and implementing strategies that embrace experimentation, transformation, and failure.

> Unlike in slow-changing and predictable environments, successfully competing in VUCA environments requires transformative strategizing that embraces complexity, rather than traditional strategizing that aims to reduce complexity.

Transformative strategizing

What are transformative strategies and transformative strategizing?

A business *strategy* refers to the long-term visions, objectives, and courses of action regarding how to compete in the marketplace and *strategizing* is the process of developing the business strategy. Strategizing requires consideration of the organizations' main areas of operation and the developments in its environment that stand to affect its functioning. Strategizing in environments that change slowly or in predictable ways is well understood by management thinkers and practitioners alike. Management ideas and practices over the last century allowed the maturation of understanding the best practices and the appropriateness of various strategies. What is immeasurably more challenging and less understood is how to develop strategies in VUCA environments, as many of the existing strategies developed for stability and predictability are likely to lead modern organizations to obsolescence. In a VUCA environment, traditional strategies can be ineffective, as quick environmental changes can make existing business models obsolete.

Put simply, even if an organization is best-in-class at doing something, it is in danger of becoming obsolete overnight as new technologies, markets, and (de)regulations make alternative business models more competitive. Consequently, even best-in-class organizations need to continuously explore, experiment, and develop new resources that make their own best-in-class capabilities antiquated. While organizations that focus exclusively on exploiting current capabilities face the risk of being left behind by market changes, organizations that focus exclusively on developing new capabilities face the risk of not fully benefiting from their investments (O'Reilly and Tushman 2004). Thus, for long-term survival it is essential that organizations employ strategies that incorporate the tension between the present and future.

'Transformative Strategizing' comprises reflexive actions and initiatives that embrace strategic and organizational contradictions to allow organizations to compete in environments characterized by drastic, rapid, and unpredictable change.

Transformative strategizing requires a focus on duality and reflexive action to successfully navigate dynamic, disruptive, and unpredictable environments. This stands in contrast with traditional thinking, which aims to reduce complexity by offering clear strategic directions and implications. Transformative strategizing aims to incorporate strategic contradictions that direct organizations to focus both on exploiting current capabilities and on developing new, potentially incompatible, ones. The goal is to build organizations that are ready to not only benefit in the present, but also to be prepared for an unexpected future or, more ambitiously, to create the very future that makes current capabilities obsolete. In periods of rapidly advancing technologies, business models, and global competition, organizations require transformative ways of strategizing and strategy implementation (Volberda et al. 2018). To be able to engage in transformative strategizing, organizations need to encourage their members to identify, discuss, and embrace tensions. As Lewis, Andriopoulos, and Smith (2014: 58) put it, 'strategic agility is inherently contradictory'. Because organizations and individuals prefer to engage in the activities they are best at doing (Levinthal and March 1993; March 1991), transformative strategizing pushes organizations and their employees outside of their comfort zone to combine what they are good at doing with enacting new and often uncomfortable behaviors.

Consequently, formulating and implementing a transformative strategy - the set of actionable reconciliatory solutions - must account for (alleged) contradictions at various organizational levels. At the top management team level, organizations need to implement processes that encourage voicing dissenting opinions and discussing all facets of issues facing the organization (Mihalache et al. 2014). At the team level, multi-functional teams, such as new product development teams, need to engage in initiatives aimed both at improving the current product offering and coming up with ideas to develop new products and services (Jansen et al. 2016). Further, even individuals need to internalize and solve tensions as they engage in efforts to further existing organizational activities and come up with ideas for new business directions (Gibson and Birkinshaw 2004). Thus, since tensions are present at different organizational levels, transformative strategizing entails an inclusive and comprehensive process that incorporates perspectives from multiple hierarchical levels and business areas. Transformative strategies refer to the outcome of this process.

Importantly, transformative strategies are unique to each organization as opposed to traditional, off-the-shelf solutions. The common denominator of transformative strategies is that they are built on the principles of incorporating and reconciling tensions. Since organizations differ in their resources and capabilities, in their perceptions of the environment, and in their goals, the outcome of the strategizing process needs to result in unique approaches to deal with the complexities each organization faces. Consequently, in this book, we focus on developing the principles underlying the strategizing process rather than providing prescriptive strategies. By shifting the perspective to the process rather than the content of strategies, we hope that decision-makers can develop strategies that are uniquely attuned to their own situation.

'Transformative Strategies', as the manifestation of transformative strategizing, incorporate and reconcile tensions across organizational challenges. Transformative strategies are unique to each organization rather than off-the-shelf solutions.

What is different about transformative strategizing and strategies?

Transformative and traditional strategizing draw on a different set of principles (see Figure 1.1). Whereas traditional strategizing values stability, consistency, linearity, and simplicity, transformative strategizing draws on principles such as continuous change, inconsistency, nonlinearity, and complexity. These principles are not categorical, but should rather be seen on a continuum. The underlying principles are important because they affect the key elements of strategizing: view on change, strategic thinking, decision-making rationale, managerial bias, strategic leadership and organization, and coping with tensions (see Table 1.1). Existing theories about strategy-making and competition are located at various places on this continuum, with some elements distinct and others overlapping with our notion of transformative strategizing. For instance, theories such as Transaction Cost Economics (Williamson 1975; Williamson 1981), Industrial Organization (Porter 1980), and the Resource-Based View (Barney 1991; Rumelt 1984; Wernerfelt 1984) tend to be developed more on traditional principles, while theories such as Strategic Agility (Weber and Tarba 2014) and Strategic Renewal (Schmitt, Raisch, and Volberda 2018) tend to draw to a higher degree on principles we associate with transformative strategizing (see the Appendix for a concise overview of the main theories). Next, we explain how the different underlying principles affect elements of traditional and transformative strategizing.

Figure 1.1 Strategizing continuum

Table 1.1 A polarized comparison of traditional and transformative thinking

Traditional strategizing	⇔	*Transformative strategizing*
Deterministic Decision-makers are constrained by pre-set change plans	**View on change**	**Voluntaristic** Decision-makers have choice in how to strategize change
Linear Strategizing - formulation and execution - entails a formal and controlled process	**Strategic thinking**	**Circular** Strategizing - formulation and execution - entails a non-linear, adaptive, and reflexive process
Economic rationality Decision-making based on logical considerations and complete information	**Decision-making rationale**	**Bounded rationality** Decision-making based on limited information-processing capacity and incomplete information
Manageable The impact of cognitive bias on strategic decision-making is mitigated	**Managerial bias**	**Unavoidable** Cognitive bias is inherently tied to strategic decision-making
Objectivist Leaders design and guide organizations to serve (financial) performance	**Leadership & Organizing**	**Subjectivist** Leaders create and enact organizations to serve a multitude of interests
Favoritism Tensions exist between opposing forces; strategic responses typically favor one force over the other	**Tensions**	**Reconciliation** Tensions exist between opposing forces; strategic responses typically reconcile opposing forces

View on change. Traditional strategizing tends to postulate that strategy and strategizing are embedded in an instrumental - deterministic - view. Strategic actions are seen as determined by and reacting to structural constraints (that is, market structure, organizational design), with limited possibility of choice; strategy is constrained by a pre-set solution set (Astley and Van de Ven 1983). For example, drawing on the structure-conduct-performance (SCP) model (Bain 1959), Porter's (1980) view on competition stipulates that performance heterogeneity between firms can be explained by a firm's ability to occupy a unique market position in an industry. However, the range of options and constraints facing a firm is defined by the attributes of the industry within which this firm operates. Strategic change approaches tend to be built on normative analytical frameworks to initiate intense, organization-wide programs that enhance performance and boost organizational health (Bladek et al. 2019). In contrast, our view of transformative strategizing builds on a voluntaristic perspective; decision-makers challenged to make decisions are autonomous, proactive, self-directing agents (Astley and Van de Ven 1983) who can construe and effectuate solutions. The conception of choice (versus determinism) is part of an ongoing debate in the strategic management field; see, for example, strategic choice (Child 1972), organizational adaptation (Barnett and Carroll 1995), and (neo-)contingency theory (Donaldson 2001). In our view, transformative strategizing advances this debate, as this practice recognizes that different leaders may interpret a more or less similar reality differently, but still arrive at decisions that steer them and their organizations toward success.

Strategic thinking. Enacting transformative strategies puts forward the idea that, in the current environment, reconsidering strategic thinking is critical to organizational success. Traditional principles inform a view of strategic thinking as a linear and stepwise approach (Steptoe-Warren, Howat, and Hume 2011). For example, decision-makers should: (1) adopt a holistic view on the internal and external factors; (2) create fit between resources and opportunities; (3) align internal actions with external rival moves; (4) reduce risk and develop alternative options; and (5) leverage and capitalize on strategic opportunities. However, unforeseen adversities, economic uncertainty, digitalization, environmental and social issues, and globalization dynamics force companies to face unique strategic problems that cannot be resolved by mechanistic approaches. Under these conditions, transformative strategizing is more likely to be effective. Transformative strategizing adheres to a process view on strategy, a process during which decision-makers enact continuous cycles of acting, reflecting, learning, and adaptation. Transformative strategizing does not render step-wise approaches obsolete, but it does suggest that traditional strategizing needs to be complemented with an ability to shift between perspectives, conduct experiments, learn from failure, and progress without complete certainty.

Decision-making rationale. Strategic management theories, including Transaction Costs Economics (Williamson 1981), Agency Theory (Jensen and Meckling 1976), and Game Theory (Von Neumann and Morgenstern 1944), assume (to varying degrees) economic rationality. The economic rationality principle stipulates that decision-makers behave in rational ways and consider alternatives and choices within logical structures of thought, as opposed to incorporating emotional, moral, or psychological elements. Transformative strategizing builds on the idea that decision-makers are subject to bounded rationality. When individuals make decisions, the boundaries of the decision problem, the cognitive limitations of the mind, and the time available to make the decision affect their choice (Simon 1955). Decision-makers, in this view, act as satisficers, seeking a satisfactory solution rather than an optimal one, as per economic rationality. A key implication for transformative strategizing is that the focus shifts from making sense of the 'knowns' (that is, providing answers) to embrace and understand the 'unknowns' (that is, asking questions) to guide strategizing.

Managerial bias. Cognitive biases affect decision-making with regard to formulating and executing strategies. Cognitive biases are mental shortcuts (known as heuristics) that enable decision-makers to engage in accurate and expedient strategizing, but also make them prone to errors. Prior experiences and expertise can cause 'errors' that limit decision-makers' ability to think divergently, causing them to jump to less-than-optimal outcomes (see Box 1.2). For example, a confirmation bias suggests that a decision-maker favors information that that confirms pre-existing beliefs or preconceptions. As such, solutions tend to corroborate existing beliefs that then challenge them, thus overlooking new opportunities. Strategizing that draws on traditional principles considers cognitive bias as manageable. Through techniques such as team-based decision-making, checklists, and external consultants, decision-makers attempt to minimize the risk of a cognitive bias. In contrast, transformative strategizing acknowledges that cognitive bias is unavoidable. Prior experiences and expertise simply cause 'errors' that limit decision-makers' abilities to think divergently, causing them to adopt less than optimal outcomes. To deal with these cognitive limitations of leaders, transformative thinking values experimentation and the decentralization of decision-making to those closest to the problem, or to communities of experts inside and outside the organization.

Box 1.2 Decision-making biases

Understanding, identifying, and resolving cognitive biases are critical tools in the decision-maker's tool box. Below is a concise overview of critical cognitive biases.

Confirmation bias:	Looking for solutions that confirm beliefs rather than challenge them; rejecting new possibilities.
Conformity bias:	Groupthink suppresses outside opinions, leading to self-censorship and loss of independent thought.
False causality bias:	Citing sequential events as evidence, i.e. the first caused the second; leads to tackling the wrong problems
Self-serving bias:	Favoring decisions that enhance self-esteem. Decisions are driven by personal agendas, not business interests.
Framing bias:	Being influenced by the way in which information is presented rather than the information itself.

Source: Pinder (2020)

This promotes, lateral, associative, and inclusive thinking to resolve challenges, rather than opting for quick fixes without reflexivity.

Strategic leadership. Transformative strategizing embraces the unknown and thus departs from prescriptive notions associated with theories such as strategic design (Chandler 1962) and industrial organization (Porter 1980) that draw on traditional principles. Within predictable and stable environments, strategizing entails a top-down activity exercised by leaders, often construed on the notion that firms have successfully aligned strategies and organizational designs with their environments. The task of decision-makers is to conduct comprehensive assessments of the internal and external environments, articulate the strategy, and develop long-term plans. Strategic analytical tools, like forecasting and scenario planning, are adequate techniques for unraveling future developments, and strategy execution is simply about carefully implementing plans. Although this approach does not become obsolete in a VUCA world, their application value becomes (very) limited. It is difficult to predict how the business environment will develop, let alone formulate future-proof strategies. Building on the principles of continuous change and complexity, transformative thinking views strategizing as a decentralized process involving divers, internal and external actors who are exposed to different stimuli and can contribute complementary insights. This does not mean that leaders do not play a role in strategizing, but rather that their role has shifted from creating the strategy to that of facilitating strategy-making and implementation. Such decentralization in strategizing associated with transformative thinking is necessary because various parts of the organization may be vulnerable to different forces and may see different opportunities in today's complex and volatile world.

Organizing. Whereas theories based on traditional principles tend to assume an objective view on organizations – organizations can be designed, human labor is a commodity, and (financial) performance (such as shareholder value) represents the ultimate objective - transformative strategizing adopts a subjectivist view of organizing and organizations. Organizations are subject to continuous change, humans attribute meaning to their work, and performance entails a wide-range of stakeholders' interests. Under a subjectivist assumption, strategizing is both a dynamic competence and a relational process (Lewis, Andriopoulos, and Smith 2014). Unlike a top-down-design view on organizing, transformative strategizing entails the ability to identify and leverage opportunities and threats, and to exploit internal and external capabilities. Leaders set a vision for their followers, foster commitment to strategy execution, and fuel imagination in the process of reconciling contradictory demands.

View on tensions. Differences in the consistency-inconsistency and simplicity-complexity principles give rise to different approaches to dealing with tensions between traditional and transformative strategizing. Whereas traditional approaches aim for simplicity and consistency, they also aim to reduce tensions between strategic alternatives and tend to commit organizational resources to a particular strategic alternative. In contrast, transformative strategizing adopts tensions rather than eliminating them. Framing strategic decisions as a tension holds promise for decision-makers, as resolving tensions will help decision-makers make sense of an apparently unexplainable and often seemingly irrational contemporary world (Smith et al. 2017). Confronted with scarce resources, a need to accelerate change, and mounting pressures in a VUCA world (Smith and Lewis 2011), approaching strategic decisions with a tension-lens enables decision-makers to shift between perspectives rather than remaining in their comfort zone. As such, transformative strategizing shares, for example, with a strategic agility approach (Lewis, Andriopoulos, and Smith 2014) that tensions and contradictions - such as stability-flexibility - guide decision-making. Competing demands pose challenges that require leadership practices with a focus on seeking creative, reconciliatory solutions that can enable fast-paced, adaptable decision-making. A transformative decision-maker builds and leverages an ability to identify opposing forces, reconcile contradictions, articulate creative solutions, and implement them responsibly and effectively.

Studying transformative strategizing

Traditional methods of learning strategic management - with a focus on specific topics such as industrial organization, the Resource-Based View of the firm, and analysis of the external environment - do not address how managers in real businesses work and, perhaps even more importantly, do not address the business needs in the current era of rapid and drastic change. Changing demands of future professionals and digitalization of learning tools require new ways of (strategic management) teaching that extend beyond traditional educational reading and formats. Readers look for learning experiences that mimic the strategic challenges they confront in their future professional careers. The challenges are often fuzzy, unclear, complex, and tend to involve multiple and opposing stakeholders' interests, all of which presents decision-makers with tensions that can only be resolved by strategizing the unknown. Thus, this book draws on: (1) a tension-based pedagogy; (2) contemporary strategic management topics to detail on tensions; and (3) provides real-life business illustrations.

Tension-based pedagogy

A key message of the book is that decision-makers need to enact transformative strategizing - by engaging in creative and tension-based thinking - to develop viable solutions to deal with strategic and organizational challenges. This means that decision-makers need to embrace tensions instead of the traditional 'piece of the puzzle' or 'either/or' thinking (Trompenaars and Hampden-Turner 2004). Within the academic and professional literature, however, there

Box 1.3 Tension studies in the management sciences

With foundations in philosophy and psychology that include the works of Aristotle, Confucius, Freud, Hegel, Jung, Kierkegaard, Lao Tsu and others, tensions - in the form of trade-off, dilemmas, and paradoxes - were, are, and will remain inherently part of organizations and organizing. Unsurprisingly, management research has embraced a tension perspective to understand the interplay between cooperation and competition, exploration and exploitation, stability and change, novelty and usefulness, learning and performance, etc. Below is an arbitrary overview of influential academic works.

In their compendium *Paradox and Transformation: Toward a Theory of Change in Organization and Management*, Quinn and Cameron (1988) suggested that to navigate the complexity and dynamics of organizations, the identification and reconciliation of paradoxical problems is pivotal to enact the smooth management of change. Their work offers several applications (such as just-in-time manufacturing), but also details on how transformational thinking can be embedded in education.

Van de Ven and Poole (1989) argued that theory-building strategies help researchers take advantage of theoretical tensions. Specifically, they developed four different modes of working with paradoxes: (1) accept the paradox and use it constructively; (2) clarify levels of analysis; (3) temporally separate the two levels; and (4) introduce new terms to resolve the paradox. These four modes of paradox resolution are illustrated by application to the action-structure paradox in organizational theory.

Smith and Lewis (2011) presented a dynamic equilibrium model of organizing that depicts how cyclical responses to paradoxical tensions enable sustainability - peak performance in the present that enables success in the future. The model provides the foundation of a theory of paradox. Smith (2014) put organizational leaders at the center of such a theory of paradox, viewing them as responsible for managing paradoxes by supporting a consistently inconsistent pattern of adopting tensions.

Based on a literature review encompassing 25 years of management science research, Schad and colleagues (2016) concluded that management research simplified the paradox phenomena. In response, they proposed an integrative perspective on paradox research and indicated that, to advance theorizing, a meta-theory of paradoxes in management science is required. Such a meta-theory would account for the nature of a paradox (that is, the type and relationships), the paradox approaches (that is, individual and collective), and the impact (that is, outcomes and dynamics).

exists some conceptual ambiguity with regard to the differences and similarities between tensions, dilemmas, trade-offs, and paradoxes (De Wit and Meyer 2004). Throughout this book, we purposively use the term *tension*, as our conceptualization of a tension-based pedagogy encompasses trade-offs, dilemmas and paradoxes (see Box 1.3).

A dilemma is a decision-making situation that has only two possible solutions, neither of which is logically the best (De Wit and Meyer 2004). Dilemmas confront decision-makers with difficult either/or choices, each with its own advantages and disadvantages, but neither is clearly superior to the other. In contrast, trade-offs and paradoxes depict decision-making situations in which there are multiple possible solutions. A trade-off refers to independent oppositions that can be solved with an either/or resolution. A decision-maker needs to allocate scarce resources to particular activities, knowing that a suboptimal resource allocation (as resources are invested elsewhere) may have adverse consequences. A paradox is a decision-making situation in which two seemingly contradictory, or even mutually exclusive, forces appear to be true at the same time (De Wit and Meyer 2004). A problem that is a paradox has no real solution. Rather, resolving a paradox requires decisions that aim to achieve one of many possible creative reconciliations of the two opposing forces, as there is no logical way to integrate the two opposites into an internally consistent understanding (Van de Ven and Poole 1989).

Our tension pedagogy acknowledges that the way in which a decision-maker frames a tension will determine whether his/her frame fits with a dilemma, trade-off, or paradox view. For example, in Chapter 9, Trompenaars elaborates on leadership 'dilemmas', though his view of a dilemma resembles how others may view a paradox. In any case, we proffer that framing strategic decisions as tensions will stimulate creative reconciliation and thinking out of the box, rather than simply seeking a balance between two opposing forces. A tension mindset is key to unlocking synergies (Miron-Spektor et al. 2017) and allows decision-makers to deal effectively with increased uncertainty, irrationality, and absurdity. In other words, our tension-based pedagogy enables readers to shift from dichotomized thinking (such as exploring *or* exploiting) to transformative thinking (such as exploring *and* exploiting; exploring through exploiting), which enables them to replace mono-theoretical explanations and solutions (for example, the Resource-based View *or* Industrial Organization) with multi-disciplinary ones, (for example, the Resource-based View *and* Industrial Organization). This will stimulate readers to formulate solutions that creatively reconcile opposing forces.

Theme-driven approach

Traditionally, strategic management literature draws on theoretical perspectives to provide answers to questions about explaining performance differential between firms. More recently, insights have been offered on strategy formulation, execution, and change (strategic agility, renewal, learning, etc.), but these advances also tend to be theoretically driven, and therefore have limited affinity for the challenges confronting decision-makers. In this book, we take a different approach.

First, as a point of departure, we start with contemporary themes that appear on the decision-makers' to-do list. What are these themes? PricewaterhouseCoopers (PwC) conducted a Global CEO Survey and found that CEOs expect an economic downturn in the near future, but that opportunities (and challenges) exist with regard to sustainability, digitalization, and upskilling (PwC 2020). In a report by EY, top priorities included board effectiveness, climate change, sustainability, and digital business transformation (Jégourel 2020). Other survey reports corroborate these insights, but also suggest that board diversity and corporate innovation (McCann 2020), uncertain decision-making and diverse strategic thinking (Gill 2020), and cultivating new leaders and global trade developments (Price 2020) are important concerns and priorities. Drawing on these insights, we detail themes such as global competition, business model transformation, digital strategizing, business ecosystems, corporate social responsibility, top management team dynamics, and strategic leadership in a globalized world.

Second, we abandon the traditional idea that (corporate) strategizing entails an exclusive top-management activity. In line with an emergent view on strategy – as opposed to a deliberate view (Mintzberg 1990), we proffer that transformative strategies unfold at different levels with organizations and involve different people. Global competition and venture growth entail a corporate-level dialogue; business model transformation represents a business-unit discussion; digitalization, collaboration, and CSR concern corporate and business-unit levels; whereas team dynamics and leadership center on individuals and groups within organizations. Transformative strategizing (and the required competency) therefore is relevant to current and future business leaders as well as all organizational members.

Case-application approach

Throughout this book we challenge readers to solve real problems that companies face by reconciling their inherent tensions. Our approach takes real problems as the starting point for the learning journey and guides students to acknowledge the broader context in which organizations operate and to analyze the problem from multiple perspectives. The implication of this approach is a differentiating characteristic of our book; we aim to provide readers with a way of developing strategies that fits their own complex situation rather than providing off-the-shelf solutions. The dialogues, cases, questions, and examples serve as a foundation to on the one hand design high-quality instructional and learning environments and on the other to offer the reader with an opportunity to practice transformative strategizing.

Structure of the book

The book comprises four parts, each presenting two chapters. Each part associates with a cross-section between the four developments – globalization, disruption, collaboration, and social responsibility – representing the decision-maker's business environment (see Figure 1.2). Each chapter details a unique tension, such that the book presents a set of tensions in eight contemporary strategic themes (see Table 1.2).

Part 1: globalization and disruption

Part 1 introduces and discusses transformative strategies that organizations may develop to resolve the strategic tensions inherently associated with global growth endeavors.

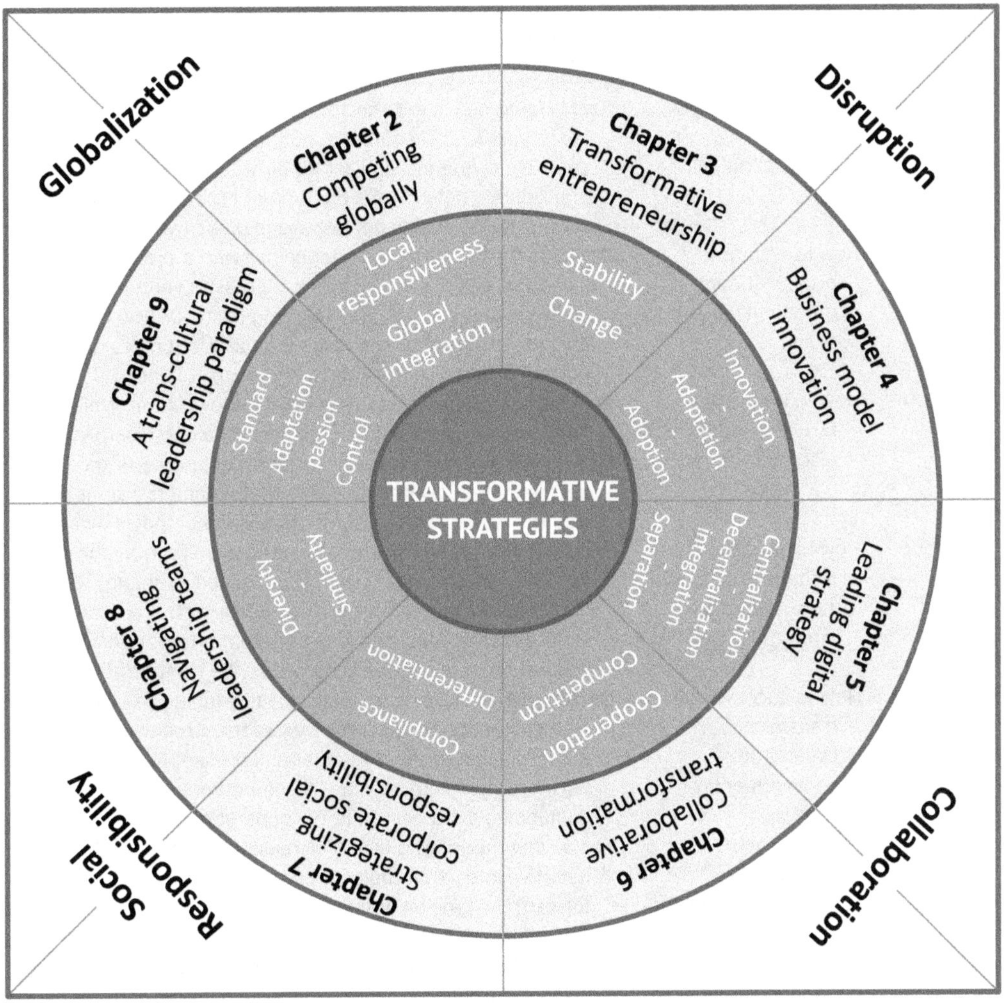

Figure 1.2 Structure of the book

Furthermore, it provides details on transformative entrepreneurship, viewed as the creation and growth of new ventures in increasingly disruptive competitive environments.

- ***Chapter 2*** discusses how organizations can compete on the global arena and the opportunities and challenges of doing business across borders. Success in the global arena belongs to those companies that are best able to manage a specific tension: local responsiveness versus global integration. This chapter describes the respective benefits of responsiveness and integration, their paradoxical relationship, and ways in which companies can manage the tension.
- ***Chapter 3*** focuses on the key question of how new ventures (i.e. small firms) grow and what is the role of strategic elements, and entrepreneurial roles. Firm growth requires a

Table 1.2 Chapters: guiding questions and chapter case

	Guiding question	*Case*
Chapter 2	How to successfully compete in a globalized world?	***Kraft Heinz*** needs to cater to the different expectations of its customers in 200 countries, but also identify ways to reduce costs by leveraging similarities between consumers. This has implications not only for the type of products sold, but also for how value chains are organized globally.
Chapter 3	How to ensure organizational growth in (small) firms?	***Optics11*** started with a founder/owner with a promising invention and has grown into a successful venture comprised of two business units. Transitioning from start-up to mature company necessitated change in organization design and entrepreneurial roles while maintaining stability.
Chapter 4	How to innovate a business model in disruptive times?	***TomTom*** has been able to reinvent itself over time. While TomTom may appear fortunate from the outside, this is because of the long-term preparation, perseverance, determination, as well as agility that helped the company to ride the waves and transform its business models over time.
Chapter 5	How to successfully formulate and execute digital strategy?	***Ericsson AB*** has successfully enacted a digital transformation. To cope with the uncertainties and speed of change, Ericsson launched numerous centralized and decentralized initiatives, while simultaneously making sure that integration and separation of initiatives occurred at the right time.
Chapter 6	How to successfully transform collaborative arrangements?	***Netflix*** rose to global prominence by leveraging key partnerships with content providers. However, as the streaming business model started to show its potential, some of Netflix's main partners started to become its competitors; continuously demanding a reassessment of cooperation and competition.
Chapter 7	How to enact responsible corporate social responsibility practices?	The ***airline industry*** is facing increasing criticism for its negative impact on the environment. The case brings forward the tension airline companies face between continuing with their existing business model and responding to calls from stakeholders concerned about the climate crisis.
Chapter 8	How to design and manage effective leadership teams?	The TankTerminal ***international joint venture*** is managed by an executive coordination committee. Confronted with different goals, cultural backgrounds and expertise areas, this leadership team overcame team challenges and steered the joint venture towards success.
Chapter 9	How to become an effective strategic leader in a globalized world?	***Manager or Leader in the 21st Century?*** This case presents the challenges leaders face when overseeing employees in multiple countries. Drawing on different expectations of leadership across the globe, the case highlights how different values and norms require different leadership approaches.

solution to a key tension: stability vs. change. Stability ensures the exploitation of existing capabilities, whereas change promotes the exploration of new capabilities; although both are necessary for long-term firm survival, the two activities are difficult to reconcile. By combining theory and examples, this chapter analyzes how entrepreneurial role transformation enables and inhibits firm growth.

Part 2: disruption and collaboration

Part 2 of the book focuses on transformative strategies that organizations may develop to cope with the strategic tensions inherently associated with emerging and disruptive technologies. In addition, this part focuses on how disruptive forces trigger companies to change their business models to fit with a connected world.

- ***Chapter 4*** introduces the concept of business models and discusses the challenges of business model transformation. The discussion is centered on the underlying tension among innovation, adoption, and adaptation. Further, the chapter presents the dynamic capability framework and stakeholder theory as providing the theoretical lenses for addressing this central tension of business model transformation as business model innovators interact with their environment to challenge established industry players.
- ***Chapter 5*** focuses on strategizing in a digital world. The chapter discusses changes in the strategy process, content, and context associated with digital transformation. The chapter also addresses how strategy changes to account for new competitive dynamics such as platform competition and ecosystem development. Chapter 5 discusses these topics around the key tensions that firms need to overcome: centralization versus decentralization and integration versus separation.

Part 3: collaboration and responsibility

Part 3 of the book focuses on transformative strategies that organizations may enact in order to cope with the strategic tensions inherently associated with transformation shaped and caused by inter-firm collaboration. This part also focuses on the requirements for practicing strategic corporate social responsibility (CSR), as it entails a reconciliation between internal practices and external stakeholder pressure.

- ***Chapter 6*** focuses on how companies use collaborative arrangements to their advantage and use these external relations to enhance their organizations' responsiveness. Chapter 6 details four types of collaborative arrangements: alliances, alliance portfolios, alliance networks, and business ecosystems. This is followed by a theoretical-driven elaboration on change and transformation perspectives. The chapter concludes with an analysis of how each type of collaborative arrangement is subject to different transformational logics.
- ***Chapter 7*** addresses the increasing expectations that companies have responsibilities towards the society. The chapter discusses various CSR approaches as influenced by a compliance-differentiation tension. Furthermore, the chapter presents several relational tactics that help organizational leaders to garner support for and acceptance of their CSR actions.

Part 4: responsibility and globalization

Part 4 of the book focuses on the top-management team (TMT) and strategic leadership implications of transformative management. As modern organizations operate in a globalized and connected world, the composition of TMTs and boards have become more diverse, while their tasks and responsibilities have become more demanding.

- ***Chapter 8*** explores issues related to what makes leadership teams (such as boards and top management) effective by considering how team composition and team process affect the performance in a global context. The tension under investigation pertains to diversity and similarity and this chapter combines insights with regard to team composition (fault-lines), team embeddedness (multi-team system), and team context (transactive memory system) to explain how leadership teams can effectively navigate the diversity-similarity tension.
- ***Chapter 9*** present a trans-cultural leadership paradigm that views dilemma reconciliation as an integral part of a leaders' trans-cultural competence. Leaders are confronted with a wide-range of universal dilemmas, and building and using a trans-cultural competency is paramount for leaders to guide their organizations and teams, effectuate change, and enact leadership as learning in global organizations. To this end, the chapter juxtaposes this new paradigm with traditional leadership views.

The book concludes with reflective thoughts on strategizing the unknown, the need for transformative strategizing, and the need to change strategic thinking and learning. With transformative strategizing, managers can address contemporary questions, extending beyond the topics discussed in this book.

How to read this book

Each chapter is preceded by a case in which a tension is introduced. The purpose of the prelude is to articulate the nature of the tension inherently tied to the chapter's topic. It provides readers with insights into how thinking strategically may lead to differing perspectives on the same issues, pointing to a need to deal with uncertainty. Following the prelude, the learning objectives of each chapter are described. We then provide a background to the topic of the chapter, i.e. the definition, scope, and key issues are presented. We then provide detail on the tension, followed by a discussion on relevant theoretical perspectives and frameworks. In a subsequent section, reflection, we discuss implications. Together, the prelude, background to the topic, theoretical perspectives, and the reflection offer a foundation to prepare readers to develop solutions that fit their own complex problems. Each chapter ends with an overview of learning, a case exercise, and reflective questions.

References

Astley, W. G. and Van de Ven, A. H. (1983) 'Central perspectives and debates in organization theory'. *Administrative Science Quarterly*, 28: 245-273.

Bain, J. S. (1959) *Industrial Organization: A Treatise*. New York: John Wiley.

Barnett, W. P. and Carroll, G. R. (1995) 'Modelling Internal Organizational Change'. *Annual Review of Sociology*, 21: 217-236.

Barney, J. B. (1991) 'Firm resources and sustained competitive advantage'. *Journal of Management*, 17(1): 99-120.

Bennis, W. and Nanus B. (1985) *Leaders: The strategies for taking charge*. New York: Harper & Row.

Bladek, O., Deighton, J., Dunn, A., Huizenga, T., and Walden, W. (2019) '*The wisdom of transformations: How successful CEOs think about change*'. New York: McKinsey & Company.

Chandler, A. D., Jr. (1962) *Strategy and Structure: Chapters in the History of the American Industrial Enterprise*. Cambridge, MA: MIT Press.

Child, J. (1972) 'Organization structure, environment and performance: The role of strategic choice'. *Sociology*, 6: 1-22.

Christensen, C., McDonald, R., Altman, E., and Palmer, J. (2018) 'Disruptive innovation: An intellectual history and directions for future research'. *Journal of Management Studies*, 55: 1043-1078.

De Wit, B. and Meyer, R. (2004) *Strategy process, content, context: An international perspective* (3rd ed.). London: Thomson Learning.

Donaldson, L. (2001) *The Contingency Theory of Organizations*. Thousand Oaks, CA: Sage.

Gibson, C. B. and Birkinshaw, J. (2004) 'The Antecedents, Consequences, and Mediating Role of Organizational Ambidexterity'. *Academy of Management Journal*, 47(2): 209-226.

Gill, A. (2020) 'Top five boardroom priorities for 2020. Available online at https://bvalco.com/top-five-boardroom-priorities-for-2020/ (accessed 25 June 2020).

Jansen, J. J., Kostopoulos, K. C., Mihalache, O. R., and Papalexandris, A. (2016) 'A socio-psychological perspective on team ambidexterity: The contingency role of supportive leadership behaviours'. *Journal of Management Studies*, 53(6): 939-965.

Jégourel, J. Y. (2020) 'Board Agenda 2020: Eight priorities for boards as they tackle the COVID-19 crisis'. Available online at https://www.ey.com/en_gl/board-matters/board-agenda-2020-eight-priorities-for-boards-as-they-tackle-the-covid-19-crisis (accessed 25 June 2020).

Jensen, M. C. and Meckling, W. H. (1976) 'Theory of the firm: Managerial behavior, agency costs and ownership structure'. *Journal of Financial Economics*, 3(4): 305-360.

Levinthal, D. A. and March, J. G. (1993) 'The myopia of learning'. *Strategic Management Journal*, 14: 95-112.

Lewis, M. W., Andriopoulos, C., and Smith, W. K. (2014) 'Paradoxical leadership to enable strategic agility'. *California Management Review*, 56(3): 58-77.

March, J. G. (1991) 'Exploration and exploitation in organizational learning'. *Organization Science*, 2(1): 71-87.

McCann, D. (2020) 'What are the top concerns for boards in 2020?' Available online at https://www.cfo.com/governance/2020/01/what-are-the-top-concerns-for-boards-in-2020/ (accessed 25 June 2020).

Mihalache, O. R., Jansen, J. J., Van den Bosch, F. A., and Volberda, H. W. (2014) 'Top management team shared leadership and organizational ambidexterity: A moderated mediation framework. *Strategic Entrepreneurship Journal*, 8(2): 128-148.

Mintzberg, H. (1990) 'The design school: Reconsidering the basic premises of strategic management'. *Strategic Management Journal*, 11(3): 171-195.

Miron-Spektor, E., Ingram, A., Keller, J., Smith, W. K., and Lewis, M. (2017) 'Microfoundations of organizational paradox: The problem is how we think about the problem'. *Academy of Management Journal*, 61(1): 26-45.

O'Reilly, C. A. III. and M. L. Tushman. (2004) 'The ambidextrous organization'. *Harvard Business Review*, 82(4): 74-81.

Pinder, M. (2020) '16 cognitive biases that can kill your decision making'. Available online at https://www.boardofinnovation.com/blog/16-cognitive-biases-that-kill-innovative-thinking/ (accessed 25 May 2020).

Porter, M. E. (1980) *Competitive strategy*. New York: Free Press.

Price, N. J. (2020) 'Top concerns for U.S. CEOs in 2020'. Available online at https://insights.diligent.com/ceo/top-concerns-us-ceos-2020 (accessed 25 June 2020).

PwC (2020) '23rd Annual Global CEO Survey'. Available online at https://www.pwc.com/gx/en/ceo-agenda/ceosurvey/2020.html (accessed 25 June 2020).

Quinn, R. E. and Cameron, K. S. (eds) (1988) 'Ballinger series on innovation and organizational change'. In *Paradox and transformation: Toward a theory of change in organization and management*. Cambridge: Ballinger Publishing Co/Harper & Row Publishers.

Rumelt, R. P. (1984) 'Towards a strategic theory of the firm'. In *Competitive strategic management*, Lamb R. B. (ed). Upper Saddle River, NJ: Prentice-Hall, 556-570.

Schad, J., Lewis, M. W., Raisch, S., and Smith, W. K. (2016) 'Paradox research in management science: Looking back to move forward'. *Academy of Management Annals*, 10(1): 5-64.

Schmitt, A., Raisch, S., and Volberda, H. W. (2018) 'Strategic renewal: Past research, theoretical tensions and future challenges'. *International Journal of Management Reviews*, 20: 81-98.

Simon, H. A. (1955) 'A behavioral model of rational choice'. *Quarterly Journal of Economics*, 69: 99–118.

Smith, W. K. (2014). 'Dynamic decision making: A model of senior leaders managing strategic paradoxes'. *Academy of Management Journal*, 57(6): 1592–1623.

Smith, W. K., Erez, M., Jarvenpaa, S. L., Lewis, M. W., and Tracey, P. (2017) 'Adding complexity to theories of paradox, tensions and dualities of innovation and change: Introduction to organization studies special issue on paradox, tensions and dualities of innovation and change'. *Organization Studies*, 38(3-4): 303–317.

Smith, W. K. and Lewis, M. W. (2011) 'Toward a theory of paradox: A dynamic equilibrium model of organizing'. *Academy of Management Review*, 36(2): 381–403.

Steptoe-Warren, G., Howat, D., and Hume, I. (2011) 'Strategic thinking and decision making: Literature review'. *Journal of Strategy and Management*, 4(3): 238–250.

Tallman, S., Luo, Y., and Buckley, P. J. (2018). 'Business models in global competition'. *Global Strategy Journal*, 8(4): 517–535.

Trompenaars, F. and Hampden-Turner, C. (2004) *Managing people across cultures*. Chichester: Capstone Publishing Ltd.

Van de Ven, A. H. and Poole, M. S. (1989) 'Using paradox to build management and organization theories'. *Academy of Management Review*, 14(4): 562–578.

Volberda, H. W., Baden-Fuller, C., Birkinshaw, J., Khanagha, S., and Mihalache, O. R. (2018) 'Strategizing in a digital world: Implications for strategy process, content and context'. *Long Range Planning*, Special Issue Call for Papers.

Von Neumann, J. and Morgenstern, O. (1944) *Theory of games and economic behavior*. Princeton, New Jersey: Princeton University Press.

Weber, Y. and Tarba, S. (2014) 'Strategic agility: A state of the art: Introduction to the special section on strategic agility'. *California Management Review*, 56(3): 5–12.

Wernerfelt, B. (1984) 'A resource-based view of the firm'. *Strategic Management Journal*, 5(2): 171–180.

Williamson, O. E. (1975) *Markets and hierarchies: Analysis and antitrust implications*. New York: Free Press.

Williamson, O. E. (1981) 'The economics of organization – The transaction cost approach'. *American Journal of Sociology*, 87(3): 548–577.

PART 1

Globalization and disruption

2 Competing globally

Oli Mihalache

Summary

The chapter starts with a case detailing the challenges of competing on a global scale. In a world of falling trade barriers and in which technology increasingly provides access to customers and suppliers in far-away countries, competition has moved from the domestic to the world stage. Success in the global arena belongs to those companies that are best able to manage a specific tension: local responsiveness versus global integration. This chapter describes the respective benefits of responsiveness and integration, their paradoxical relationship, and the ways in which companies can manage this tension. We provide a discussion of the tension in the fundamental context of increasing sales versus increasing efficiency. We then take the discussion in the direction of the new context of global strategic change. Building on the key insight of the book, that to survive companies need to respond to disruption in their environment, we discuss the challenges that the responsiveness-integration tension poses to the attempts of global organizations to change, and challenge the reader to consider ways to reconcile them.

Case: Kraft Heinz – competing globally in the food and beverage industry

In 2015, Kraft Foods Group, Inc. and H. J. Heinz Company merged into The Kraft Heinz Company to become the fifth-largest company in the global food and beverage industry worldwide. The merger provided the new company with a truly global reach by combining Kraft's North American market with Heinz's foreign brands. In 2018, Kraft Heinz had US$26 billion in net sales with US$20 billion from the United States and Canada, US$2.7 from Europe, the Middle East, and Africa, and US$3.3 billion from the rest of the world.

As Kraft Heinz sells its products in close to 200 countries, how can it best compete in the global market? Devising an appropriate competitive strategy is a complex task that reduces to three fundamental choices: increasing revenues, reducing costs, or both. The starting point to devising an effective global competitive strategy is understanding the environment in which the company operates, primarily the degree to which consumer needs are aligned or differ between its diverse consumer bases.

To increase revenues, Kraft Heinz tries to respond to customer differences by developing products tailored to the specific needs of customers from different countries. While this strategic option can help to increase revenues, as it provides the products that consumers want, it comes with an increase in costs. To capture the differences in customer needs, Kraft Heinz also sells products specifically designed for certain countries and sold under local brands. For instance, in the Netherlands, it is very common for people of all ages to eat chocolate sprinkles on sliced bread instead of jam or chocolate. Kraft Heinz addresses this peculiar taste through a local brand called De Ruijter. Another local brand sold in the Netherlands is Karvan Cevitam, through which it sells juice concentrate. These products allow Kraft Heinz to maximize revenues in a certain location as it customizes products for local tastes. However, addressing local tastes increases costs as Kraft Heinz needs to invest in local research and development and marketing.

A second strategic option for Kraft Heinz when competing globally is to focus on cost reduction and increased efficiency. This requires focusing on the similarities between consumers in different countries. When customers have similar needs, companies can reduce costs, as by providing standardized products they benefit from economies of scale. Kraft Heinz addresses similarities between consumers through its global brands, such as Kraft (mostly with a low-cost positioning), Heinz (mostly with a premium positioning), or Philadelphia. These global brands allow Kraft Heinz to leverage its global scale and reduce costs. For instance, as ketchup is a standard product, Kraft Heinz does not need to develop a new formula when entering a new market. It can also reduce its marketing costs, as many consumers are familiar with the brand and there is therefore no need to invest in the development of new ads.

The third strategic option addresses both similarities and differences between customers in different countries. Kraft Heinz does this by using a global brand, but allowing for adaptations to local tastes. A case in point is the entry of Oreo on the Chinese market. In response to surprisingly low sales, Kraft Heinz engaged in local research to understand that Chinese customers had different expectations of the product. The local research team made several changes to the classical Oreo cookie: they made it less sweet, introduced a variety with wafers, and provided smaller packages. The marketing team supported these efforts with locally adapted advertisements, using the Oreo concepts but centered on Chinese instead of American families. Consequently, sales soared.

Importantly, Kraft Heinz's competitive strategies are not limited to customer-facing activities, but also include other value-chain activities, such as manufacturing or administrative activities. In manufacturing, Kraft Heinz aims to increase efficiencies by aggregating its manufacturing activities in larger and more technologically advanced factories that produce for many countries. For instance, in November 2015 Kraft Heinz announced that it would close its Canadian factory in St. Marys, Ontario. The senior vice-president of corporate and government affairs, Michael Mullen, motivated this decision by stating that it is 'a critical step in our plan to eliminate excess capacity and reduce operational redundancies for the new combined company'

(Canadian Grocer). Similar decisions were taken at the time regarding six factories in the United States.

Another way in which Kraft Heinz aims to gain efficiency is by implementing standardized practices across its global operations. As an effort in this direction, in 2018 Kraft Heinz established a Global Center of Excellence in Amsterdam, the Netherlands. Through this center, Kraft Heinz aims to improve its efficiency by identifying and implementing best practices globally. Standardized practices can help to reduce costs by ensuring that different locations across the globe adopt the practices of the highest performers.

The success of Kraft Heinz, like that of other global companies, depends on its ability to understand in which aspects its customers differ and in which aspects they are similar. Consequently, Kraft Heinz needs to both cater to the different expectations of its global customers, while at the same time identifying ways to reduce costs by leveraging similarities between consumers. This has implications not only for the type of products sold but also for how value chains are organized globally.

Questions:

1 What are Kraft Heinz's strategic options for competing globally?
2 Which strategic options should Kraft Heinz focus on and why?

Learning objectives

The objectives of this chapter are to:

1 Explain the main opportunities and challenges of doing business across borders
2 Introduce readers to what it means to compete globally
3 Present the different strategic options organizations have when competing globally
4 Describe the local responsiveness - global efficiency tension underlying global competitive options - and discussing ways to reconcile this tension

Introduction to global competition

In the 21st century, the competition moved from the domestic to the global arena. It is difficult to conceive of any business that is not affected by the international environment. Even those businesses whose owners or managers have no ambition to venture outside of their country should understand that they are part of a global marketplace, as local competitors can get ahead by taking advantage of foreign resources and global competitors can try to challenge them in their domestic market. Global competition is the reality of our days and businesses are better off when they acknowledge this in their strategizing.

The rise of global business is due to geopolitical and technological developments that took place over the past few decades (see also Tallman et al. 2018). Globally, in the past 50 years, there has been increasing trade liberalization with falling barriers to the flow of goods. The establishment of international organizations such as the World Bank and the World Trade

Organization (WTO) have further contributed to the rise in international trade by providing checks and balances in the global marketplace. The rise of membership in these organizations shows an increasing ease in trade between more countries. For instance, the precursor of WTO, the General Agreement on Tariffs and Trade (GATT) had only 43 members in 1948, while the WTO has 163 member countries as of 2019.

Another factor that contributed significantly to the rise in global trade is the integration of emerging and developing economies in the global marketplace. The adoption of pro-market reforms allowed emerging countries such as Brazil, Russia, India, and China, as well as many Latin American countries to join in global trade. Deregulation and industrialization of emerging economies made it possible not only for foreign organizations to establish operations there but also for emerging market companies to venture into developed economies. As more than 85 percent of the world's population lives in emerging economies (Muller 2018), their increased participation in the global marketplace had a major impact on global business dynamics.

Alongside these geopolitical developments, technological developments stimulated increased global connectivity. Advances in transportation accelerated the flow of trade and movement of people. The introduction of containerization and super-freighters facilitated the shipment of goods across the globe, and the development of commercial flying significantly reduced travel time. Furthermore, advances in telecommunication accelerated the flow of information and data, making it easier for an organization to connect employees from offices around the world. Overall increased global connectivity means not only that businesses can trade more, but, perhaps more importantly, that they have a new way to create value through innovative business models that allow them to link people and resources from diverse locations in unique ways. As a result of these developments, we are experiencing a rise in firms engaged in international business.

A firm *internationalizes* when it ventures outside its national boundaries. This can be to various degrees and in various ways. Some organizations make only small steps abroad by trying to sell their products to foreign consumers or sourcing products abroad without making direct investments in foreign operations. On the other extreme, there are true multinational enterprises (MNE). An MNE is an organization that has substantial direct investment in foreign countries (not just trading relationships of export business), actively manages its offshore assets (not simply holding them as a passive financial portfolio), and engages in the active coordinated management of its operations located in different countries (i.e., strategic and organizational integration) (Bartlett and Beamish 2018). That is, there is a degree of internationalization ranging from firms making their first steps across borders to true MNEs.

The defining characteristic of global firms is that they are operating in multiple countries. This is important because managing a global firm requires an understanding of the differences between countries. Countries differ in many aspects. First, countries differ in terms of the institutional environment. Institutions provide the rules according to which firms operate as they determine which behaviors are possible. Institutions can be formal or informal. ***Formal institutions*** comprise the laws and regulations set by the government or its delegate authoritative bodies. An example could be regulation regarding copyright protection. The fact that intellectual property laws and the enforcement of these laws differ from country to country can affect firms' choices regarding what products to sell, produce, or develop in a country.

Informal institutions include the culture and norms of countries. Informal institutions (unlike formal ones that are coercive) are normative and cognitive. If we return to the intellectual property point, individuals in different countries have different perspectives on the ethicality of copying somebody else's work. That is, the perception of right versus wrong affects how one might engage with a foreign firm's technology. Culture can also affect success in different countries, as it determines how customers perceive the attractiveness of products and services. Even when it comes to modes of transportation, culture affects what is perceived as acceptable or preferable. While someone from North America might consider driving as the preferred mode of transportation, people living in the Netherlands tend to prefer riding a bicycle, as driving is perceived as a sign of laziness. Such differences in accepted behaviors affect all aspects of doing business, such as how an international firm engages with its foreign customers or employees and how it interacts with its competitors and suppliers.

Countries also differ in terms of their factor endowments, such as the labor force characteristics (amount, type, and productivity), land, or capital. For instance, Romania is becoming a hotspot in Eastern Europe for IT work due to a large pool of university graduates and lower wages than in Western European countries. Factor endowments can change over time as more firms enter. For instance, the wages for manufacturing work in China are rising due to an increase in demand as more organizations are trying to leverage China's manufacturing capabilities. Variations in factor endowments imply that different countries are attractive for different types of activities, providing opportunities for companies to engage in arbitrage.

Considering that global organizations operate in multiple countries and that countries differ, then competing in the global arena requires organizations to not only overcome challenges associated with the differences between countries, but also to leverage these differences. That is, to successfully compete on the global area, organizations need to develop an understanding of whether and in which ways countries differ and to develop capabilities to understand whether they can gain benefits from exploiting differences versus similarities between countries.

Managing global organizations

Managing global organizations requires companies to understand and leverage the differences between countries, as these can provide many potential benefits for companies that can overcome their associated challenges. Between-country differences enable organizations to increase their revenues by entering new markets. Differences in customer sophistication and market development allow organizations to increase revenues and allow growth, even when their home market has matured (Levitt 1965). A classic example is that of the TV industry. When the US market became saturated, companies grew by selling TV sets to customers in less developed markets.

However, an important challenge is that firm-specific advantages may not be relevant, and the organization might not be able to appropriate value from these advantages when moved to a foreign location (Lessard, Lucea and Vives 2013). Many organizations internationalize to exploit their existing capabilities, but differences between countries can affect their ability to transfer firm-specific advantages abroad. Cultural differences can create different customer needs and expectations such that a successful product or service at home might not be relevant in a different location. For instance, a TV show might be very successful in one country, but, due to its high cultural embeddedness, it might not find the same success when transferred abroad. Furthermore, institutional differences might affect the degree to which the benefits from transferred firm assets can be appropriated in a foreign country. For instance, even if a TV show might be well-received in a different country, lack of copyright protection leading to peer sharing makes it difficult to appropriate benefits. These issues apply not only on the product side, but also in terms of transferring internal formulas for success abroad. For instance, a global organization might not be able to transfer its successful employee-reward policy abroad due to cultural acceptance or institutional constraints. That is, between-country differences can create challenges when interacting with both customers and employees.

Differences between countries also fuel resource-seeking internationalization, as firms venture abroad to tap into foreign resources not available at home. Some organizations go abroad to enter foreign clusters that give access to the latest know-how. For example, electronics companies may choose to open a research and development office in Silicon Valley to access the latest technological developments, or apparel manufacturers may open design offices in Milan to gain access to the latest fashion trends. As an alternative to locating abroad, companies can also tap into foreign capabilities by contracting foreign firms such as in the case of manufacturing contracts that allow firms to tap into China's manufacturing prowess – Apple contracting Foxconn to manufacture its iPhone is a prime example. This practice of leveraging between-country differences by choosing to perform activities in the countries that have a comparative advantage is called 'arbitrage' (Ghemawat 2007).

In summary, since global firms operate in multiple countries, succeeding in the global arena requires managers to leverage the similarities and differences between countries.

Tension: local responsiveness versus global integration

International strategy boils down to whether firms can get more benefits from leveraging: (i) similarities; (ii) differences; or (iii) both similarities and differences between countries. As the goal of the strategy-making is to drive profits, the starting point to understand the international strategies available is the profit formula:

$$\textit{Profit} = \textit{Revenues} - \textit{Costs}$$

There are two levers to increase profit: (i) increase revenues; or (ii) decrease costs. How can multinational organizations achieve these goals? Multinational organizations can:

(i) Increasing revenues through local responsiveness

To maximize sales, firms need to tailor products and services to the needs of customers in each country. Adaptation of the product and service offering increases sales, as customers are more likely to purchase products when those products meet their needs and expectations.

Take, for instance, Kraft's expansion in emerging markets. In 2011, the then-CEO Bill Johnson described his approach of customizing the product offering to grow revenues from emerging markets: 'You have to make sure the product suits the local culture. We do sell some ketchup in China, but the dominant condiment there is soy sauce; if we're to compete in sauces, that's what we need to offer.... The first time I visited the Philippines and tasted the ketchup, I found that it was very different from American ketchup. It turned out that it was made from bananas. It didn't suit me, but it's what Filipino consumers want, so it's applicable' (Johnson 2011). By offering banana-based ketchup instead of its regular tomato-based ketchup, Kraft is more likely to achieve higher sales in the Philippines, as it provides a product that satisfies the special customer tastes.

(ii) Decreasing costs through global efficiency

Firms can minimize costs by focusing on global efficiency, which can be achieved through standardization and global integration. When selling a standardized product, firms can lower their costs due to economies of scale. When producing larger volumes of the same product, the cost per unit decreases because the fixed costs are spread over a larger number of units, there are lower prices when purchasing inputs in higher volume, and learning increases efficiency. An example of global integration in manufacturing activities is Tesla's battery Gigafactory, which opened in 2014 Sparks, Nevada. Intending to manufacture sufficient batteries to outfit its target production of 500,000 vehicles a year, the building of the Gigafactory allows Tesla to enjoy higher efficiencies when compared to building multiple smaller battery factories around the world (Tesla 2014). A similar logic underlies Ben & Jerry's (owned by Unilever since 2001) approach to manufacturing ice cream in only three factories in the US and then shipping it to the 38 countries in which its 600 shops operate, instead of manufacturing close to the point of sale (Schug 2017).

Choosing and implementing strategic options

The goal is to choose a strategy that makes an organization successful when competing on the global stage. Three elements need to fit for organizations to successfully compete globally: strategy, environment, and organizational design. The international strategy needs to fit the environment of the organization and the strategy needs to be supported by an appropriate organizational design. That is, choosing an appropriate strategy for the environment in which the organization competes needs to be complemented by the implementation of an appropriate organizational design, which allows the execution of the strategy.

So, when should organizations choose local responsiveness versus global integration? To answer this question, organizations need to analyze their environment to understand whether they are facing pressures for local responsiveness or global integration.

The environment and strategic options. To a large extent, the relative benefits of the two strategic alternatives depend on the characteristics of the industry in which firms operate. For instance, in the food industry there tend to be high benefits arising from local

Figure 2.1 Local responsiveness-global integration tension

responsiveness. Since there is a high difference between countries in tastes due to cultural differences and religion, maximizing revenues requires adaptation to local tastes, as the previous example of Kraft selling banana-based ketchup in the Philippines shows. Furthermore, in the food industry, there are relatively fewer benefits potentially arising from global integration. The lower costs of producing in a large efficient factory might be reversed by high costs of transportation or tariffs, and expiry dates might make shipping to a far location impossible.

On the other hand, some industries face pressures for global efficiencies such as the consumer electronics industry. With only minor differences between the needs of consumers in different countries, there are little benefits to be obtained from local adaptation; there are, however, benefits to be obtained from global integration. In the case of cellphones, centralized manufacturing can significantly reduce costs. In the case of Apple, cellphone assembly is integrated by using two Taiwanese firms, Foxconn and Pegatron.

So far, we have addressed the strategic choice as either local responsiveness or global efficiency. But wouldn't it be even better if organizations would try to both increase revenues and decrease costs by pursuing (i) local responsiveness *and* (ii) global efficiency? This is a very challenging approach because of the tension between local responsiveness and global efficiency (see Figure 2.1)

While companies trying to maximize profit from global operations want to pursue both local responsiveness and global efficiency, they might not be able to do so, as these two strategic alternatives are conflicting. Actions aimed at increasing local responsiveness oftentimes lead to a decrease in global efficiency. For instance, a company might attempt to increase local responsiveness by developing a marketing campaign tailored to a specific country. However, developing country-specific marketing campaigns increases costs as it involves production expenses and potentially hiring internal marketing staff in each country, thus reducing global efficiency. For maximizing global efficiency, a single marketing campaign would be developed in a location that offers a comparative advantage and then rolled out in every country in which the firm operates. Similar tensions can be experienced with other functions, such as research and development (R&D) or manufacturing. Local R&D teams in each country might be able to develop the most relevant products for those markets, but they come at the cost of efficiency due to the duplication of activities. Therefore, while companies might want to both increase revenues and reduce costs, they are facing a tension between local responsiveness and global efficiency.

Strategic options and organizational design. To devise organizational design appropriate for the implementation of the different strategic options, three elements need to be considered: (i) structural anatomy; (ii) process physiology; and (iii) cultural psychology (Bartlett and Beamish, 2018). The structural anatomy refers to how assets and responsibilities are distributed and are generally represented by the organizational chart. Akin to the human skeleton, while providing the fundamental shape of the organization, the organizational structure does not fully describe how an organization behaves. Two organizations with similar structures might behave differently because of differences in how the information flows between its different parts. That is, the physiology of the organization affects the relationships between the different parts of the organization and the subsequent information flows. The final element of the organizational design is the organizational culture, which comprises the mentality and values of the organization. The organizational culture is important as it influences how organizational members interpret events and the responses they devise.

When considering the organizational design of multinational organizations, a defining element is a relationship between the headquarters (HQ) and foreign subsidiaries. The relationship between the HQ and each subsidiary can be described in terms of three governance mechanisms: (i) centralization (i.e., the hierarchical level in the organization where formal authority resides); (ii) formalization (i.e., the level of bureaucracy or the extent to which behavior is controlled through formal rules and regulations); and (iii) normative integration (i.e., the extent to which the behavior of organizational members is controlled through shared beliefs and values). When analyzing the entire multinational organization there can be different patterns of relationships between the HQ and the foreign subsidiaries. This relationship can be described in terms of two factors: (i) structural differentiation; and (ii) structural integration (Ghoshal and Nohria 1993). Structural differentiation refers to the extent to which the subsidiaries vary in their relationship to the HQ, and structural integration refers to the strength of organization-wide integrative mechanisms. Different patterns of structural differentiation and structural integration will be more appropriate to leverage different strategic options - local responsiveness versus global integration.

Now that we have discussed the two strategic options and the environment in which they can be applied as well as the organizational design building blocks, we can continue to a discussion of how all these elements fit together. That is, what are the different strategies for when organizations compete in the global arena and how can these strategies be implemented?

Strategies for competing on the global arena

Based on the two conflicting environmental pressures, there are four strategies that companies can employ for global competition. Figure 2.2 provides an overview of the global strategic space that incorporates the four ideal-types strategies and Figure 2.3 is a depiction of the HQ-foreign subsidiaries' relationships appropriate for each one of the strategies.

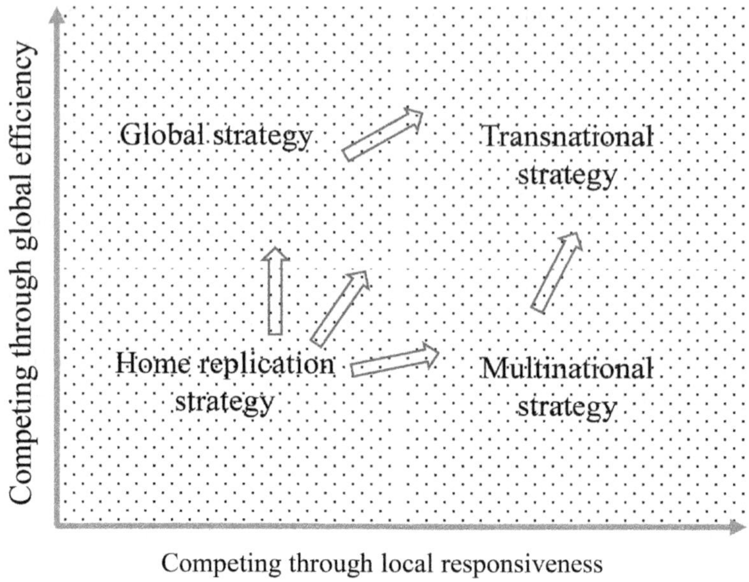

Figure 2.2 The global competitive space

Source: Based on Ghoshal and Nohria (1993)

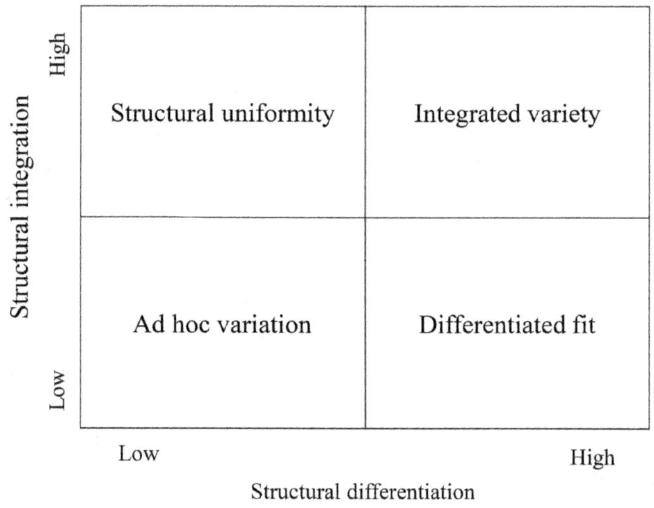

Figure 2.3 The HQ-foreign subsidiaries relationship

Source: Reproduced from Ghoshal and Nohria (1993)

1. Home replication strategy

With this strategy, organizations compete in the global arena by leveraging their competencies developed at home. They attempt to increase revenue through international sales by providing a product or service developed for domestic consumers. The 'home replication strategy' label describes the form of the organization abroad, as its foreign subsidiaries tend to look like mini versions of the domestic organization. Organizations adopting this strategy exhibit low levels of local responsiveness and low levels of global efficiency. Some industries might indeed not provide potential benefits from either one of the strategic options. An example might be the cement industry, where there might not be many differences between customer needs, but also there might not be many opportunities to increase global efficiency through integration as transportation costs can be prohibitive for such a product with a low price per weight ratio. However, many organizations employ this strategy not because of industry characteristics, but as a first foray into international markets. It can be perceived as a low-cost way to enter the global arena, as it does not imply the development of new products or services. So, while it allows the exploitation of a firm's capabilities, it does not provide an opportunity for learning abroad as the foreign subsidiaries are generally used only as pipelines.

The ***organizational design for the home replication strategy*** tends to be one of the simplest relative to the designs for the other strategies. Oftentimes, the home replication strategy is implemented using the current organizational structure to which an *international department* is added to oversee the international operations. Since the home replicating strategy is oftentimes used at the beginning of the internationalization journey, the addition of an international division allows the implementation of the strategy without disturbing regular business operations.

The HQ-foreign subsidiaries' relationship tends to be low on both structural differentiation and structural integration, a patterned called 'ad hoc variation'. That is, usually, there is a rather uniform relationship between the HQ and foreign subsidiaries and the subsidiaries' operations are not integrated. Although the foreign subsidiaries are under the control of HQ, they are not required to act in unison because they operate as pipelines for the HQ. This is because the flow of resources is from the HQ to the foreign subsidiaries rather than from the subsidiaries to the HQ or between the subsidiaries.

2. Multinational strategy

With this strategy companies compete by attempting to maximize revenue by adapting to local markets. As markets differ, foreign subsidiaries develop solutions for their customers. With its emphasis on differentiating the product offering between countries, this strategy decreases the extent to which firms can obtain economies of scale. Furthermore, a multinational strategy makes it difficult for organizations to transfer knowledge between subsidiaries, because knowledge or products from one country might not be perceived as relevant in another country. Many companies in the food industry find it beneficial to employ this strategy due to the high forces for local responsiveness they face.

The ***organizational design for the multinational strategy*** needs to emphasize the importance of foreign regions. The organizational structure that fits a multinational strategy is organized around geographical divisions. This structure divides the worldwide operations based on geographical regions, with the heads of the regions reporting to the CEO. Since the strategy emphasizes differences between countries/regions, using geographic divisions allows the organization to respond to the different needs of these regions.

The relationship between HQ and the foreign subsidiaries tends to be high on structural differentiation and low on structural integration, a pattern called 'differentiated fit'. There is variation in the relationship between HQ and the foreign subsidiaries because the implementation of the multinational strategy requires foreign subsidiaries to adapt to their local environment. This means that different governance mechanisms need to be used. The structural integration is low because the organization does not need to act in a coordinated fashion when each subsidiary adapts to the local context. On the contrary, what is important is that the HQ gives control to the subsidiaries to operate as is most appropriate in their environment.

3. Global strategy

Companies employing a global strategy compete through cost reduction. They develop a product or service for a 'global' consumer as they view the world as one unit of analysis. Through the sale of a standardized product designed around the common features desired by most consumers around the world, companies can enjoy the benefits of economies of scale. To increase global efficiency, this strategy maximizes world-scale systems, such as concentrated manufacturing or global R&D operation performed in a location with comparative advantages.

The ***organizational design for the global strategy*** needs to emphasize efficiency, which is achieved by a focus on the products or services. As such, the appropriate organizational structure is based around product divisions. By focusing on the products or services, the structure allows a focus on the similarities rather than the differences between countries, as it encourages the development of standardized products or services. Product division focuses organizational attention on how the products or services can be most efficiently brought to the market. Differences between locations are also important when implementing a global strategy; however, they are important primarily when it comes to deciding where to perform various activities (i.e., the location of resources). To maximize efficiency, organizations need to perform activities in locations that provide advantages. For instance, the mega-factory producing the standardized products needs to be placed in a location that has comparative advantages rather than in, say, the hometown of the organization's founder.

The relationship between HQ and the foreign subsidiaries tends to be low on structural differentiation and high on structural integration, a pattern called 'structural uniformity'. For maximizing efficiency, there is little variance in how the different subsidiaries are managed as a common governance model is adopted for all foreign subsidiaries. As there needs to be integration between the global operations, there is high centralization. This leads to uniform subsidiaries that efficiently implement the centrally devised strategy.

4. Transnational strategy

With this strategy, companies try to compete through both local responsiveness and global efficiency. That is, they aim to balance global and local concerns (Begley and Boyd 2003). The strength of this strategy is that companies actively pursue both cost reduction through economies of scale and revenue maximization through adaptation to the local market. Despite its

Box 2.1 Philips towards local responsiveness and global integration

Philips is a Dutch technology conglomerate headquartered in Amsterdam with operations in more than 100 countries and 2019 revenues in excess of US$36 billion. It has three main areas of operations: consumer health, professional health, and consumer well-being. Philips was established in 1891 in Eindhoven and began operations by producing light bulbs. Philips developed multiple new technologies, such as the compact disc or the home video-cassette recorder.

In its early internationalization, Philips was notorious for its local responsiveness as many of its technologies were developed for the local needs of customers in foreign countries with the resources available in those locations. For instance, its first color TV was produced and sold in Canada, the first stereo TV was developed in Australia, and the Teletext TV in the UK (Bartlett and Ghoshal 1990). Already in the 1980s, it became obvious to Philips' management that local responsiveness without global integration made it very difficult to compete, especially with its major rival Matsushita (i.e., the Japanese company today operating as Panasonic). Matsushita was competing using a global strategy by developing products at its central research facility in Japan and selling highly standardized products through its global subsidiaries. Philips' local adaptation implied that its value chains were largely replicated in the countries in which it operated, duplicating many of its costs. Such realization led to organizational restructuring, as Philips embarked on a journey of aggregating its worldwide operations.

In the 2000s, Philips' aimed to compete with a more transnational strategy as it attempted to 'achiev[e] global scale with local relevance' (Editor 2015). For instance, in 2013 Wiebo Vaartjes stated: 'We are a global brand and we want to be perceived as a global brand'. The decision to compete by combining local relevance with efficiency saw changes in its organizational design to increase global integration. When it comes to its manufacturing facilities, Philips attempted to concentrate production in fewer factories. In 2018, Philips had only 50 manufacturing facilities in 26 countries and plans to further reduce this number to 30 (Meijer 2019). An example is its planned closure of the UK manufacturing facility for baby care products and the move of production to its Drachten factory in the Netherlands. Such global integration attempts are taking place in its research and development activities. Philips now has only nine research centers worldwide. The foreign research centers complement research efforts in its central research facility in Eindhoven, the Netherlands, by providing either specialized knowledge or regional insights and adaptation. This dual role of the foreign research facilities is evident in Philips Research China's description: 'We are an integral part of Philips' international Research organization and have extensive collaborations with Philips' innovation teams across the world. We also aim at forging integrated digital solutions across businesses for the Chinese market with "last mile" engineering to realize local-relevant solutions for our partners and customers by collaborating with the China Digital Innovation team'.

Philips' attempt to compete by engaging in both local responsiveness and global integration shows the importance of both focusing on increasing revenues and decreasing costs for long-term survival. Competing with a transnational strategy requires managers to design an organization that supports both strategic actions.

appeal, a transnational strategy is difficult to implement in practice due to the tension between local responsiveness and global integration.

The ***organizational design for the transnational strategy*** is more complex than the ones for the other strategies. As it implies the incorporation of inconsistent competitive logics, the implementation of a transnational strategy requires organizational design solutions that allow for coordinated action while at the same time providing sufficient flexibility for local responses. The organizational design solution for the transnational strategy is described in detail in the next section.

So, which strategy to pursue? The above strategies all have their strengths and weaknesses and they might be more appropriate in different situations. The starting point for strategy choice is considering whether competing based on efficiency versus differentiating offering for local demands is more appropriate (as discussed in the previous section). However, the pursuit of revenues without any consideration of costs might be irresponsible, and the pursuit of efficiency without any consideration for differences in customer needs might be leaving on the table important revenue streams. Therefore, how can an organization overcome the tension between global efficiency and local responsiveness and implement a transnational strategy?

Implementing transnational strategies: overcoming the tension between local responsiveness and global efficiency

To manage the tension between global efficiency and local responsiveness, organizations need to move away from an either/or perspective to embrace the complexity of pursuing multiple conflicting goals. To this end, organizations need to adopt a mentality shift in global strategizing and to implement organizational design solutions.

Mentality shift in global strategizing. The starting point is the realization that the four strategies described above are ideal types. However, in practice, companies do not pursue them in pure forms. The strategies' practical usefulness increases when they are considered in terms of degrees rather than presence versus absence. That is, instead of thinking of the strategies in a 2x2 matrix (i.e., Figure 2.2), considering them in a continuous space provides more nuance. Companies can be positioned in a two-dimensional space defined by local responsiveness vs. global efficiency.

Furthermore, global strategizing needs to be considered as dynamic rather than static. While an organization might have a predominant way to compete globally, it should be considered in a state of flux. That is, the strategy changes over time. One organization might predominantly compete based on local adaptation and gradually increase efforts to reduce costs through initiatives that emphasize efficiency. This might be in response to more intense competition or to the realization that there are additional benefits to be captured.

> Transformative strategizing for competing globally is a dynamic process that requires organizations to adopt a continuous improvement mentality that incorporates rival logics of increasing revenues and lowering costs.

Box 2.2 Global supply chain resilience

Companies operating global supply chains should learn a lesson from the COVID-19 crisis of 2020: they should fundamental change and prepare their supply chains for future shocks. The pre-Covid-19 design of global supply chains has not been able to deal effectively with volatile changes in consumer demand - either exponential growth or decline - highlighting how vulnerable global value chains are. In the future, inter-state conflicts, extreme weather conditions, shifting local government policies and regulations, staffing challenges, sustainability concerns, and data threats may all undermine a global value chain's efficacy. Next, some guidelines to boost supply chain resilience:

- Activate a global supply chain task team, preferably a cross-functional task team. The goal of the task team is to actively seek real-time information and feed it into an agile response planning and execution process.
- Proactively communicate with critical suppliers to determine inventory levels and potential issues in the short and long term. Also, focus on your customers, under-promise with a realistic expectation, and over-achieve where possible.
- Monitor supply disruptions in the short term and reprioritize available supply and inventory accordingly. Run multiple, real-time fact-based scenarios to 'stress test' the supply chain and better understand how daily demand fluctuations will affect your suppliers, customers, and revenue at risk.
- Involve the entire ecosystem. Increase end-to-end supply chain visibility and enhance sharing of information, connect to partners' data sources in all directions. To minimize latency of information from suppliers, manufacturers, freight partners and third-tier suppliers, establish a standardized - data-driven - working environment (e.g., common documents).

Source: Martinez (2020); Tucker (2020)

In addition to providing a more practical interpretation of strategies available for multinational organizations, thinking in terms of degrees along with the local responsiveness and global integration dimensions, pushes organizations to consider how to overcome the tension between the two strategic actions. Thinking in terms of degrees instead of dualities can make organizations strive to increase revenues through local adaptation or to reduce costs by searching for global efficiency. For instance, Kraft Heinz, while adopting an adaptation strategy by altering its product offering to fit the tastes of consumers in different locations, might also attempt to increase efficiency by grouping countries with similar characteristics and integrating some activities (i.e., common marketing campaign).

Therefore, considering a continuous strategy space, organizations can stimulate a continuous improvement mentality to adjust their strategy by adopting competing dominant competitive logic. However, implementing a strategy that comprises contradictory strategic logics is not easy, especially when organizations are operating in multiple and geographically distant locations.

Organizational design solutions. To support contradictory competitive logics, organizations need to implement organizational design solutions. To be able to execute a transnational strategy, the following three elements of organizational design need to be used to manage the tension between local responsiveness and global efficiency.

(i)The structural anatomy for transnational strategy

The organizational design solutions need to be developed by considering the entire global footprint of organizations. At the foundation of any organizational design solution, rests the understanding of the differences between the countries in which the organization operates. In other words, differences between countries inform the global distribution of assets. To resolve the tension between local responsiveness and global efficiency, organizations can localize some activities and globally integrate others. For this, they need to start with an analysis of their value chain. The value chain can be broadly thought of as comprising front-end and back-end activities.

To enhance local responsiveness, organizations can localize front-end activities. Generally, front-end activities such as sales and marketing are good candidates for localization because these are the activities that most often come in direct contact with the customers. As such these activities are best positioned to allow the organization to understand idiosyncratic customer needs and how to address them. To be able to adapt to local needs, foreign subsidiaries performing front-end activities need to be decentralized. As for local adaptation, subsidiaries need to be able to behave in ways appropriate for their local context and to engage with local customers. That is, subsidiaries performing front-end activities need to have the freedom to adapt to local needs. This means that their behavior cannot be controlled from the HQ, since the HQ does not understand the specific needs of the different country subsidiaries.

To enhance global efficiency, organizations can globally integrate back-end activities such as IT, R&D, purchasing, etc. For this, organizations need to disaggregate their value chain and perform activities in the locations that provide the most advantages, a concept known as arbitrage (Ghemawat 2007). The functions in the value chain can be further divided into smaller activities, which can then be performed in different locations. Instead of considering where to perform the R&D function, a more fine-grained perspective would differentially locate its different component activities. For instance, Vestas Wind Systems A/S, a Danish manufacturer of wind turbines, performs the main development activities in Denmark, aero-mechanical structural design and analysis in the UK, and has an R&D back-office in India. Such operations that take advantage of location advantages can become centers of excellence and be leveraged or disseminated throughout the global organization (Frost, Birkinshaw, and Ensign 2002). Credit Suisse, a US financial services company, took advantage of the higher level of education and relatively low salaries in Poland to establish a back-office as a center of excellence that supports its global operations (e.g., support for trading, HR service, law, and design services).

After the value-chain functions have been disaggregated and dispersed around the globe, the organization needs to put in place mechanisms to coordinate these activities (Kumar and Puranam 2011). This is where the other two organizational design elements - process physiology and cultural psychology - come into play.

(ii)The process physiology for the transnational strategy

Organizations can establish information flows to coordinate specialized activities by employing formal and informal coordination mechanisms. Formal channels for coordination include the assigning of specific integration roles such as Program Manager. To bring together the required knowledge to develop and deliver a new product or service, organizations can establish global virtual teams. That is, establishing teams based on their members' competencies regardless of the geographical location in which they reside. Furthermore, distances can be bridged by putting in place direct communication channels.

In addition to formal coordination mechanisms, organizations can stimulate coordination through tacit mechanisms. A primary way to stimulate coordination is by connecting geographically distant employees by using IT systems that allow the monitoring of work as it is being performed. In this way, members of the global team can know who is working on what and the progress their colleagues are making.

(iii)The organizational culture for the transnational strategy

To coordinate the geographically dispersed and specialized assets of organizations using a transnational strategy, organizational culture plays a major role. That is, to make the localized front-end operation work in tandem with the globally integrated back-end activities the organizational culture needs to stimulate cooperation and knowledge transfer. The strength of the organizational culture can influence the extent to which organizational members understand their membership in the global organization rather than the local subsidiary in which they work and whether they perceive other parts of the organization as competitors rather than complementors. To be able to coordinate globally, the organizational culture needs to be strong and to emphasize common goals. A way to achieve this is by ensuring that the organization's mission and values are clear and shared throughout the global organization. The organizational values can be used to communicate desired behaviors from organizational members. Values around knowledge transfer and common goals can stimulate employees to engage in these types of behaviors, which are required for globally coordinating work. The organizational culture can be supported through socialization processes that teach organizational members 'how we do things around here'. Socialization can happen, for instance, through management development programs offered by the learning and development department. These programs can emphasize the importance of collaboration for achieving organizational goals and for professional development.

In addition, the organizational culture can be strengthened to stimulate coordination through personnel policies and practices. A practical example of a personnel policy could be to include in the yearly evaluation of employees a measure regarding collaboration with colleagues from other countries. There could be items based on providing knowledge as well as seeking knowledge from foreign colleagues. Such measure shows the need to go outside national borders to achieve organizational goals.

Furthermore, top managers can play an important role in stimulating collaborative behaviors throughout the organization. As organizational members often take behavioral cues from the behavior of higher-ranked managers, top managers need to exemplify the desired collaborative behaviors. That is, top managers can contribute to an organizational culture that encourages collaboration by making it visible to the rest of the organization that they, too, collaborate. For this to be effective, the top management team must include managers from different geographical regions of the organization. Only then it can become obvious that different parts of the organization are important and that all need to be working together.

The relationship between the HQ and the foreign subsidiaries appropriate for the implementation of a transnational strategy tends to exhibit high levels of both structural differentiation and structural integration, a pattern called 'integrated variety'. High structural differentiation means that different foreign subsidiaries will have a different relationship with the HQ depending on the functions they are performing. As discussed in the structural anatomy section, some subsidiaries will be more decentralized to allow for a local response, while others will be more centralized to increase global efficiency. However, since the organization requires high levels of coordination to function properly, there should also be high structural integration. Such integration is best achieved through normative mechanisms or through different levels of rules and regulations for different parts of the organization, since uniform formal rules and regulations restrict local responsiveness. For instance, subsidiaries performing back-end operations to support global operation might be guided through more formal rules and regulations than sales subsidiaries that need to engage with local customers.

Reflection

As organizations increasingly compete in the global arena, they need to understand their strategic options. The main ways in which organizations can compete is either by attempting to maximize revenues through local adaptation or by attempting to minimize costs through global efficiencies. Ideally, organizations would capture the benefits of both strategic options. However, there is a tension between global efficiency and local adaption such that the pursuit of one tends to come at the expense of the other - this is the central tension organizations face when competing globally.

This chapter argues that due to an increasingly competitive business environment, organizations need to pursue both strategic options, although there might be a dominant one. That is, organizations can consider the strategic space and should ask whether they can improve their competitive positioning by increasing either local responsiveness or global efficiency. Regardless of which way they choose to further increase their competitiveness, they need to overcome the tension between local responsiveness and global efficiency. While difficult, the tension can be managed by: (i) promoting a mentality shift in global strategizing to incorporate strategic dualities; and (ii) implementing organizational design solutions. Organizations that can pursue both local responsiveness and global integration are competing using a transnational strategy. Although implementing a transnational strategy is very complex, it is very appealing to obtain the benefits of both strategic options.

The chapter also discussed in detail the organizational design solutions for overcoming the tension between local responsiveness and global efficiency. The fundamental logic is that the organizational design for the transnational strategy requires a varied set of structures and relationships. To stimulate local responsiveness, front-end operations can be decentralized, while to stimulate global efficiency, back-end operations can be globally integrated (e.g., using centers of excellence that leverage the advantages of a location throughout the global organization). Then, these globally dispersed operations need to be coordinated using formal and tacit coordination mechanisms and through the organizational culture.

Overall, while challenging, the tension between local responsiveness and global integration can be managed.

Future challenges

Looking to the future, organizations competing globally need to consider a few key points when devising and executing their transnational strategy.

Organizing for Global innovation. Increasingly, the survival of organizations depends on their ability to innovate. Even the best products and services become obsolete because the environment changes over time. So, the ability to compete with a transnational strategy is intrinsically linked with the ability to innovate. By design, organizations that can pursue both local responsiveness and global efficiency are well-positioned to innovate. However, not all can take advantage of their position due to several barriers to knowledge transfer.

There are three main activities required for innovation: (i) sensing a need; (ii) responding by garnering required resources; and (iii) implementation by bringing to market the new product or service. Transnational organizations have an international footprint and an organizational design that allows them to engage in these three activities in various patterns. The decentralized customer-facing subsidiaries can act as a sensing mechanism to provide information on different customer needs. Then, specialized resource can be brought together from various locations to develop a new product that can then be sold to customers in various countries. However, while there is great potential for innovation, the extent to which this potential is realized depends on whether organizations can overcome barriers to innovation (Mihalache et al. 2012).

The challenge for the transnational organization is to stimulate knowledge transfer. This is not an easy feat as there are many barriers related to both the willingness and ability to seek and provide help (Hansen and Nohria 2004). For many organizations, it is very challenging to put in place the proper incentives to convince people to share knowledge, as many perceive that providing knowledge results in loss of power. Similarly, some people are wary of asking for knowledge because this can signal that they are somehow deficient. There are also issues related to the ability to find the knowledge required. Due to geographical and cultural distance, people who look for knowledge might not know who to ask for help. The reverse is also true, as organizational members might be willing to provide help, but they don't know who would need the information they have.

Therefore, transnational organizations can leverage their international footprint to engage in global innovation, as this allows them to sense new customer needs, deploy global resources to develop products and services that satisfy those needs, and then leverage the new offering in a multitude of countries. However, to be able to do this, organizations need to implement mechanisms to overcome barriers to knowledge transfer.

'The only constant is change'. As the old saying states, the environment continuously changes. This poses challenges for both devising an appropriate strategy and for its global implementation. The biggest implication is that both strategy choice and implementation need to be considered as dynamic rather than static. Organizations, even when performing well, should not become complacent and consider their strategic position as ideal. A continuous improvement mentality is required for sustained performance and even survival. Take, for instance, the situation of changing customer tastes. Due to advancing globalization and ever greater media pervasiveness, in some industries, there is a homogenization of customer tastes. This means that organizations might be able to improve their performance by modifying their competitive positioning to adopt a position lower on local responsiveness and perhaps higher on global integration. However, this competitive move might find strong resistance from some organizational members. For instance, country managers might oppose moving decision-making from the country to the regional level. Such a strategic adjustment might also imply that country-level marketing staff are no longer needed, as a marketing campaign will be designed at the regional level. Change is difficult.

Furthermore, environmental change poses some very real issues for the implementation of the transnational strategy. As a fundamental principle of the transnational strategy is that organizations take advantage of country advantages, when these relative country advantages change there are tangible consequences for the organizational design. An example of this is raising wages in manufacturing hot spots. This was observed in China for instance, which experienced a sharp rise in wages over the last two decades. It can also happen that other locations develop new capabilities and challenge existing hot-spots, as is perhaps the case of the Philippines as a new rising location for outsourced IT work, or Vietnam for apparel manufacturing. The consequences of such changes in the comparative advantages of locations have implications for the execution of strategic options, as organizations might have to relocate operations to maximize their global efficiency (Mihalache and Mihalache 2016).

Therefore, managers should continuously consider the appropriateness of their organization's position in the global competitive space and challenge themselves to find ways to improve it. As environmental dynamism intensifies, the importance of making organizations more flexible will increase.

Learning and discussion questions

1 Why has there been an increase in organizations competing globally?
2 In what ways do countries differ?
3 What is different about competing globally versus competing domestically?
4 How do organizations choose between strategic options?
5 What are the four strategies for competing in the global arena?
6 What are the appropriate organizational designs for each of the four strategies?
7 How can the central tension of competing globally be resolved?
8 What are some future challenges of organizations competing globally?

Exercise: the international expansion of Tony's Chocolonely

Tony's Chocolonely is a chocolate producer headquartered in Amsterdam, the Netherlands. It was established in 2005 by Dutch investigative reporter Teun (Tony) van de Keuken with the ultimate mission of eliminating child labor and slavery from the chocolate industry. Tony made the decision to establish Tony Chocolonely when doing research on the cacao plantations in Ghana and the Ivory Coast and finding out that they used child slave labor. To fight against such practices, the three journalists wanted to show the world that you can be successful in the chocolate industry when acting ethically by creating a slave-free chocolate bar. To reflect this shift in practices, the company's stated mission is 'Together we'll make chocolate 100% slave-free'. To drive home to consumers that there is injustice in the chocolate industry, and by extension the world, Tony's signature chocolate bar has unequally divided pieces and includes a map of Western Africa.

Tony's Chocolonely has had great success and became the largest chocolate brand in the Netherlands with a 19% market share. To achieve its mission, the company must expand outside its home borders and it has started to do so aggressively. Following its first foray in international markets in 2005 in the US, Tony's entered Belgium, Denmark, Finland, Germany, Sweden, the United Kingdom, and Romania. As it continues its foreign expansion, Tony's Chocolonely is going to have to carefully consider its competitive strategy. Its ability to make the appropriate choices regarding its local responsiveness and global efficiency will affect whether it will be successful in achieving its mission of eliminating slavery from the chocolate industry.

Case questions

1. What key challenges will Tony's Chocolonely face when it further expands into new countries?
2. Which five countries would you advise Tony's to expand into?
3. What benefits can Tony's enjoy from local responsiveness? What about from global efficiency?
4. How can Tony's become more locally responsive while at the same time increase its global efficiency?

References

Bartlett, C., and Beamish, P. (2018). *Transnational Management: Text and Cases in Cross-Border Management* (8th ed.). Cambridge: Cambridge University Press.

Bartlett, C. A. and Ghoshal, S. (1990) 'Managing innovation in the transnational corporation'. In Bartlett, C. A., Doz, Y., and Hedlund, G. (eds.), *Managing the Global Firm*. Routledge: London, (215-255).

Begley, T. M., and Boyd, D. P. (2003) 'The need for a corporate global mind-set'. *MIT Sloan Management Review*, 44(2): 25.

Canadian Grocer. 'Kraft Heinz to shut Ontario factory'. Available online at http://www.canadiangrocer.com/top-stories/kraft-heinz-to-close-ontario-factory-59284 (accessed 25 May 2020).

Editor, B. (2015). 'Philips Lighting: achieving global scale with local relevance'. *Business Chief*. Available online at https://europe.businesschief.com/Philips-Lighting/profiles/116/Philips-Lighting:-achieving-global-scale-with-local-relevance (accessed 25 May 2020).

Frost, T. S., Birkinshaw, J. M., and Ensign, P. C. (2002). 'Centers of excellence in multinational corporations'. *Strategic Management Journal*, 23(11): 997-1018.

Ghemawat, P. 2007. 'Managing differences: The central challenge of global strategy'. *Harvard Business Review*, 85(3): 58–68.

Ghoshal, S. and Nohria, N. (1993). 'Horses for courses: Organizational forms for multinational corporations'. *Sloan Management Review*, 34(2): 23.

Hansen, M. T. and Nohria, N. (2004). 'How to build collaborative advantage'. *MIT Sloan Management Review*, 46(1): 22.

Johnson, B. (2011). 'The CEO of Heinz on powering growth in emerging markets'. *Harvard Business Review*, 89(10): 47–50.

Kumar, N. and Puranam, P. (2011). 'Have you restructured for global success?' *Harvard Business Review*, 89(10): 123.

Lessard, D., Lucea, R., and Vives, L. (2013). 'Building your company's capabilities through global expansion'. *MIT Sloan Management Review*, 54(2): 61–67.

Levitt, T. (1965). 'Exploit the product life cycle'. *Harvard Business Review*, 43: 81–94.

Lu, J. and Beamish, P. (2004). 'International diversification and firm performance: The S-curve hypothesis'. *Academy of Management Journal*, 47(4): 598–609.

Martinez, R. (2020). 'Top 10 global supply chain risks. Supply Chain Digital'. Available online at https://www.supplychaindigital.com/top10/top-10-global-supply-chain-risks (accessed 25 June 2020).

Meijer, B. (2019). 'Philips to close its UK factory in 2020, with loss of 400 jobs'. *Reuters*. Available online at https://www.reuters.com/article/us-philips-restructuring-eu/philips-to-close-its-uk-factory-in-2020-with-loss-of-400-jobs-idUSKCN1PB201 (accessed 12 March 2020).

Mihalache, O. R., Jansen, J. J., Van Den Bosch, F. A., and Volberda, H. W. (2012). 'Offshoring and firm innovation: The moderating role of top management team attributes'. *Strategic Management Journal*, 33(13): 1480–1498.

Mihalache, M. and Mihalache, O. R. (2016). 'A decisional framework of offshoring: integrating insights from 25 years of research to provide direction for future'. *Decision Sciences*, 47(6): 1103–1149.

Muller, D. (2018). 'Emerging Markets – Powerhouse of global growth'. Available online at http://www.ashmoregroup.com/sites/default/files/article-docs/MC_10%20May18_2.pdf (accessed 30 July 2020).

Schug, D. (2017). 'How Ben & Jerry's successfully manages its plants'. *Food Engineering Magazine*. Available online at https://www.foodengineeringmag.com/articles/97116-how-ben-jerrys-successfully-manages-its-plants (accessed 20 March 2020).

Tallman, S., Luo, Y., and Buckley, P. J. (2018). Business models in global competition. *Global Strategy Journal*, 8(4): 517–535.

Tesla. (2014). 'Gigafactory Tesla'. Available online at https://www.tesla.com/fr_FR/gigafactory?redirect=no (accessed 10 January 2020).

Tucker, R. (2020). 'Biggest supply chain risks in 2020'. *MXmove*. Available online at https://www.mixmove.io/blog/biggest-supply-chain-risks-in-2020?gclid=EAIaIQobChMIy-OQvIHt6gIVmrp3Ch1egI1EAAYAiAAEgInQfD_BwE (accessed 25 June 2020).

3 Transformative entrepreneurship

Enno Masurel[1]

Summary

Chapter 3 focuses on transformative entrepreneurship during the life cycle of the (small) firm, i.e., how the roles exercised by the entrepreneur transform as the firm develops, or should transform in order to avoid tension within the firm. Specifically, the chapter details how the relationship among entrepreneurial roles, strategic elements, and firm size develops as time moves on, and what kind of instability appears when the proper balance between these three phenomena does not take place. Subsequently, to grasp transformative entrepreneurship, the basic concept of the life cycle of the small firm is explained, followed by a discussion on the tension between stability and change. This foundation makes it possible to make inferences about three sets of iterative relationships: (1) firm size and strategic elements; (2) firm size and entrepreneurial roles; and (3) strategic elements and entrepreneurial roles. Extending beyond these insights, we reflect on freedom of choice for entrepreneurs, followed by the transformative entrepreneurship lessons.

Case: the development of Optics11

In 2016, Optics11 was one of the most innovative small- and medium-sized enterprises (SMEs) in the Netherlands. In that year the firm ranked seventh in the Netherlands and second in Amsterdam on the list of the most innovative SMEs compiled by the Dutch Chamber of Commerce and the leading Dutch newspaper *De Financiële Telegraaf*. Since then, the firm has continued to improve its innovative character.

Optics11 was founded in April 2011 by physical scientist Davide Iannuzzi and serial entrepreneur Hans Brouwer. Hans and Davide met for the first time in 2010. At the time that Optics11 was founded, Davide was an assistant professor (he is currently a full professor at Vrije Universiteit, Amsterdam, a position he has held since 2013) who saw an opportunity to valorize (or commercialize) his academic knowledge together with Hans. At that time, Hans was (and remains) a serial entrepreneur who had developed multiple businesses and saw a good business opportunity in starting Optics11 together with Davide. The two had an instant sense of mutual trust, despite Davide being clearly more academically oriented than business-oriented, and Hans being the opposite. Davide had already been thinking seriously about starting his own firm for a long time, even before 2011. Nevertheless, he acknowledged that his great academic interest and his predominantly risk-averse attitude might not be conducive for starting and developing his own firm. However, these drawbacks were greatly reduced by the collaboration with Hans, who clearly had the entrepreneurial talent to overcome them.

The business model of Optics11 is grounded in one of Davide's major scientific inventions, which allows scientists to assess the mechanical properties of cells and tissues with an easy, fast, and reproducible approach. Thanks to Optics11's instruments, researchers all over the world have been able to perform novel experiments that have contributed to a better understanding of the role of mechanics, especially in the life sciences. Optics11 aims to build optical fiber-sensing systems that are best-in-class, and also easy and flexible to use, by building on its core technologies, which are fiber interferometry and micro-manufacturing. One of the major strengths of Optics11 is its fast and lean product development, which is enabled by its broad range of engineering skills, mainly fiber optics, analog and digital electronics, software, micro-manufacturing, mechanics, and mechatronics.

Optics11 currently consists of two business units, each with its own research and development (R&D) group and its own sales team. The 'life sciences' business unit is the oldest and most developed one of the two units. The 'remote sensing' unit is the younger of the two, but is developing more than the life sciences unit. The user and buyer markets for the two business units differ significantly, and the technology used by both business units overlaps only partially. A typical example of the life sciences unit is a table-top measurement instrument, while a typical project in the remote sensing unit is a feasibility study.

The first row in Table 3.1 shows the development of Optics11 in terms of its number of employees. The table shows that, after a cautious start, the growth curve of Optics 11 becomes much steeper. The same situation applies to the level of sales (see Table 3.1, second row): again, after a cautious start, the growth curve of Optics11 rises steeply. Optics11 started with 100 percent of its sales from the life sciences unit. In 2016, the life sciences unit represented approximately 80 percent of total sales, with the remote sensing unit accounting for the other 20 percent. In 2017, the estimated shares were two-thirds and one-third, respectively. This development of the two business units symbolizes an increasing diversification in the sales composition of Optics11.

In 2017, Optics11 had 18 full-time equivalent employees, two-thirds of whom were technical employees (approximately 80 percent development staff and 20 percent production staff). In 2017, fewer than 25 percent of Optics11's employees were working as sales staff, and about 10 percent worked as support staff. The main development in the employment of Optics11 over the years has been the growth in the share of the support staff.

Table 3.1 Development of Optics11 (2011-2017)

Year	2011	2012	2013	2014	2015	2016	2017 est.
Employees	0	1	2.5	4.7	5.9	11.7	18.0
Sales (€1,000)	0	67	18	297	487	1,043	1,600

Questions:

1 As Optics11 grew, how did the founders' roles change and how would this have impacted organizational change?
2 Growth requires change, yet unlimited change may invoke instability. Focusing on Optics11, what could the founders have done to resolve this tension?

Source: Masurel (2017).

Learning objectives

After studying this chapter, the reader will have:

1 A basic understanding of transformative entrepreneurship and the life cycle of the small firm.
2 A deeper insight in the stability-change tension inherently tied to firm growth.
3 An understanding of the iterative relationships among firm size, strategic elements, and entrepreneurial roles.
4 Knowledge of lessons for entrepreneurs of small and established firms with regard to adopting entrepreneurship practices.

Introduction to transformative entrepreneurship

In the United States, 44 percent of all start-ups fail within the first five years of their existence (measured over the period 2014-2018; Mansfield 2019). Why is this number so high? The main standard explanations are 'no market need' (42 percent), 'ran out of cash' (29 percent), and 'not the right team' (23 percent) (Mansfield 2019). These explanations may sound obvious, but there could be other reasons. Firm termination may result from misalignment between the size of the firm and the characteristics of the firm and the role(s) that the entrepreneur of the firm exercises, as time passes. That is, firms fail to survive when they fail to successfully manage transitions through their life stages as they grow.

The ***essence of entrepreneurship*** is the 'identification and exploitation of previously unexploited opportunities' (Hitt et al. 2001: 480). Pursuing new opportunities implies a focus on growth. However, as this chapter shows, entrepreneurial firms' ability to grow depends not only on identifying and pursuing opportunities, but also on how the change associated with growth is balanced with the stability required for exploiting firm competencies. In other words, to be able to grow and survive, an entrepreneurial firm must balance change with stability. This is an existential challenge because attempting to change as part of the process of pursuing new opportunities can create an internal imbalance with the current way of operating. This imbalance is based on the iterative relationships among firm size, strategic elements, and entrepreneurial roles.

Ensuring alignment among firm size, strategic elements, and entrepreneurial roles refers to the processes that underpin transformative entrepreneurship; namely, the right balance of the roles exercised by the entrepreneur against the background of his/her firm. If the right balance is not found, firm termination is likely; this is, in fact, a disruption of the life cycle of the small firm. A deeper understanding of the aforementioned iterative relationships may lead to a decreased failure rate of small firms during the early days of their existence, but also to an increase of the wellbeing of the main people behind these small firms; that is, the entrepreneurs or the owner-managers. The latter are explicitly mentioned here because the failure of small firms is not an abstract phenomenon, but this failure may have dramatic and stressful consequences for the lives of the most involved people in this context: the entrepreneurs who once owned and managed these firms. These consequences occur in both their professional lives and their personal lives.

Like a living organism, the small firm is conceived at a certain moment in time and then develops through a number of consecutive stages. In general, these stages are start-up, scale-up (also called growth), maturity, and decline. These four stages are not just clinical distinctions; going through these stages brings about major changes in the firm, in terms of sales diversification, employment dispersion, and financing structure. These four stages also involve (or, at least, should involve) major changes in the roles that entrepreneurs exercise, in terms of being a professional, a leader, and a manager.

Whereas extant studies have investigated the influencing role of entrepreneurship for firm growth (see, e.g., Zhou, Huang and Kuo 2018), the present chapter also takes the reversed pattern into account, i.e., the influencing role of firm growth for entrepreneurship. Akin to McKelvie and Wiklund (2010), we make a distinction between growth as an outcome - in which firm growth is in fact the dependent variable, where the focus is on the factors that determine firm growth - and the outcome of growth - in which firm growth is the independent variable, where the focus is on the changes that result from firm growth.

Tension: stability versus change

The well-known axiom that 'the only constant is change' reflects the fact that firms move through different stages as they grow. Long-term survival requires firms to successfully transition through the various life stages. That is, even firms that provide products and services desired by the market can become extinct if they fail to manage life-stage transitions. This is particularly difficult because of the underlying tension between stability and change.

This central tension is caused by the fact that long-term survival requires firms to engage in both advantage-seeking and opportunity-seeking (Ireland and Webb 2007). Whereas advantage-seeking is associated with stability and exploitation of current capabilities, opportunity-seeking is associated with change and growth from new opportunities. These two activities contradict one another because one reinforces the status quo, while the other challenges it. Since neither activity alone is sufficient for long-term survival, firms need to find ways to manage the tension in order to survive.

This ***stability-change tension*** is perhaps most clearly felt as a small firm grows and attempts to transition through the life stage. As the firm is structured in a way that is appropriate for its current way of operating, growing requires it to adopt different structures that are incompatible with the current situation. Disruption of the life cycle of the small firm is caused by an imbalance between firm size (as a result of firm growth), strategic elements, and exercised entrepreneurial roles.

The stability-change tension materializes in an imbalance in the organizational structure, as growth comes with new organizing logics that can be incompatible with existing ones as the entrepreneurial firms attempt to move through their life stages. For instance, the need for centralization vs. decentralization in the organizational structure depends on the firm's current life stage. As entrepreneurial firms aim to balance opportunity-seeking with advantage-seeking, they need to resolve the tension in their structure as the former requires less centralization and the latter requires more centralization (Jansen, Van Den Bosch and Volberda 2006). As it transitions through the life stages, the entrepreneurial firm must adjust its structure. While most firms tend to focus on opportunity-seeking during the start-up stage, they can benefit from more decentralized ways of organizing to help with opportunity recognition and faster action. However, advancing through the life stages, as they also need to shift attention to exploiting current capabilities, the need for centralization rises, as it allows for increased efficiency. The stability-change tension as it manifests in the need to balance centralization-decentralization is also felt during the maturity stage of the firm, as it attempts to prevent decline by combining the exploitation of current opportunities with the exploration of new ones.

The stability-change tension also materializes in tensions in the roles and expected competencies of organizational members. The stability-change tension creates an imbalance in the leadership roles required as the firm shifts its focus between opportunity-seeking and advantage-seeking. An example of this is the appropriateness of different leadership styles. Research shows that transformation leadership is more effective in stimulating exploratory activities associated with change, while transactional leadership is more effective for exploitation activities associated with stability (Jansen, Vera and Crossan 2009). Extending this to entrepreneurial firms as they transition through the life stages, the roles of the leaders (who are often the founders) need to transform.

Thus, in order to survive in the long-term, entrepreneurial firms need to manage the stability-change tension as they grow and transition through the life stages. This requires an understanding of the dynamics between the firm's size and structure and entrepreneurs' roles. The next section describes the firm's life stages and the interplay between the firm's elements as underpinned by the stability-change tension.

Understanding the firm's life cycle

The origins of thinking in terms of a life cycle of the small firm go back to the biological sciences, the branch of science that can be seen in general as the science of life. The biology sciences study living organisms and how living organisms develop through different stages in time, from cradle (and even before) to grave (and beyond).

In general, a firm is an organizational entity, but it can also be interpreted as a place of working. Frequently used synonyms for the noun *firm* are *company*, *venture*, and *business*. However, the focus in this chapter is not on the firm in general, but on the small firm. Small firms can be distinguished from large firms in terms of size, along with quantitative aspects such as the number of employees, level of sales, and value of assets.

Along with quantitative aspects, the qualitative aspects of small firms can also be distinguished: apart from their size, how do small firms look different compared to large firms?

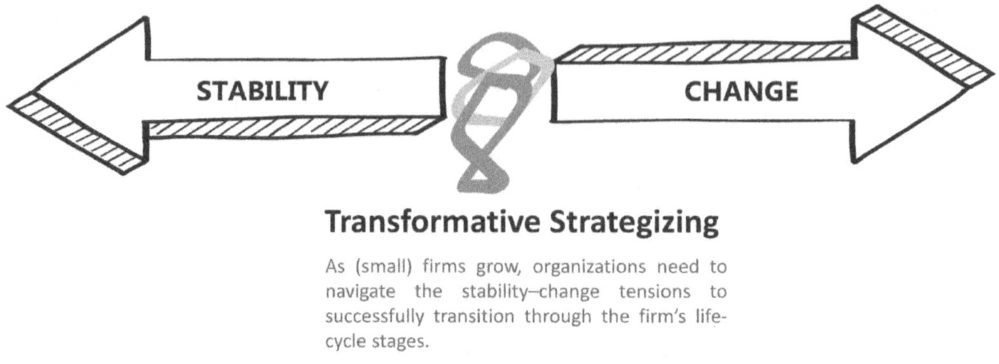

Figure 3.1 Stability-change tension

Several decades on, the title of the paper by Welsh and White (1981) remains telling: 'A small business is not a little big business'. The authors emphasized the role of resource poverty for small firms, but there is more to being small in this context. There are eight main, general, and interacting qualitative aspects of small firms (see also Masurel 2019: section 1.4.2): (i) the prominent role of the entrepreneur (as he/she is both the owner and the daily manager of the firm); (ii) the focus on the short-term (although small firms may live for a long time); (iii) the strong regional/local focus (small firms comprise part of the regional/local landscape); (iv) the complicated performance measurement (small firms use a broad palette of performance measures); (v) the high prevalence of family businesses (despite the lack of consensus on the best definition of a family business); (vi) the simple organograms or organization charts (as small firms do not have a complicated way of doing business); (vii) the low degree of formalization (because of the small firm size and the direct role of the entrepreneur in the daily process); and (viii) the high importance of umbrella organizations (like trade-associations and business incubators, in order to create scale economies).

The general concept of the life cycle of the small firm is presented in Figure 3.2. As well as being based on the biological sciences, this approach of the life cycle is also based on the product life cycle concept that is often used in marketing in order to analyze the rise and fall of products. The key to this approach of the life cycle of the small firm is that the small firm, when it develops, follows a combination of time and size, the two factors that are represented on the horizontal axis and the vertical axis, respectively. Time and size can be interpreted as abstract measures, but they can also be interpreted in a more, or even very, concise way. Concerning the horizontal axis, years and months are the most obvious and specific measures of time in this context. Concerning the vertical axis, Shepherd and Wiklund (2013) argued that sales and employment[2] are the most frequently used measures of growth of firms (growth is delta size, so to say), followed by profit and equity/assets. Development of firm size always needs time, but time does not necessarily need development of firm size nor does time necessarily lead to development of firm size. Therefore, in the remainder of this chapter, we do not refer to development of size in time, but only of development in size, or in similar terms.

After its conception, a small firm generally passes through four distinct stages: (i) start-up; (ii) scale-up (or growth); (iii) maturity; and (iv) decline. The scale-up stage is different from the start-up stage in the sense that both time and size have progressed. The maturity stage is different from the scale-up stage, again in the sense that both time and size have progressed, also when compared with the start-up stage. The decline stage is different from the maturity stage in the sense that time has progressed but that size has regressed. The difference in time also counts for the comparison with the start-up stage and the scale-up stage, but then the difference in size is not always clear. In other words, firms in the decline stage are smaller than firms in the maturity stage, but not much can be said about whether firms in the decline stage are smaller or bigger than firms in the start-up stage or in the scale-up stage.

This distinction into the four stages of start-up, scale-up, maturity, and decline is more or less the standard when discussing the life cycle of the small firm (on the basis of the literature from previous decades). In practice, however, a number of different indications and labels are used as well, such as courtship, infant organization, go-go, adolescent, entrepreneurial stage, collectivity stage, formalization and control stage, structure elaboration and adaptation stage, survival, expansion, high growth, existence, disengage, early growth, rapid growth, early diversification, formation, late growth, and stability (see Masurel and Van Montfort 2006). Some of these terms even go back decades (the seminal work in the life cycle of the small firm is most probably that of Churchill and Lewis 1983). According to Levie and Lichtenstein (2010), the majority of studies in stages models include three, four, or five stages. However, the present chapter sticks to the more-or-less standard approach of start-up, scale-up, maturity, and decline.

However, this ***life cycle approach*** to the small firm hardly has any predictive value for the sequence of the four development stages. That approach does not imply that the scale-up stage automatically follows the start-up stage, nor that the maturity stage automatically follows the scale-up stage, nor that the decline stage automatically follows the maturity stage. The start-up stage may be followed or interrupted by a maturity stage

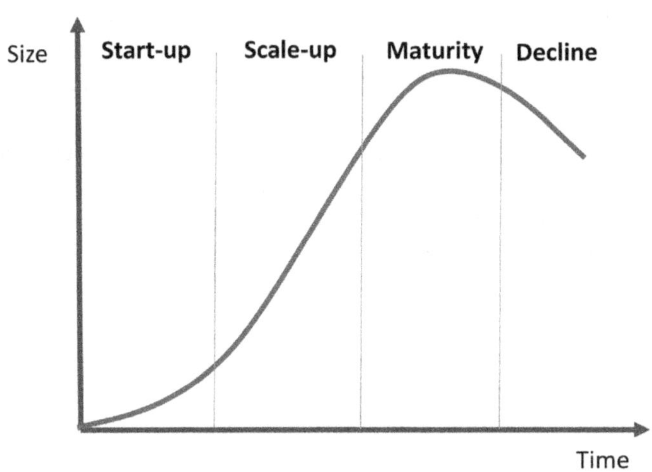

Figure 3.2 The life cycle of the small firm

or even by a decline stage, instead of being followed by the scale-up stage. The scale-up stage may be followed or interrupted by a decline stage or a new start-up stage, instead of being followed by the maturity stage. The maturity stage may be followed or interrupted by a new scale-up stage or a new start-up stage, instead of being followed by the decline stage. The decline stage may be followed or interrupted by a new maturity stage, a new scale-up stage or a new start-up stage, instead of being followed by the finalization of the small firm. All in all, prematurity and relaunch are also options in the life cycle of the small firm.

As with any life cycle, obstacles may be encountered with the further development of the small firm. According to Lougui and Nyström (2014), the main obstacles that entrepreneurs encounter when starting and running a business are general information and training, taxes, permits and laws, and consulting requests. Also as with any life cycle, the life cycle of the small firms ends with the exit. Detienne (2010: 204) called this the 'entrepreneurial exit' and defined it as 'the process by which the founders of privately held firms leave the firm they helped to create; thereby removing themselves, in varying degree, from the primary ownership and decision-making structure of the firm'. She mentioned three forms of entrepreneurial exit: market exit, technological exit, and form exit.

Box 3.1 Upscaling and unicorns

In contemporary business literature, upscaling is considered a critical strategic topic. Upscaling a business (unit) means that growth is accelerated without suffering in other areas (such as employee turnover because of heavy workloads or a product that cannot be produced quickly enough to meet demand). When companies upscale, they add revenue at a faster rate than they take on new costs. The company's gains outpace its losses. The key to upscaling is that a business attracts and keeps the right people to protect the company's core values, creates a truly differentiated strategy, drives flawless execution, and has deep pockets to maintain investment levels. To effectively scale up, the organizational infrastructure needs to be able to handle growth, and the business needs to address competitive pressures that build (and erode) margins as scaling progresses.

A specific manifestation of successful upscaling has been termed a ***unicorn***, which refers to a privately owned start-up with a valuation exceeding US$1 billion. Notable examples of unicorns include home-sharing giant Airbnb, video game company Epic Games, and fintech companies Robinhood and SoFi. Aileen Lee first wrote about unicorns in her article 'Welcome to the unicorn club: learning from billion-dollar startups'. She investigated software start-ups founded in the 2000s and estimated that only 0.07 percent of them ever reach US$1 billion valuation; finding such a start-up is therefore similar to finding a mythical unicorn. Since then, the term unicorn has become widely used to refer to start-ups in the technology sector.

Source: Lee (2013)

Different strategic elements

As a small firm develops through the different stages of its life cycle, the firm will not remain the same; on the contrary, the firm will change, content-wise. It was already within the definition of the life cycle of the small firm that different stages connected different ages and different sizes of the small firm. In other words, as a small firm develops during its life cycle, it becomes older and larger, and in the end it becomes older and smaller. In this section, the focus is on the change in three strategic elements during the respective life cycle stages - namely, alteration of diversification of sales, alteration of dispersion of employment, and alteration of the financing of the firm.

A first element is the ***diversification of sales***. At its conception, a small firm generally starts with only one target group or market, or at best a very limited set of target groups or markets. As the firm grows bigger, from start-up to scale-up to maturity, more risk reduction within the firm is needed so that the firm does not become too vulnerable. This increase in risk reduction can be achieved by diversification of sales over multiple markets. In the decline stage, the older firm reduces its size and goes back to a very limited set of markets, or perhaps even to only one market. This pattern of sales diversification (working at more markets as the small firm develops from start-up to maturity, through scale-up, and finally working in fewer markets as the small firm develops from maturity to decline) is empirically confirmed in the paper by Masurel and Van Montfort (2006).

Consider the example of a painter who starts his/her own painting company. At the start of the firm, the founder only paints houses, but then, as the firm grows, starts painting office buildings and factories as well. In the decline stage, the company reduces the number of types of objects that it paints, and in the final days of the firm, the painting company returns to only painting houses, as it had in the start-up stage.

The second strategic element that changes during the life cycle of the small firm is ***dispersion in employment***. If the firm is founded by just one person, then the dispersion in employment by definition is zero. As sales diversification increases as the firm grows, different employees must be attracted in order to service the different markets and to exercise the different activities; these are not so much clones of the current people, but real different people. In the decline stage, fewer markets are serviced (or even only one market is serviced) and fewer activities are exercised (or even only one activity is exercised), so fewer different people are needed to maintain the company. This pattern of employment dispersion (more diverse employment as the firm develops from start-up to maturity, through scale-up, and less diverse employment as the small firm develops from maturity to decline) is also empirically confirmed in the paper by Masurel and Van Montfort (2006).

In the abovementioned example of the painting company, specialists are attracted by the firm, to paint the office buildings and the factories, along with the founder, who is a specialist in painting houses only. Also, the office of the painting company has to be staffed when the firm develops; for example, with an office manager and a bookkeeper. In the decline stage, the company reduces the types of objects that it paints and, in the final days of the small firm, only paints houses again; the specialists who were once attracted to paint the office buildings and the factories have left the firm, leaving the founder alone. The increasing sales diversification and employment dispersion, as the firm develops, are confirmed in the first case in this chapter (about Optics11).

The third strategic element of the small firm that changes during the life cycle is the formality of the ***financing of the firm***. Jones, MacPherson, and Jayawarna (2014) presented an interesting overview of financing the small firm in the next sequence in time: seed → start-up → early growth → established (the horizontal axis was labeled 'stage of development of entrepreneurial firm' and can also be interpreted as simply 'time'). The authors suggested a decreasing level of informality (or, an increasing level of formality) with the investors of the firm during the life cycle of the small firm, because the level of investment risk assumed by investors (the entity on the vertical axis) decreases as the firm develops; in fact, as the firm proves its viability over time.

Jones et al. (2014) distinguished the next sequential string of financing forms, without really defining most of them (most additions below are by the author of the present chapter): personal finance (such as personal savings or a mortgage on the own house of the founder of the firm); family and friends (apparently because they want to help their family member or their friend, not so much because they expect that it will make them rich); bootstrapping ('a range of activities aimed at absorbing and borrowing resources at no/low financial cost from the entrepreneur's social networks', Jones et al. (2014: 127)); internal funding (also called retained earnings or profits that are kept within the firm); seed capital (public/grant funding, according to Jones et al. 2014); business angels (independent individuals who provide capital for the development of small firms); formal venture capitalists (professionals investors that invest in small firms with high growth potential); non-financial corporations (that do not specifically focus on small firms to invest in, but do so because it fits in their interests); commercial banks (regular banks); and finally initial public offering (IPO: going to the stock exchange). The decline stage is not incorporated in Jones et al.'s (2014) overview. However, it can be assumed that when the small firm declines, the rather informal forms of financing - internal funding, bootstrapping, family and friends, and personal finance - gain importance again, as investors that are more formal will not have much confidence in the future of the declining firm.

Different entrepreneurial roles

However, it is not only the characteristics of the small firm that change as it develops through the different stages of its life cycle; the entrepreneur also transforms (or, at least, should transform) as the small firm develops through the different stages of its life cycle. Next, we focus on the transformation of the roles of the entrepreneur that he or she exercises during the life cycle of the small firm, namely, the roles of professional, leader, and manager.

As a ***professional***, the entrepreneur works directly on the job and takes care of the sales himself/herself. Among the other main activities of the entrepreneur in the professional role are quality control and keeping up to date with industry developments. As a ***leader***, the entrepreneur gives direction to the development of the firm and formulates the long-term goals of the firm. Another important activity is conducting analyses of the firm (such as SWOT analyses, where S = current internal strengths of the firm, W = current internal weaknesses of the firm, O = future external opportunities to the firm, T = future external threats to the firm). As a manager the entrepreneur ensures that the firm's employees come into daily action and do the things that they have to do. Other main activities of the entrepreneur in the management role are to control and to solve conflicts, both within the firm and in relation to the firm towards stakeholders, and to create decision-making processes at the firm level.

> The roles exercised by the entrepreneur are, like the firm itself, dynamic and not static. This is also known as transformative entrepreneurship.

However, it is important to realize that the roles that are exercised by the entrepreneur are connected to the development stages of the firm. In other words, the roles exercised by the entrepreneur are, like the firm itself, dynamic and not static. This is also known as transformative entrepreneurship. In this context, three propositions can be defended. First, in the start-up stage, the entrepreneurial role of the professional is the most important one. In this stage, the entrepreneur is often the only employed person at the firm, or one of the few employed persons, yet the daily work still has to be done, so it is obvious who has to do that. While the entrepreneurial role of the professional is the most important one at this stage, this positioning does not exclude minor entrepreneurial roles of the leader and the manager. During the growth stage, the entrepreneurial role of the leader is the most important one, as the entrepreneur must make important choices about the future development of the firm. However, this positioning does not exclude minor entrepreneurial roles of the professional and the manager. In the maturity stage, as the entrepreneur has attracted an increased number of employees, the entrepreneurial role of the manager is the most important one. However, this positioning does not exclude minor entrepreneurial roles of the professional and the leader in this stage.

The situation is somewhat more complicated during the decline stage, as the firm is often in jeopardy and busy with ceasing operations. In principle, however, the entrepreneurial role of the professional is the most important one in this stage, as the entrepreneur is one of the few remaining employed persons, if not the only one, and daily work remains to be done. In this sense, the decline stage is quite similar to the start-up stage. However, this positioning does not exclude minor entrepreneurial roles of the leader and the manager. Because what is happening in the decline stage is rather unpredictable, this stage in the life cycle of the small firm is not considered in the remainder of this chapter. This is also the reason why the life cycle of the small firm in Figure 3.1 ends somewhere in the air: the decline may be abrupt or smooth, delayed, or accelerated.

The interplay among firm size, strategic elements, and entrepreneurial roles

Now that we have discussed the differences in the strategic elements and the differences in the entrepreneurial roles in the different combinations of age and size of the firm, it is time to look at the causal relationships: to what extent do more sales diversification, more employment dispersion, more finance formality, and a greater leadership and management role lead

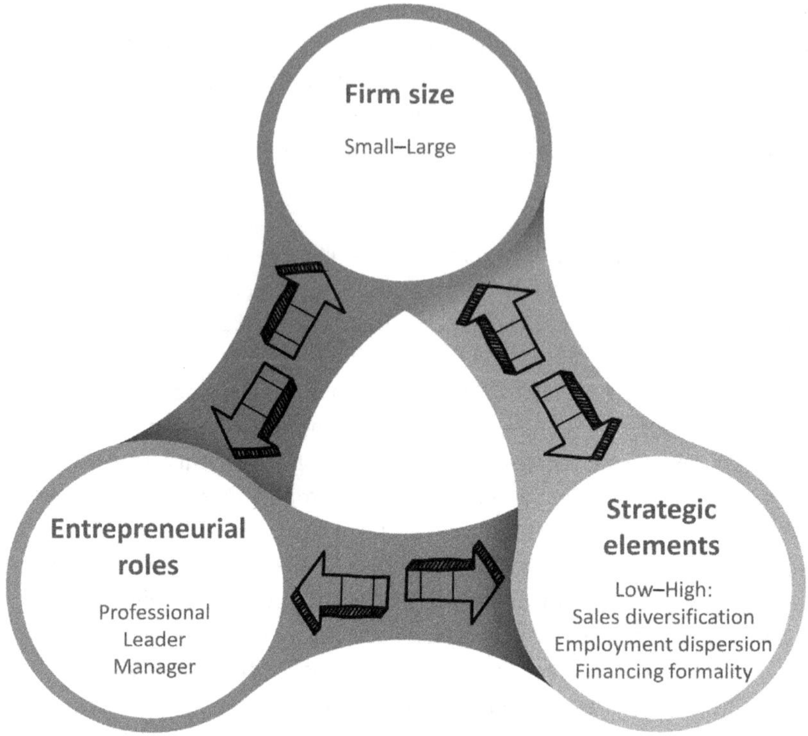

Figure 3.3 The interplay between firm size, strategic elements, and entrepreneurial roles

to an increase in firm size? Or is the situation reversed: does an increase in size of the firm lead to more sales diversification, more employment dispersion, more finance formality, and a greater leadership and management role? And how about the causal relationship between the strategic elements and the entrepreneurial roles between themselves? Each of the next three sections will deal with one these three causality issues. Figure 3.3 provides a visual of the relationships.

Iterative relationships #1: firm size and strategic elements

The first important reflection to be made in the context of this chapter concerns the following causality: does the development of the small firm in its life cycle lead to change in the strategic elements, or, conversely, does change in the strategic elements of the firm propel the development of the small firm in its life cycle?

First, it makes sense to defend the proposition that an increased size of the small firm enables sales diversification of the firm, because the grown small firm is able to enter more markets and markets are, by definition, not homogenous. There is also an incentive for the grown small firm to increase sales diversification, and that is risk-reduction; in other words: to reduce the risk by working with a portfolio of multiple markets.

Second, it also makes sense to defend the proposition that increased size of the small firm enables employment dispersion of the firm, because the grown small firm is able to hire more employees and employees are, by definition, not homogenous. There is also an incentive for the grown small firm to increase employment dispersion, and that is division of labor over different kind of employees, in order to improve the productivity of the firm.

Third, it also makes sense to defend the proposition that increased size of the small firm enables more formality in financing of the firm, because the grown small firm has proven its right to exist over time, which makes the firm more attractive to investors, especially those that are more formal. Put another way, the firm has proven its rationale for existence, which decreases the level of investment risk assumed by investors.

However, this raises the question of whether it also works in the other direction? Do more sales diversification, more employment dispersion, and more financing formality lead to small-firm growth? The direction of the answer to these questions is again positive, as the next three propositions can be defended as well. That is:

- More sales diversification contributes to growth of the small firm in time, as more markets can be tapped
- More employment dispersion contributes to growth of the small firm, as more segments in the labor market can be tapped
- More financing formality contributes to growth of the small firm, as more financing institutions can be tapped.

Therefore, we can speak of an iterative relationship between the development of the small firm in terms of size, on the one hand, and the change of the small firm in terms of sales diversification, employment dispersion, and more formal investment, on the other. In brief: A leads to B and B also leads to A. The question arises as to where the relationship between the development of the small firm in terms of size, on the one hand, and change in the strategic elements, on the other, starts? Does the relationship start with the development of the small firm in terms of size, or does it start with change in the strategic elements? This iterative relationship is something of a chicken-and-egg question.

Iterative relationships #2: firm size and entrepreneurial roles

The second important reflection to be made in the context of this chapter concerns the following causality: does size development of the small firm lead to the exercising of different roles by the entrepreneur, or, conversely, does the exercising of different roles by the entrepreneur lead to size development of the small firm?

First, it makes sense to defend the proposition that increased size of the small firm leads to more leadership by the entrepreneur, because the grown size of the small firm offers more room for leadership activities. There is also an incentive for more leadership within the larger firm, as the entrepreneur needs to make more strategic choices. The increasing importance of the leadership role comes at the cost of the professional role when the small firm grows over time, but does not necessarily exclude the professional role. This is because, the entrepreneur may choose to attract staff with complementary skill sets, enabling her/him to remain committed to her/his profession.

Second, it makes sense to defend the proposition that increased size of the small firm thereafter leads to more management by the entrepreneur, because the grown small firm offers more room for management activities. There is also an incentive for more management with the larger small firm, as a larger firm requires more control, including procedures, rules, regulations, and monitoring. The increasing importance of the management role comes at the cost of the leadership role, as it is difficulty to enact management and leadership simultaneously; that is, each role necessitates unique and distinct skills. Nonetheless, a management role does not necessarily exclude the leadership role or the professional role.

However, questions again arise as to whether it also works in the other way. Does more attention for leadership by the entrepreneur lead to more firm growth? Does more attention for management by the entrepreneur lead to more firm growth thereafter? The direction of the answer to these questions is again positive, as the next two propositions can be defended as well:

- More leadership contributes to growth of the firm as a leader makes strategic choices to further the development of the firm
- More management contributes to growth of the firm as a manager makes coordination choices to further the control of the company.

Therefore, we can again speak of an iterative relationship, now between the development of the small firm in terms of size and transformation of the roles that are exercised by the entrepreneur. In brief, A leads to C and C also leads to A. A related question then arises, as it did with the first causality issue: where does the relationship start between the development of the firm and the transformation of the roles that the entrepreneur exercises? Does the relationship start with the development of the firm in terms of size or with the transformation of the roles that the entrepreneur exercises? This is another chicken-and-egg question.

Iterative relationships #3: strategic elements and entrepreneurial roles

The third important reflection to be made in the context of this chapter refers to the following causality: does change in the strategic elements lead to the exercising of different roles of the entrepreneur? Or, conversely, does the exercising of different roles of the entrepreneur lead to a change in the firm's characteristics?

First, it makes sense to defend the proposition that change in the strategic elements leads to different roles of the entrepreneur. Specifically, a small firm with higher sales diversity needs a leader who is able to make strategic choices (i.e. push new markets and offerings) for the development of the firm. Similarly, a small firm with higher employment dispersion needs a manager who is able to efficiently organize the company, to maintain cost efficiency. A small firm with higher finance formality does not thrive with somebody in charge who is primarily a professional. Instead, investors tend to favor charismatic leaders who are able to lead an efficient organization.

Second, it makes sense to defend the proposition that different roles of the entrepreneur also lead to a change in the strategic elements. A leader makes strategic decisions that seek to increase sales diversity, instead of remaining with the original focus of the small firm. Or, a manager imposing control to the company after the dynamic road of the growth stage may invoke employee dispersion (i.e. new units and hierarchical layers). However, a professional works directly on the job and therefore may not have a clear eye on sales diversity, on employment dispersion, or on ways to attract more formal financers to the firm.

Therefore, we can again refer to an iterative relationship, now between change in the strategic elements and the exercising of different roles by the entrepreneur. In brief, generally speaking, B leads to C and C also leads to B. As with the two previous causality issues, the chicken-and-egg question arises as to where the relationship starts between the change in the strategic elements and the transformation of the entrepreneurial roles. Does it start with the change of strategic elements or with the exercising of different roles by the entrepreneur?

Reflection

The need for growth?

Overall, a system of three iterative relationships appears when the firm grows. Changes in firm size, strategic elements, and entrepreneurial roles intervene with each other. The three causal relationships all appear to be iterative relationships, with causality running in both directions. These iterative relationships explain why and how the business model changes over time when the small firm grows.

Now that it has been reasoned how and why the changes during the life cycle of the small firm take place, the question remains as to whether it can be stated that these changes *should* take place, in a normative way. Are these changes unavoidable? If so, what are the consequences if these changes do not take place? It is obvious that a growing firm needs more diversification in sales, needs more dispersion in employment, and needs more formal forms of financing, because otherwise the firm gets out of balance. It is also obvious that a growing firm needs more leadership and more management from the entrepreneur. Otherwise, the firm may again fall out of balance, which leads to tension, and the firm may enter the decline stage prematurely and without wanting to, earlier than after the stage of maturity, as it was positioned in the life cycle of the small firm, with all its consequences for the entrepreneur.

But the small firm does not need to grow over time; there is also the option not to grow with the small firm and to stabilize in size with the small firm at a certain moment in time. Next to the limits that are dictated by the market that cause the firm not to grow, the decision not to grow (or to grow slowly) can be made by the entrepreneur himself/herself deliberately, for example because the entrepreneur acknowledges his/her own weaknesses. This is also called the horizontal growth curve, which is in fact a no-growth curve. It is important to realize that not every entrepreneur will transform from a professional to a leader and that not every entrepreneur will transform from a leader to a manager, simply because not every person is able to change himself/herself in this way. Even if the entrepreneur is able to change himself/herself in this way, not every entrepreneur is willing to do so. However, the entrepreneur can always decide not to grow further with his/her small firm and not to transform from professional to leader to manager. The entrepreneur can then decide to enter the stage of maturity prematurely, during or shortly after the start-up stage, or during the scale-up stage.

The decision for stability (i.e. limited growth) may make the entrepreneur happier than he or she would be if his/her firm was changing as he/she does not have to devote a lot of time to the required leadership role and/or the required management role. These may be roles that the entrepreneur does not enjoy and/or is unable to exercise. The entrepreneur may focus more on the role of being a professional because this is the one role that he or she wants to and/or is able to exercise. The decision for limited growth may also make the entrepreneur happy, as he/she does not have to share the equity of and the say in the small firm with another person or organization. In this way, the entrepreneur can defy the pressure from his/her business environment and remain small with his/her firm.

Surviving in the long-term

As organizational growth continues, small entrepreneurial ventures may turn into large corporations that are comprised of hierarchical layers, business divisions, and overseas operations. Although large corporations are challenged by increasing complexity, at the core the organizational challenges - as depicted in this chapter by iterative relationships among firm size, strategic elements, and entrepreneurial roles - remain valid. However, to enact transformative entrepreneurship large firms require different solutions, which are often referred to in the literature as corporate entrepreneurship and intrapreneurship.

Corporate entrepreneurship refers to the process of creating new business within established firms to enhance a company's performance and competitive position (Åmo 2010). Practices focus on how leaders can inspire followers to embrace innovation to support a company's success. Corporate entrepreneurship is typically initiated from the top; management champions the initiative, provides content, assigns project members, and allocates responsibility and resources. In contrast, corporate intrapreneurship is about innovation in organizations, where the innovation is initiated and championed by employees in a bottom-up way to exploit a given business opportunity (Åmo 2010). Management may even resist the project. The role of managers is to create organizational structures and climates that encourage experimenting, learning, and risk-taking. Self-appointed project leaders take responsibility for identifying the need for change and carry the innovation towards success. Whereas intrapreneurs occasionally seek the corporation's blessing for their initiatives afterwards, in the process of the innovation becoming institutionalized, intrapreneurs should enlist (executive) sponsors to obtain access to the company's resources and infrastructure.

Taken together, whether within established corporations new ventures originate through entrepreneurship or through intrapreneurship, each new venture is subject to the dynamics described in this chapter. Growth results from continues alignment between venture size, venture characteristics, and the roles venture owners fulfill. The key distinction is that these ventures progress within the infrastructure of the corporation, which may inhibit growth (for example, compliance to rigid bureaucratic procedures) and may also accelerate growth (for example, funding and resource availability). Therefore, to pre-emptively resolve growth tensions, large corporations may carefully select venture champions and staff, structurally disconnect ventures from the organizations (for example, incubator units), and promote entrepreneurial climates.

Some final lessons

Taken together, several key lessons emerge from this chapter:

- If a firm grows and shows changes in its characteristics, one should transform the set of entrepreneurial roles in order to maintain alignment between organizational complexity and founders'/owners' behaviors and actions
- Transformation of the set of entrepreneurial roles, in turn, may influence firm growth and changes in strategic elements
- If a founder/owner cannot, or does not want to, make the transformation of entrepreneurial roles from professional to leader to manager, they should choose not to grow the firm or to do so at a slow pace, otherwise they risk entering the stage of maturity prematurely.

Learning and discussion questions

1 In this chapter, eight qualitative aspects of the small firm are distinguished. In your opinion, what are the two most important qualitative aspects of a small firm? Why?
2 How do the strategic elements sales diversification, employment dispersion, and financing formality change during the life cycle of the firm? Give your answer in the following ways: (a) the difference between the scale-up stage and the start-up stage; (b) the difference between the maturity stage and the scale-up stage; and (c) the difference between the decline stage and the maturity stage.
3 How do the entrepreneurial roles of professional, leader, and manager transform during the life cycle of the small firm? Give your answer in the following ways: (a) the difference between the scale-up stage and the start-up stage; (b) the difference between the maturity stage and the scale-up stage; (c) the difference between the decline stage and the maturity stage.
4 Wasserman (2008) indicated that founders/owners of new ventures have to resolve the 'founder's dilemma'. That is, the founder/owner must basically choose between two options: retain own control of the firm or welcome a new shareholder on board. In your opinion, what are the best criteria to choose between the two options?
5 Picture the situation that a firm is founded by two entrepreneurs who choose different options to solve the founder's dilemma (see question 4). How would you solve this conflicting situation if the two founders cannot reach an agreement?

Exercise: firm growth and changing roles of the entrepreneur

Firms change during their life cycle, which raises the question of whether entrepreneurs change their roles according to the life cycle of their firm. This question was investigated in a joint project between EY and the Vrije Universiteit, Amsterdam (VU) (see Masurel and van der Lugt 2016) for details). The research project conducted a survey across members of the

EY Entrepreneur of the Year society – they were all finalists of the EY Entrepreneur of the Year program in the Netherlands during the period 2004–2015. Fifty-six entrepreneurs/firms participated in this research project; 48.4 percent of these firms were in the growth stage or in the start-up stage, and the remainder were in the maturity stage or decline stage. To assess how entrepreneurial roles were perceived, the participants were asked to indicate the time spent on 'professional', 'leader', and 'manager' roles in their own firm, with a total of 100 percent.

The most striking observation from this research project was that there were no significant differences between the time spent on the three different roles, between the firms that were in the growth/start-up stage and those in the maturity/decline stage. The entrepreneurs dedicated most of their time to their role as a leader (48.8 percent), followed by the role as a professional (27.6 percent) and the role as a manager (23.6 percent). However, the entrepreneurs indicated that they would like to pay significantly more attention to their role as a leader (the ideal is 56.4 percent of their time), and significantly less to their role as manager (15.5 percent of their time) than they did. The entrepreneurs were more or less satisfied with the time spent to their role as professional (28.1 percent of their time).

There seems to be no logic in the fact that there were no significant differences in time spent on different roles by entrepreneurs in firms in the growth/start-up stage and those in the maturity/decline stage. Furthermore, the entrepreneurs indicated that they would like to spend more time on leadership and less on management. Apparently, the entrepreneurs are not able to solve this issue by themselves and seem to require external assistance, for instance from a consultant.

In sum, the results of the study show that entrepreneurs of growing firms may experience difficulties with new entrepreneurial roles. There appears to be a clash between the set of entrepreneurial roles that the entrepreneur exercises in practice versus the ideal set of entrepreneurial roles according to the entrepreneur.

Case questions

1 What difficulties might an entrepreneur encounter if his/her firm grows at a higher speed compared to the transformation of entrepreneurial roles?
2 Apparently, the entrepreneur is not always capable of changing the actual situation into a preferred situation, as far as his/her entrepreneurial roles is concerned. Imagine you were hired by this entrepreneur as a consultant and that the entrepreneur has no financial budget to hire anybody else. What would you advise the entrepreneur in terms of how to change the situation? Substantiate your advice thoroughly.

Notes

1. This Chapter elaborates on Section 1.5 in the book 'The entrepreneurial dilemma in the life cycle of the small firm' by Masurel (2019). The title of that section is 'Stages in the development of small businesses (Life cycle of the firm)'.
2. Strictly speaking, Shepherd and Wiklund (2013) used the term 'employees' not 'employment'. However, the term 'employment' is preferred in this chapter because it includes not only employees as such, but also active owner-managers (even non-reimbursed people that work for

the small firm, like family members or friends, may be considered here). Ignoring the active owner-managers when counting the number of people (and the involved non-reimbursed people as well) working for a small firm may lead to serious measurement problems and incorrect analyses.

References

Åmo, B. W. (2010) 'Corporate entrepreneurship and intrapreneurship related to innovation behaviour among employees'. *International Journal of Entrepreneurial Venturing*, 2(2): 144-158.

Churchill, N. C. and Lewis, V. L (1983) 'The five stages of small business growth'. *Harvard Business Review*, 83(3): 3-12.

Detienne, D. R. (2010) 'Entrepreneurial exit as a critical component of the entrepreneurial process: Theoretical development'. *Journal of Business Venturing*, 25(2): 203-215.

Ireland, R. D. and Webb, J. W. (2007) 'Strategic entrepreneurship: creating competitive advantage through streams of innovation'. *Business Horizons*, 50(1): 49-59.

Hitt, M. A., Ireland, R. D., Camp, S. M., and Sexton, D. L. (2001) 'Guest editors' introduction to the special issue strategic entrepreneurship: entrepreneurial strategies for wealth creation'. *Strategic Management Journal*, 22(6/7): 479-491.

Jansen, J. J., Van Den Bosch, F. A., and Volberda, H. W. (2006) 'Exploratory innovation, exploitative innovation, and performance: Effects of organizational antecedents and environmental moderators'. *Management Science*, 52(11): 1661-1674.

Jansen, J. J. P., Vera, D., and Crossan, M. (2009) 'Strategic leadership for exploration and exploitation: The moderating role of environmental dynamism'. *The Leadership Quarterly*, 20(1): 5-18.

Jones, O., MacPherson, A., and Jayawarna, D. (2014) *Resourcing the start-up business: Creating dynamic entrepreneurial learning capabilities*. New York: Routledge.

Lee, A. (2013) 'Welcome to the Unicorn Club: Learning From Billion-Dollar Start-ups'. Available online at http://techcrunch.com/2013/11/02/welcome-to-the-unicorn-club/ (accessed 18 December 2020).

Levie, J. and Lichtenstein, B. B. (2010) 'A terminal assessment of stages theory: Introducing a dynamic states approach to entrepreneurship'. *Entrepreneurship Theory & Practice*, 34(2): 317-350.

Lougui, M. and Nyström, K. (2014) 'What obstacles do entrepreneurs encounter?' *Journal of Entrepreneurship and Public Policy*, 3(2): 275-291.

Mansfield, M. (2019) 'Startup Statistics: The numbers you need to know'. Available online at https://smallbiztrends.com/2019/03/startup-statistics-small-business.html (accessed 18 August 2020).

Masurel, E. (2017) 'The development of Optics11 during the life cycle of the firm' Available online at https://entrepreneurshipcases.amsterdam/wp-content/uploads/2018/11/Optics11.pdf (accessed 15 May 2020).

Masurel, E. (2019) *The entrepreneurial dilemma in the life cycle of the small firm: How the firm and the entrepreneur change during the life cycle of the firm, or how they should change*. Bingley: Emerald.

Masurel, E. and Van Montfort, K. (2006) 'Life cycle characteristics of small professional service firms'. *Journal of Small Business Management*, 44 (3): 461-473.

Masurel, E. and van der Lugt, S. (2016) *Veranderende rollen van de ondernemer tijdens de levenscyclus van de onderneming*. Amsterdam: ACE Update, mei.

McKelvie, A. and Wiklund, J. (2010) 'Advancing firm growth research: A focus on growth mode instead of growth rate'. *Entrepreneurship Theory & Practice*, 34(2): 261-288.

Shepherd, D. A. and Wiklund, J. (2013) 'Are we comparing apples with apples or apples with oranges? Appropriateness of knowledge accumulation across growth studies'. In Davidson, P. and Wiklund, J. (eds.), *New perspectives on firm growth*. Cheltenham: Edward Elgar, (115-138).

Wasserman, N. (2008) 'The founder's dilemma'. *Harvard Business Review*, 86(2): 102-109.

Welsh, J. A. and White, J. F. (1981) 'A small business is not a little big business'. *Harvard Business Review*, 59(4): 18-32.

Zhou, H., Huang, L., and Kuo, T. (2018) 'Determinants of small firm grow: An exhaustive analyses using conceptual and statistical approaches'. *International Review of Entrepreneurship*, 16(4): 525-564.

PART 2

Disruption and collaboration

4 Business model innovation

Jingshu Du

Summary

This chapter starts with a discussion of the fundamental elements of a business model and then dives into the challenges of business model transformation. It attributes these challenges to an underlying tension between innovation-adoption-adaption. Further, the chapter presents the dynamic capability framework and stakeholder theory as providing the theoretical lenses for addressing this central tension of business model innovation, as business model innovators interact with their environment to challenge established industry players.

Case: business model innovation at TomTom

TomTom is a Dutch multinational company specialized in developing personal navigation systems (now known as GPS), location technology and consumer electronics. Founded in early 1991, it has gone through several transformations during its lifetime. When TomTom was founded, its technology was too advanced and too early for the mass market. Its meter-reading and barcode-reading technology was pioneering and cutting-edge, but the essential complementary infrastructures were lacking for the mass adoption of the technology, and the market was not yet ready. At that time, the technology was about 10 years ahead of its time. The founders of TomTom did not wait for 10 years for the market to mature, nor impatiently abandon the technology as they did not see immediate business opportunity for it. Instead, they effectuated around their technology and packed it into, at that time, the most suitable business model to unlock its potential: they marketed it as a business-to-business (B2B) solution to companies and also sold to upper-class businessmen who needed personal navigation for their busy agendas and could afford the premium price that came with the technology. This model proved to be successful as it benefited from the advanced technology of TomTom and sustained its core business even before the mass market was developed.

However, TomTom was not merely satisfied with what it had achieved in the niche market (the B2B and the upper-class businessmen); it believed in the much broader use of its technology when the market would finally become ready for it. Therefore, while its main business targeted wealthy businessmen, TomTom started experimenting the technology in a variety of (other) business applications, among which was mapping. As TomTom at that time did not know for sure whether mapping would indeed turn out to be its new growth engine on the mass market, it made maps for small areas with low quality; just as it did for its far-ahead-of-its-time meter-reading and barcode-reading technologies, it waited for the big moment to come. Very soon, mapping proved to be the right bet and it contributed to two-thirds of TomTom's revenue, and, subsequently, mapping became TomTom's main business.

In the year of 1999, however, the internet bubble burst. Again, the technology appeared too early for the mass infrastructure to be ready to couple with it: the speed of the internet was too slow, no one really saw the value in it, and no one was buying it. Worse still, changes took place in the regulatory environment. At that time, with the introduction of 3G networks, national governments saw the great business opportunity brought by the network and made the use of auctions: if one wanted to use the 3G band, one had to pay for it at a very high price. As the internet bubble collapsed, the business of TomTom (which was very much based on the internet and connectivity) was hit severely. It refocused 75 percent of the company, had to lay off two-thirds of its employees, closed its London office, and moved to Amsterdam. The organization of TomTom became very lean in order to survive all these challenges. Despite this near-death experience, however, TomTom still did not abandon its belief in navigation technology; instead, it honed its skills and waited, while continuing to invest in navigation technology. With the introduction of digital photography and then the Clinton government's more liberal policy on the civil and commercial use of the Global Positioning System (GPS) liberating the market, TomTom hit the sweet spot. From the outside, TomTom may appear fortunate, but it is because of its long-term preparation, perseverance, determination, and agility, that the company was able to ride the waves and transform itself over time.

Questions:

1 What business model innovations did TomTom undergo?
2 Why did TomTom change its business model over the years?

Learning objectives

The objectives of this chapter are to:

1 Develop understanding about business models (the definition, types, and process)
2 Introduce the concepts of business model innovation and transformation
3 Provide insights into the application of dynamic capabilities framework and stakeholder theory to business model innovation and transformation in a dynamic environment
4 Explain the innovation-adoption-adaptation tension underlying business model transformation.

Introduction to business models

In the field of management, and innovation management in particular, the literature has been progressing along two distinctive lines of research: (i) the stream of technological innovation, led by prominent intellectuals such as Schumpeter, Mansfield, Utterback, Teece, Tidd, Christensen, Tushman, and later also Schilling, Kaplan, Gambardella, Laursen, Salter, etc., which primarily focuses on understanding and harnessing the development of science and technology, as well as their related managerial issues especially for research and development (R&D); and (ii) the stream of organizational innovation, pioneered by organizational scholars such as Van der Ven, Burgelman, March, Levinthal, Cohen, and more recently also Sorensen, Stuart, Foss, etc., who center their research around organizational and strategic issues about the management of innovation. In the last decade, research on business model innovation (BMI) has emerged. Drawing mainly from studies on organizational innovation, but also tapping into the fields of strategy, operations research, and marketing, business models are generally understood as depicting the rationale of how an organization ***creates***, ***delivers***, and ***captures*** value (Chesbrough 2010; Teece 2010; Afuah and Tucci 2001; Zott, Amit, and Massa 2011). Essentially, technological innovation is primarily about the technical foundation of a business, while business model innovation pertains to the entire process transforming business input into profitable output, which also includes social benefits (e.g., for NGOs and non-profit organizations).

The traditional innovation research has been focusing on managing the balance between exploitation and exploration of technological development (e.g., March 1991; O'Reilly and Tushman 2004). However, as Chesbrough (2010) eloquently puts it, 'technology by itself has no single objective value'. The value of a technology remains latent until it is unlocked by a suitable business model. It then follows that a mediocre technology pursued within a great business model may turn out to be more valuable than an extraordinary technology exploited by a lousy business model. This line of research not only highlights BMI and puts it from the back seat in management to the front seat, but also points to the crucial balance and interplay between technology and business model.

As BMI has become increasingly popular in the field of management and strategy, some scholars have pointed out that BMI itself is a meaningful research theme in management and innovation, related or unrelated to technologies. The role of BMI is generally considered as twofold (Massa and Tucci 2013). First, BMI represents an important value-adding *vehicle* for innovation, by enabling managers and entrepreneurs to more effectively turn input into innovative output; second, BMI is also a critical ***source*** of innovation in and by itself. It represents a new dimension of innovation, alongside the classic types of innovation such as product, process, or organizational innovation (Kaplan 2012). Beyond its power to unlock the potential of technologies, BMI can support companies in exploiting new opportunities in three different ways: (i) by supporting the development of new value propositions that address an unsatisfied 'job-to-be-done' for existing customers; (ii) by tackling new customer segments that have traditionally been overlooked by existing value propositions; and (iii) by entering entirely new industries or a new terrain (Johnson 2010). In other words, the essence of a business model provides answers to the following classical questions: who is the customer; what does the customer value; how do we make profit in the business; and what is the economic logic that explains how we can deliver value to customers at an appropriate cost?

So far, the most fruitful research on BMI is embodied in two (oftentimes intertwined) streams of literature, which are pioneered by scholars such as Zott and Amit (2010) in their ***activity system view*** of BMI, and Teece (2010) and Chesbrough (2010) in their ***value chain view*** of BMI. To better understand business models, especially as a set of interdependent activities, Zott and Amit (2010) differentiate between 'design elements' and 'design themes'. The design elements display the infrastructural logic of a business model's architecture, while the design themes represent the type and style of a business model's soul.

Design elements include: the selection of activities (content); the sequencing between these activities (structure); and the choices concerning who performs which activity (governance). Design themes comprise: novelty, which inserts innovation in the content, structure or governance of the activity system; efficiency, which helps to reduce transaction costs in performing these activities; lock-in, which keeps third parties attracted as participants of the business model; and complementarities, which bundle activities within a system to produce more value than running these activities alone and separately. Zott and Amit (2010) proposed that managers can fundamentally innovate a BMI in three ways: by adding new activities; linking activities in novel ways; or changing which parties perform an activity. In other words, from a managerial standpoint, BMI consists of innovating the ***content*** (the nature of the activities), the ***structure*** (linkages and sequencing of activities), or the ***governance*** (the control/responsibility over an activity) of the activity system between a firm and its network (Zott and Amit 2010).

Teece (2010) and Chesbrough (2010) on the other hand, propose that BMI can be understood as three different and interlinked processes along the value chain: value creation, value delivery, and value capture. As Teece (2010) famously put, 'customers don't just want products; they want solutions to their perceived needs'. Therefore, in order to satisfy these needs, BMI provides a coherent system that involves business strategy, financial logics, operations structure, and organizational design, and which centers on the three phases along the value chain: value creation, delivery, and capture (see Box 4.1).

Building on Teece's (2010) and Chesbrough's (2010) view about business models, three major triggers can be identified that contribute to the ***value creation*** of business model innovation: (i) market identification; (ii) technology ignition; and (iii) ingenuity. Among these, market identification is the most common trigger for value creation in business model innovation. It can be applied in almost all types of businesses across industries and sectors. As market identification has a relatively low entry barrier for technologies, it is also more demanding for the business model to stand out and succeed. Market identification refers to creating value by developing new ways of doing business, which could either help customers to gain resources and control that they did not have before (i.e., to reach new, better, or more durable resources faster, more steadily, or in a more advanced way) or help customers to make more efficient use of the current resources and control that they already have at hand (i.e., through better resource (re)distribution, increased connections, and enhanced communications, etc.).

Technology ignition means creating value by introducing a new technology, and the subsequent development of new business models that center on the invention, interpretation and delivery of the new technology. When an innovation (especially a radical innovation) is introduced, there may be no existing business model at the time, or the business model may

Box 4.1 High-impact business transformations

The ability to transform is more critical than ever before. Which companies are best meeting the challenge? To find out, researchers evaluated the S&P 500 and Forbes Global 2000 firms along three dimensions: (i) the creation of new offerings and business models; (ii) the effective repositioning of the core business; and (iii) the attainment of robust financials. Below are the top six of firms undergoing the highest-impact transformations.

1. Netflix: Transitioned from DVD rental by mail to a global leader in video-on-demand (VOD), as well as a top original-content provider.
2. Adobe: Transitioned from a creative- and document-software company to a global leader in digital experiences, marketing, commerce platforms, and analytics, while changing its business model from packaged software to cloud subscriptions.
3. Amazon: Launched 'Amazon web services', which turned into a surprisingly lucrative profit engine. Amazon has also built an entire business ecosystem of products and services.
4. Tencent: Transformed from a niche player - online messenger and video games - to an all-around technology business that has a presence in entertainment, autonomous vehicles, cloud computing, and fintech.
5. Microsoft: Transitioned from a business model based primarily on selling products, licensees (IP), and devices to a cloud-based platform-as-a-service business.
6. Alibaba: Being an innovation powerhouse, Alibaba transformed from an internet e-commerce and retail company to an all-round technology business.

Source: Innosight (2019)

need to continuously evolve alongside the technology development. In either case, in technology ignition, technology is the primary driver for BMI.

Finally, ingenuity denotes the unexpected and unconventional combination and bridging of materials and resources (e.g., technologies as well as other tangible or intangible materials) in novel ways to create value. Neither from the market nor the technology, ingenuity typically starts with an original and unconventional idea, many times serendipitous, which is over time gradually refined and transformed into a business opportunity.

Once value is created, it needs to reach the (potential) customers in a form of ***value delivery***. The value delivery process of BMI is based on, but not constrained by, the classical value chain analysis introduced by Michael Porter (1985). The value delivery process of BMI brings a number of innovative ways to reinvent the traditional value chain depending on the *position* and the *resources* of the focal company. For example, for firms that possess full capabilities and resources from upstream (such as R&D) all the way to downstream (such as marketing and sales), direct selling could be a preferred approach to minimize transaction costs and maximize the benefits; for high-tech firms which are brilliant in developing technologies but lack downstream resources and capabilities (such as resources and capabilities in production and marketing), out-licensing could be the most valuable approach to deliver value, which allows these firms to focus on and capitalize their technological strengths; for firms whose products have a high sunk cost (and therefore also a high price), leasing can be an optimal approach to deliver value to the customers. Xerox produced the printing/copy machine model 914, which was highly successful in terms of its technology, but did not sell well due to the high price, that is, until Xerox switched to a leasing model, at which point the sales started to fly (Chesbrough and Rosenbloom 2002).

Regarding ***value capture*** of business models, it can be considered as incorporating two essential elements: value protection and value appropriation. Value protection refers to the ways that an innovative business can be protected, such as by patents, trademarks, copyrights, business secrets, lead time advantage, and so forth. Value appropriation relates to innovative ways to monetize on the novel business model. After a business gains publicity, an important step is then to design a unique way to monetize the business. A subtle balance needs to be well-managed between capturing the willingness-to-pay of the customers and keeping the long-term sustainability of the business. Sometimes tough trade-offs need to be made. For most new businesses, the first years typically require burning money. During this phase, the company needs to quickly experiment and find ways to develop money streams to sustain its business (also termed 'lean startup' in many writings). In other words, customers' willingness-to-pay needs to be designed around a certain payment model, and the users' payment behavior needs to be nurtured and further stabilized. Once both criteria are satisfied, it needs to be converted into a sustainable money stream. On the other hand, sometimes a money stream may look highly lucrative, but may be a one-off business without having long-term prospects. In such cases, the business needs to subtly balance between probing into different possibilities and stabilizing a certain choice. This can be done either by nurturing a payment model for all users as paying members or by segmenting a specific paying group which subsidizes the free use of other users.

To better depict these value capture models, different archetypes of business models are introduced. An archetype can be understood as an ideal example of a type. These archetypes are often presented with an identifying label followed by a short description of its core logic. A well-known example is the 'freemium' business model: the core logic is delivering a basic version of the product for free and charging for a premium version. This model has been successfully used by Skype and Acrobat, etc. Another type is the 'razor-and-blade' model, first introduced by Gillette: it lures customers with its cheap razors, which are paired with rather expensive blades in order for the razor to function. This model is also widely used in other industries where products such as cheap printing machines are paired with expensive cartridges, or cheap game consoles paired with expensive software games. A third widely used type is called a 'loss leader': the core logic being that it offers velocity items for a very low margin in anticipation of additional sales at a higher margin. For example, the US$1 menus. The 'long-tail' business model is based on the idea that the long tail of some distributions of numbers is the portion of the distribution having many occurrences far from the 'head' or central part of the distribution. In other words, the oftentimes ignored 'tail', and especially the accumulation of diverse items along the tail, may be far greater than the monotonous 'head'. Well-known examples include YouTube channels and Micro-breweries who do not cater to a single mainstream (the 'head') but enable a thousand flowers bloom (the 'long tail'). Finally, pricing the most cost-sensitive item as low as possible and then charge for every little extra, enables companies such as Ryanair to reap financial benefits based on the so-called 'nickel-and-dime' business model.

Table 4.1 Business model innovation: building blocks

Building blocks	*Focus*
Value creation innovation	
New capabilities	Firms need to develop and utilize new capabilities to capture opportunities that arise from external technological and market-related changes. New capabilities can be developed through training, continuous learning, and knowledge integration.
New technologies	Aligning technological developments with an adequate business model in order to be successful. Whereas new products or service offerings can require new production technology, new revenue models might require new technical systems.
New processes	Activities within a business model are connected with each other and change in the processes can impact the degree of efficiency of a new business model. The combination and integration of the processes may support a mass-customization business model.
New partnerships	Business model reconfigurations demand new partners, and so firms need to continuously search for new collaboration partners as well as maintaining their existing relationships, as partners provide access to external resources in support of a firm's effort to innovate.
Value proposition innovation	
New offerings	New offerings are among the most visible changes in a firm's business model. It relies on the development of new products and services and defines what a firm offers to solve their customers' problems or satisfy their needs in new or better ways.
New customers/markets	Business model innovation includes the redefinition of existing markets or the entering of new markets. The rationale of targeting customers or markets is determined by the question: who is willing to pay for what is offered?
New channels	New channels concerns the delivery of value to the customer, as this can be done through various means, especially for intangible goods or services. It may include offline and online combinations or direct and indirect delivery.
Customer relationships	This can be a firm's ability to build upon existing relationships or to establish new relationships with customers. Customer relationships provide information about environmental changes and (latent) market needs, and therefore trigger business model change.
Value capture innovation	
New revenue models	Revenue models can transform from transactions in which offerings are exchanged against payment into sustainable streams in which revenues are generated indirectly or over time through cross subsidization or life cycle values.
New cost structures	The cost structure determines the strategic scope of a firm's offerings. A change in the cost structure, accounting for direct and indirect costs, can support the product-market strategy and business model.

Source: adapted from Clauss (2017)

In today's fast-changing business environment, companies have to dynamically evolve their business models over time in order to match with the potential of their technologies and/or the environment they are embedded in. Business model development thus mainly refers to two situations: (i) a new business model must be created; and (ii) the business model must dynamically evolve according to the changes in the environment. For the former, it mainly pertains to businesses that are based on a (radically) new technology or aiming at tackling a new challenge in the business environment that has rarely been faced before. In these cases, as there is no readily available business model to leverage, a new model has to be envisioned and developed. In many other cases, however, the business has already an existing business model. The success then lies in the dynamic transformation and evolution of the model over time to compliment the development of the technology that it unpacks, or the environment that the company operates in.

Tension: innovation-adoption-adaptation

'*Innovation-adoption-adaptation*' is a useful framework to understand the tension between the innovator and its environment, and such tensions may arise at different points in time along the development of business models. On the one hand, BMI centers on the new ways of doing business, which holds the promise to challenge and disrupt the status quo; on the other hand, however, just exactly because of the changes the new business model may bring, it faces numerous resistances stemming from the reluctant and hesitant departure of its (potential) adopters from their deeply rooted habits and traditions. Meanwhile, the innovator needs not only to educate the market for its new offering, but also to continuously adapt itself in response to the changing environment. Many great innovators with brilliant technologies (which are oftentimes too advanced for their time) struggle to find a suitable business model to unleash their potential. Ironically enough, usually the more advanced the technology, the greater likelihood that the technology will stumble, especially in its early years.

Oftentimes, BMI triggered by technology ignition requires the focal company to skillfully master and balance multi-stakeholder relationships that are involved in the adoption process of the new technology. Take the example of JETREA® (see Box 4.2). This revolutionary medical invention was hailed by many industry experts, as JETREA® was predicted to soon become a blockbuster because of its technology excellence. However, contrary to many people's expectation, the sales of JETREA® stumbled after its debut in the market. The fundamental reason is not because of the technology - the technology was highly innovative - however, the business model accompanying the technology was rather traditional. As a result, it was very challenging for a potentially very powerful technology packed into a mediocre business model to fly. In selling JETREA® - the much safer and more efficient replacement of eye surgery for curing the symptomatic vitreomacular adhesion (VMA) - Thrombogenics used the traditional approach for marketing and sales, just as most pharmaceutical companies did: JETREA® was marketed to the eye surgeons with the hope that it would soon be picked up by the market because of its incomparable technology. The revolutionary nature of this radical technology has shown, however, that the existing business model, which is suitable for the delivery of existing technologies, may not be optimal for the delivery of a new technology. There is a fundamental power shift in the

Box 4.2 Thrombogenics: stumbled marketization of innovation

Thrombogenics is a Leuven-based Belgian biopharmaceutical company which successfully developed JETREA® - an innovative ocriplasmin to treat the symptomatic vitreomacular adhesion (VMA) of the eye by just a simple intravitreal injection. Before JETREA® was introduced to the market in 2013, the only way to treat symptomatic VMA/VMT was the surgical separation of the vitreous from the retina, called 'vitrectomy'. This treatment requires direct operations on the back of the patient's eyeball, involving taking out and putting back the patient's eyeball from his/her eye during the surgery. This type of surgical operations is very risky and can lead to several complications, such as bleeding, severe pain, and post-operative inflammation or irritation; it is also considered to be scary by the patient himself/herself. As a result, it is usually only undertaken when the patient's vision has deteriorated significantly to a certain point (e.g., in moderate to severe cases). This approach is called 'observation' or 'watchful waiting' until a patient becomes a candidate for the surgical treatment. With the invention of JETREA®, the treatment can be done with a simple injection into the eye without any surgery, thus the treatment can start much earlier, be conducted more safely, and bring much less pain and fear for the patients. This superior technology has gained many positive reactions in the industry and attracted high hopes from the business community. However, when JETREA® was introduced to the market in its first years, the sales stumbled.

stakeholder relationships, and great care should be taken when designing its (transformational) business model.

It was later found out that marketing JETREA® to the eye surgeons was considered as an 'invasion' into these surgeons' occupational territory, cannibalizing their current surgery business, and casting a long-lasting negative impact on the very bread-and-butter of the eye surgeons themselves. As a result, JETREA® was very unpopular among the eye surgeons although it did bring great benefits to the patients. It was found that in many cases, JETREA® was not even introduced to the patients at all. Instead, the traditional approach, the vitrectomy, continued to prevail as 'the only solution' to cure the symptomatic VMA. After having understood the new situation facing the company, Thrombogenics decided to market JETREA® to general practitioners instead of surgeons, at which point the business really started to take off. In most European countries, general practitioners are the first point of contact in checking most health-related issues. After seeing the patient, the general practitioner then decides which treatment the patient needs to receive, and whether the patient needs to be hospitalized or not. Before JETREA® was introduced to the general practitioners, vitrectomy was understood by them as the only approach to cure VMA, and so all patients who suffered from VMA were introduced to eye surgeons. However, now armed with information about the more powerful and more efficient alternative JETREA®, the patient can decide by himself/herself whether he/she wants to take JETREA® and have a simple injection in the eye, or whether he/she would prefer to go for the traditional vitrectomy approach

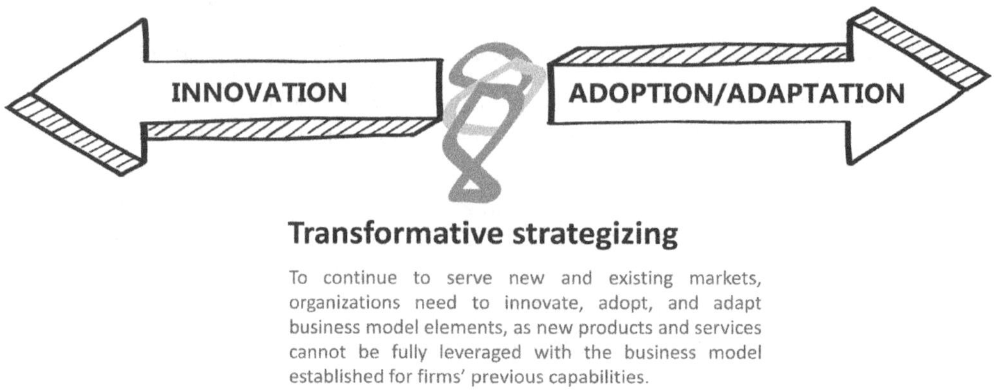

Figure 4.1 Innovation-adoption-adaption tension

performed by eye surgeons. In developing the business model accompanying an innovative technology, it is key that the shifting power balance between multiple stakeholders is carefully envisioned and managed.

Dynamic capabilities and stakeholder theory

Two theoretical frameworks - dynamic capabilities and the stakeholder theory - are particularly important in understanding business models and their innovation. In essence, both theories recognize that the entrepreneurial side of strategy, namely how significant new rent streams are created and protected, is largely ignored by many existing approaches. To address this issue, they combine perspectives from traditional models such as industrial organization, resource-based view, and cognitive theory. Moreover, the dynamic capabilities framework has a special focus on transaction cost economics and evolutionary economics, while stakeholder management further builds on institutional theory. Both theories highlight the dynamic environment of the firm, and focus on the challenges faced by entrepreneurial businesses attempting to create new markets for novel and innovative products and services (Venkataraman 1997). Especially in such dynamic markets, the business models have to adapt and evolve over time.

Dynamic capabilities framework

The ability to achieve new forms of competitive advantage can be understood as *dynamic capabilities*. It is a framework developed by David Teece (Teece, Pisano, and Schuen 1997; Teece 2007), which offers a uniquely fitting theoretical perspective to understanding business models.

According to Teece, the term 'dynamic' refers to the capacity to renew organizational competences so as to achieve congruence with the changing business environment (Teece et al. 1997). Certain innovative responses are required when time-to-market and timing are critical, the rate of technological change is rapid, and the nature of future competition and the markets are difficult to determine. The term 'capabilities' emphasizes the key role of strategic management in appropriately adapting, integrating, and reconfiguring internal and external organizational skills, resources, and functional competences to match the requirements of the changing environment. It focuses on the specifics of how organizations first develop firm-specific capabilities and how they renew their competences over time to respond to shifts in the business environment.

Extending the foundations of the resource-based view into dynamic markets (Eisenhardt and Martin 2000), the dynamic capabilities framework introduces three essential processes which are indispensable for strategy making and management in fast-changing environments: *sensing*, *seizing*, and *reconfiguring* (Teece 2007). More specifically, dynamic capabilities can be disaggregated into the capacity to *sense* and shape opportunities and threats; to *seize* opportunities that arise in the environment; and to *reconfigure* its intangible and tangible assets to maintain competitiveness through enhancing, combining, and protecting its resources and capabilities (Teece 2007). Dynamic capabilities include difficult-to-replicate enterprise capabilities that are required to adapt to changing customer and technological opportunities; they also embrace the enterprise's capacity to shape the ecosystem it is embedded in, develop new products and processes, and design and implement viable business models. Especially for BMI, as firms are proactively exploring new ways of working which would (potentially) challenge the status quo, they have to continuously sense, seize, and reconfigure in order to stay ahead of competition.

The dynamic capabilities framework is also a crucial extension of the strategy literature. As the management of R&D, product and process development, and intellectual property were often viewed as being outside of the traditional boundaries of strategy, dynamic capabilities can be seen as an integrative approach to understanding the newer sources of competitive advantage (Teece et al. 1997). More importantly, identifying new opportunities and organizing effectively and efficiently to embrace these opportunities are generally more fundamental to value creation than is strategizing (Teece et al. 1997). Indeed, particularly in rapidly changing environments, strategies are mostly emergent, rather than deliberate (Mintzberg and Waters 1985). In such an environment, creating and sustaining successful business requires the continuous interplay between the firm and its immediate and general environment, not so much with its competitors as most strategy literature would suggest.

As such, the dynamic capabilities framework is a considerably complex yet coherent whole that integrates and extends diverse research in strategy, resource-based views, evolutionary economics and organizational design to advance the field of management in general, and innovation management in particular. According to the dynamic capabilities framework, the competitive advantage of firms is seen as resting on distinctive processes (ways of coordinating and combining), shaped by the firm's specific asset positions (such as the firm' portfolio of difficult-to-trade knowledge assets and complementary assets), and the evolution path(s) it has adopted or inherited (Teece et al. 1997). In high-velocity markets where industry structure is blurring, dynamic capabilities are simple, experiential, unstable processes that rely on quickly created new knowledge and iterative execution to produce adaptive, but unpredictable outcomes (Eisenhardt and Martin 2000).

In fast-moving business environments characterized by dispersion in the geographical and organizational sources of innovation, sustainable advantage requires far more than the mere ownership of difficult-to-replicate (knowledge) assets. It also requires unique and difficult-to-replicate dynamic capabilities. The possession of such dynamic capabilities allows the firm to not only adapt to the environment, but also shape the environment.

Stakeholder theory

The stakeholder theory introduced by Freeman (1984) offers another valuable theoretical perspective in understanding BMI. Specifically, stakeholder management deals with the management of business models. Defining stakeholders as any group or individual who is affected by or can affect the achievement of an organization's objectives, the purpose of stakeholder management is to devise methods to manage the myriad groups and relationships that leads to strategy (Freeman and McVea 2001). Instead of only focusing on those immediately relevant and the most commonly referred stakeholders of the firm (such as shareholders) stakeholder theory suggests the management should actively explore its relationship with all stakeholders in order to develop business strategies. Rather than maximizing the position of one group within limitations provided by the others, stakeholder theory sees the support of all stakeholders as central to the success of the firm. Further, reaching beyond the generic stakeholder groups such as the broad customers, suppliers, or investors, the stream of stakeholder management research proposes to give a 'name and face' to each individual stakeholder and to customize the interactions with each of them in order to gain valuable information and develop close relations (McVea and Freeman 2005).

In its essence, the stakeholder theory suggests that managers must formulate and implement processes that satisfy all and only those groups that have a stake in the business. The central task in this process, therefore, is to manage and integrate the relationships and interests of shareholders, employees, customers, suppliers, communities, and other groups in a way that ensures the long-term success of the firm. A stakeholder approach is even more appropriate to today's fast-changing business environment, as it suggests that stakeholder relationships can be created and influenced, not just taken as given. Further, it is pointed out that 'stakeholder migration' is a critical issue in today's economy. A simple and accurate description of stakeholders by neat categories is becoming increasingly more difficult, as stakeholders have begun to challenge the borders between traditional stakeholder groups and started to migrate from one traditional group to the other. As the boundaries between stakeholder groups are becoming blurred, stakeholder relationships are becoming more complex (McVea and Freeman 2005).

Reflection

Throughout history, the business journeys of many great firms were breathtaking. Many firms with great technological endowment struggled to justify their existence, while other seemingly mediocre firms took the helm and reign. While people adored the overnight success of a few high-fliers, the business headlines were also glutted with epic tumbles. The traditional strategy literature offers little help in dynamic markets, as studies have been mostly focusing on explaining competitive advantage and relative firm performance in a stable setting. Shane and Venkataraman (2000) pointed out that it offers only an incomplete explanation of business strategy. For a start, such an approach presupposes the existence of products, firms, and markets and thus precludes an understanding of the creation of fundamentally new opportunities. Further, it is also common knowledge that even the most strategic firms could hardly survive and thrive for a long time, as many of them eventually disappeared despite their glitters along the way.

Many scholars then turn to innovation for answers. In the innovation literature, it is recognized that invention and innovation by themselves are insufficient to generate success (Teece 1986). For firms to succeed in the long run, they have to rely on the combination of both technology and the way of working (business model) and dynamically evolve them over time. It is proposed that it is the development and exercise of dynamic capabilities that lies at the core of enterprise success and failure (Teece 2007). The dynamic capabilities framework analyzes the sources and methods of essential BMI issues, such as value creation, delivery, and capture by enterprises operating in environments of rapid technological change (Teece et al. 1997), and it shifts the focus from outperforming competitors in stable markets to creating new development engines in dynamic environments. Whereas according to Porter the essence of strategy formulation is 'coping with competition' (Porter 1991: 11), in the dynamic capabilities tradition the essence of strategy involves selecting and developing technologies and business models that build competitive advantage through assembling and orchestrating difficult-to-replicate assets, thereby shaping competition itself. As such, dynamic capabilities are the drivers behind the creation, evolution, and recombination of other resources into new sources of competitive advantage (Eisenhardt and Martin 2000).

> For long-term success, organizations have to rely on the combination of both technology and the way of working (business model) and dynamically evolve them over time.

In essence, dynamic capabilities theory does not only provide a management framework for operating in the fast-changing environment, it is in itself also a useful set of methodology for practices. By introducing a dynamic view of the company and its surrounding environment, it helps to overcome pitfalls, such as strategic myopia and core rigidities, and prompts companies to stay alert and agile, which are especially relevant qualities for BMI. Indeed, overcoming a narrow search horizon is extremely difficult and costly for management teams that are tied to established problem-solving competences (Teece 2007).

Applying dynamic capabilities requires widely scanning and prospecting opportunities in the environment, as well as addressing opportunities by maintaining and improving technological competences and complementary assets. When the opportunity is ripe, invest heavily in the particular technologies and designs most likely to achieve marketplace acceptance (Teece 2007). Besides the firm's own resources and capabilities, the complementary assets (which may or may not owned by the focal firm) support and enable the use of these resources and capabilities and are thus critical to the success of the business. Take the example of TomTom; the company does not only stay alert of the opportunities that arise in its environment but is also very agile in reconfiguring its internal resources and capabilities to respond to those opportunities. For example, it did not passively wait until the opportunity emerged and then try to seize it, but TomTom envisioned the possible opportunity well before it eventually arrived (e.g., mapping). Sometimes, the dynamic power shift may come from the regulatory environment, which is difficult to envisage beforehand and for which companies need to carefully prepare in advance during the transformation. While it was waiting for the 'big moment' to come for its mapping technology, TomTom kept experimenting with its mapping technology in smaller scale and with lower quality, while deriving revenue stream from its more traditional, mainstream technologies. When the complementary assets for mapping were finally in place (i.e., the 3G network and the wide use of private cars), TomTom could quickly seize it and take off.

In managing business models, the role of various stakeholders related to the business are crucial (Freeman 1984). Within the dynamic capabilities framework, the environmental context is not that of the industry, but that of the business ecosystem, the community of organizations, institutions, and individuals that impact the firm and the firm's customers and suppliers. The relevant community includes complementors, suppliers, regulatory authorities, standard-setting bodies, the judiciary, educational and research institutions, and so on. According to stakeholder theory, prioritizing stakeholders that are related to the business is more than a complex task of assessing the strength of their stake on the basis of economic or political power (Freeman and McVea 2001). The values and the enterprise strategy of a firm may assign priorities to particular partnerships and discourage others. Thus, the firm needs to continuously assess and balance the priority of its stakeholders during its business model innovation process. More importantly, stakeholders must not only be understood in the present, they must also be managed over the long run.

Svendsen (1998) concludes that in an increasingly volatile world 'the ability to balance the interests of all stakeholders' will be a defining characteristic of successful companies. The key insight of stakeholder theory lies with the managers or entrepreneurs who have to put together a deal that simultaneously satisfies those who can affect or be affected by what the company does (McVea and Freeman 2005). A managerial approach would, therefore, focus on how managers make decisions that create value, while taking account of the interests of all the stakeholders affected by the decision. In the example of Thrombogenics, initially the company did not consider general practitioners (the first contact point of patients) as a vital stakeholder, this mis-focus passed the power to eye surgeons, who are actually not that important a player in the new business environment. It is only after a few trial-and-error experiments that Thrombogenics found that its stakeholders had changed because of its new technology, and it had to devise new ways of delivering value in its BMI.

Indeed, ***stakeholder migration*** is a critical issue in today's economy, especially for BMI. Stakeholders have begun to challenge the borders between traditional stakeholder groups. Numerous examples across all stakeholder boundaries suggest that a fundamental shift in stakeholder dynamics is occurring. A simple and accurate description of stakeholders by neat categories is becoming more and more difficult, particularly in the most entrepreneurial sectors of the economy, such as high technology and medical sciences. The boundaries between stakeholder groups are becoming blurred, and stakeholder relationships are becoming more complex, which will have long-term consequences for (and especially value delivery of) BMI.

Learning and discussion questions

1 Explain the main elements of a business model.
2 Discuss what business model transformation is and why it is important.
3 What is the essence of the dynamic capabilities framework and stakeholder theory, respectively? How do they differ and what do they share in common?
4 Discuss the *'innovation-adoption-adaptation'* tension and list three major challenges a company needs to deal with regarding its business model innovation (or transformation). Also, discuss solutions based on the dynamic capabilities framework and stakeholder theory for dealing with these challenges.

Exercise: business model innovation at ING Bank

ING is a global financial institution with a strong European base, offering banking services through its operating company ING Bank. The purpose of ING Bank is empowering people to stay a step ahead in life and in business. At present, ING Bank's more than 53,000 employees offer retail and wholesale banking services to customers in over 40 countries. With total assets of US$1.1 trillion, it is the bank with the most assets in the Netherlands, and one of the biggest banks in the world. It is also among the top 10 in the list of largest European companies by revenue. Since 2012, ING Bank has been on the list of global systemically important banks.

With the advent of advanced technologies such as AI and big data, the emergence of fintech, as well as increasing competition with both local and international players in the finance sector, the banking industry is facing numerous challenges. The company believes that it must learn and develop what customers really want through continuous validation and is drastically changing the way in which it develops products and services. This is done through the ING innovation methodology PACE, which combines design thinking, lean start-up, and agile scrum principles in a structured process. In a nutshell, it believes that the company has to accelerate innovation and develop more customer-centric products and services because of rapid technological change and shifting customer expectations. Above all, it has to learn and develop what customers really want, as too often solutions are/were not really the solutions customers are looking for, and therefore companies may not use their resources in an efficient way. This means the company needs to constantly validate whether customers like and want what it's developing. This, in turn, results in changing the way ING develops them.

Case questions

Based on what was described above and combined with your own desk research about this company, please answer the following questions:

1 What has changed in the environment for ING, what is changing, and what will (may) change?
2 What kind of opportunities are there in the market that may be relevant for ING?
3 How can ING seize these opportunities?
   a) Are there new ways to create value for ING (potential) customers? If so, what are they?
   b) Are there new ways to deliver value to ING (potential) customers? If so, what are they?

   c) Are there new ways to capture value from ING (potential) customers? If so, what are they?

4 What kind of resources and capabilities of ING need to be changed/reconfigured in order to adapt to the opportunity/opportunities? How should ING dynamically evolve the company to reach its goal?
5 Who are the (most important) stakeholders for ING? Is there a change of priority among its traditional stakeholders? Are there new stakeholders emerging? If so, what has changed? If not, why not?
6 How can ING engage these stakeholders?

References

Afuah, A. and Tucci, C. L. (2001) *Internet business models and strategies: Text and cases*. New York: McGraw-Hill.

Chesbrough, H. and Rosenbloom, R. S. (2002) 'The role of the business model in capturing value from innovation: evidence from Xerox Corporation's technology spin-off companies'. *Industrial and Corporate Change*, 11(3): 529–555.

Chesbrough, H. (2010) 'Business model innovation: opportunities and barriers'. *Long Range Planning*, 43(2-3): 354–363.

Clauss, T. (2017) 'Measuring business model innovation: conceptualization, scale development, and proof of performance'. *R&D Management*, 47: 385–403.

Eisenhardt, K. M., and Martin, J. A. (2000) 'Dynamic capabilities: what are they? *Strategic Management Journal*, 21(10–11): 1105–1121.

Freeman, R. E. (1984) *Strategic management: A stakeholder approach*. Cambridge: Cambridge University Press.

Freeman, R. E. and McVea, J. (2001) 'A stakeholder approach to strategic management'. In Hitt, M., Freeman, E. and Harrison J. (eds.), *The Blackwell handbook of strategic management*. Oxford: Blackwell Publishing, (189-207).

Innosight (2019) 'The Transformation 20: The Top Global Companies Leading Strategic Transformations' Available online at https://www.innosight.com/insight/the-transformation-20/ (accessed 25 July 2020).

Johnson, M. W. (2010) *Seizing the white space: Business model innovation for growth and renewal*. Boston, MA: Harvard Business Press.

Kaplan, S. (2012) *The business model innovation factory: How to stay relevant when the world is changing*. New York: John Wiley & Sons.

March, J. (1991) 'Exploration and exploitation in organizational learning'. *Organization Science*, 2: 71–87.

Massa, L. and Tucci, C. L. (2013) 'Business model innovation'. *The Oxford Handbook of Innovation Management*, 20(18): 420–441.

McVea, J. F. and Freeman, R. E. (2005) 'A names-and-faces approach to stakeholder management: How focusing on stakeholders as individuals can bring ethics and entrepreneurial strategy together'. *Journal of Management Inquiry*, 14(1): 57–69.

Mintzberg, H., and Waters, J. A. (1985) 'Of strategies, deliberate and emergent'. *Strategic Management Journal*, 6(3): 257–272.

O'Reilly, C. A. and Tushman, M. L. (2004) 'The ambidextrous organization'. *Harvard Business Review*, 82(4): 74.

Porter, M. E. (1985) *Competitive Advantage: Creating and Sustaining Superior Performance*. New York: Simon and Schuster.

Porter, M. (1991) 'How competitive forces shape strategy'. In Montgomery, C. and Porter, M. (eds.), *Strategy: Seeking and securing competitive advantage*. Boston, MA: Harvard Business School Press.

Shane, S. and Venkataraman, S. (2000) 'The promise of entrepreneurship as a field of research'. *Academy of Management Review*, 25(1): 217–226.

Svendsen, A. (1998) *The stakeholder strategy: Profiting from collaborative business relationships*. San Francisco: Berrett-Koehler Publishers.

Teece, D. J. (1986) 'Profiting from technological innovation: Implications for integration, collaboration, licensing and public policy'. In Teece, D. J. (ed.), *The transfer and licensing of know-how and intellectual property: Understanding the multinational enterprise in the modern world*, 15: 67–88.
Teece, D. J. (1993) 'Profiting from technological innovation: Implications for integration, collaboration, licensing and public policy'. *Research Policy*, 22(2): 112–113.
Teece, D. J. (2007) 'Explicating dynamic capabilities: the nature and micro-foundations of (sustainable) enterprise performance'. *Strategic Management Journal*, 28(13): 1319–1350.
Teece, D. J. (2010) 'Business models, business strategy and innovation'. *Long Range Planning*, 43(2-3): 172–194.
Teece, D. J., Pisano, G., and Shuen, A. (1997) 'Dynamic capabilities and strategic management'. *Strategic Management Journal*, 18(7): 509–533.
Venkataraman S. (1997) 'The distinctive domain of entrepreneurship research: an editor's perspective'. In Katz, J. and Brockhaus, R. (eds.), *Advances in entrepreneurship, firm emergence, and growth*. Greenwich, CT: JAI Press.
Zott, C. and Amit, R. (2010) 'Business model design: an activity system perspective'. *Long Range Planning*, 43(2-3): 216–226.
Zott, C., Amit, R., and Massa, L. (2011) 'The business model: recent developments and future research'. *Journal of Management*, 37(4): 1019–1042.

5 Leading digital strategy

Saeed Khanagha

Summary

The current business environment is affected by rapid and radical technological advances. This chapter focuses on how companies formulate and execute digital-based strategies. Digital technologies create new possibilities regarding how companies may develop new strategies as they broaden the pool of potential participants (e.g., employees, customers, and suppliers) in the strategy making and provide increased processing power. Moreover, new technologies change the actual content of strategy to account for new competitive dynamics, such as platform competition and ecosystem development. The chapter discusses the topics revolving around the key tensions that firms need to overcome when attempting to embrace digital technologies to upgrade their strategy process and contents.

Case: digital transformation at Ericsson AB

Ericsson has been in the midst of its digital transformation journey, from the introduction of new managerial practices to the adoption of new digital business models. The telecommunication industry has traditionally been populated by a few infrastructure providers that enable mobile service providers (mobile operators) in different countries and regions to provide telecommunications services to individuals and enterprises. The infrastructure providers have some degree of control over technological development and deployment because of their installed-base (i.e., the number of units of Ericsson products in use) and the dependence of mobile service providers on their technologies. The so-called 'digital disruption', due to technologies such as artificial intelligence (AI), cloud, and internet-of-things (IoT), is expected to put an end to many of the existing business models and technologies in the telecommunication sector and engender new ones. Ericsson's experience of digital transformation indicates several changes in companies' approaches towards strategy making and implementation, approaches that increasingly become critical for effective management during and after digital transformation.

Digital transformation mandates quick responses to external market changes and preparation for the highly uncertain future. Like many other incumbents, Ericsson utilizes planning cycles, growth plans, business plans, and roadmaps that are on a yearly basis or longer. With the increased speed of change on the one hand and complexity of interactions in digital ecosystem on the other, these cycles increasingly become ineffective. Managers feel an ever-increasing need for real-time analysis of internal and external information to make decisions and allocate resources. Under such conditions, a constrained and top-down approach to strategy making is likely to make the company blindsided to the rapid changes that are happening in different markets and technologies. Thanks to the advances in IT tools, it has become possible for Ericsson to engage a large group of middle managers in the process of corporate level strategy formulation.

Competitiveness and survival in the new landscape requires interactions, communication, and collaboration with numerous actors across different industries and institutions. The need for engagement with a wide scope of industries and institutions requires many new capabilities and competences. Hence, there will be a need for partnerships with other players, including competitors, in order to succeed in the digital ecosystems. Similarly, acquisition of smaller firms is essential for securing access to competences that do not exist in the firm. Strategy managers at Ericsson increasingly feel the need for dedicating a larger proportion of their time to thinking and acting beyond the organizational boundaries. Collaborations with many different actors requires new processes and practices to deal with the challenges associated with such interactions.

Separating future-oriented activities from old businesses has been Ericsson's conventional approach for dealing with new trends. In such settings, one part of the organization continues to drive the core business as is, catering for existing customers with existing values in a more traditional way; the other part adapts to new ways of working with more risk-taking to expand into new areas. The problem is that no 'core business' is expected to remain safe from disruption by new digital competitors. So, Ericsson follows an integrative approach to ensure organic transformation of its core businesses. The inflexibility of the traditional hierarchical command and control culture is increasingly taking its toll on Ericsson.

Traditionally, for Ericsson, there have been two paths to growth and to respond to pressures to perform. Either ongoing planning processes seeking new technology or market opportunities to invest in them for internal development, or to perform acquisitions within the telecommunication industry. As digital transformation unfolds, in order to cope with the uncertainties and speed of change, Ericsson finds it more effective to run hundreds of parallel experimental projects with small cross-organizational teams to see what gains traction. These experiments are not chosen because of potential market size, existing assets, or a view of adjacent markets; they are chosen based on factors such as passion of the people wanting to run them, how cheaply they can be run, how quickly success or failure can be decided, or how disruptive they can be in the marketplace.

Engagement with numerous ecosystem actors for a large company like Ericsson with in-house assets and employees is becoming expensive, slow, and cumbersome. Traditionally Ericsson operated with a few thousand registered suppliers. This number is expected to increase exponentially during the coming years and as a result of digital transformation. Ericsson finds it crucial to have application programming interfaces (APIs) for tens of thousands of partners to make it easy for them to co-create and automate business together with Ericsson. This will create a remarkable change in Ericsson's processes and systems. Google, for example, has access to millions of website owners and advertisers (such as customers) and conducts a more or less automated API business with them, which is the reason why it has outperformed the legacy advertising industry.

The approach towards standardization is an important aspect of change in managerial practices revolving around innovation processes. It is widely believed that finding a new approach to standardization is the key to realizing the full potential of IoT, in terms of data, analytics, and artificial intelligence. Traditional standardization facilitated by standardization bodies is not suitable for all businesses within the broad realm of IoT. Working with alliances and open source are two other, potentially quicker and more effective, ways of setting best practices for technology.

Ericsson's measure of growth had traditionally emphasized metrics such as subscribers, bandwidth, and traffic (and their market share tied to those metrics). Prevalence of this approached proved to be problematic in seizing opportunities that come with digital transformation because of the excessive focus on providing wireless connectivity as the main means for value creation. There are examples at Ericsson today where a new kind of metric has given a different perspective on the business. For example, in connection with the company's m-commerce activities, a new way for looking at success has been developed by transitioning from a model of systems installed to a model that counts both active wallets and actual transactions. Ericsson has realized the need for incentive systems that focus on entrepreneurial behavior and initiative taking to seize opportunities associated with digital transformation. Through new managerial innovation, such as Ericsson Garage, Ericsson's leadership attempts to foster an environment in which entrepreneurs can make a difference.

Questions:

1 What were the reasons for Ericsson's digital transformation?
2 In which areas did Ericsson make major changes in its digital transformation?
3 What were some key challenges Ericsson faced in its digital transformation?

Learning objectives

The objectives of this chapter are to:

1 Recognize and evaluate the distinct nature and dimensions of strategic management of digital business and the dilemmas associated with the new dimensions of strategies
2 Identify the tensions revolving around strategizing in digital ecosystems
3 Understand the challenges of traditional approaches to strategy making and recognize the alternative approaches and their challenges
4 Recognize and evaluate the change process to implement new processes and dimensions for strategy.

Introduction to corporate strategy in a digital era

New digital technologies, such as social media, mobile data analytics, and cloud computing, challenge existing ways of doing business, and organizations stand to rise to prominence or disappear depending on their ability to strategize within this new competitive landscape. With advances in digital technology, the very nature of strategizing is changing. First, digital technologies enable change in the process of strategy making and implementation by providing new ways to connect with employees, customers, and suppliers, and a greater capacity for data gathering and analysis that will support more inclusive, agile, and informed strategic decisions and actions (Khanagha, Volberda, and Oshri 2017). Second, by altering the competitive dynamics, new digital technologies change the content of strategy, with new concepts such as digital ecosystems and digital platforms claiming a central spot in firms' competitive strategies. Third, advances in digital technologies determine the context for strategic change, as firms face the need to transform their business models to remain relevant in the emergent digital economy (Khanagha, Volberda, and Oshri 2014). This chapter illuminates these three categories of tensions and issues.

Successfully competing in the digital era requires organizations to implement changes in the strategy process, content, and context.

Strategy process

Advances in digital technologies are creating new possibilities and challenges for strategy making and implementation processes. First, the volume of information available to decision-makers is exponentially increasing and this is consequential for the longstanding theories of managerial cognition and action (Van Knippenberg et al. 2015). Second, new technologies such as big data provide new ways for tackling management problems (George, Haas, and Pentland 2014). The new social media technologies and interdependent ecosystems all favor more transparent and inclusive approaches to strategy (Hautz, Seidl, and Whittington 2017). However, the current understanding of the potential of digital technologies for strategic management only scratches the surface. While it seems to be useful for strategy managers, leveraging digital technologies enhances the effectiveness of firms' strategy-making process and subsequent strategy implementation proves to be difficult. New roles and responsibilities will be needed to clarify who - professional strategist or broader set of employees - should be the strategists. While technological advances make it possible to engage in participative strategy making, when should strategy making remain in the realm of the upper echelons and when should it be open. Another issue is related to identifying effective ways to motivate organizational actors at different organizational levels to effectively utilize the digital infrastructure.

The approach to strategy process has an important bearing on how established firms set the organization to overcome the broader set of tensions during digital transformation. Managers need to make some important choices when attempting to organize for major transformation in response to industry and technology changes. One key question is the degree of centralization, or how much authority remains within the realm of top management. Another key consideration is the choice between separation of the transformation efforts by creating a new unit or delegating the responsibility to existing structures. These alternative options come with certain benefits, but each have their own disadvantages, creating dilemmas for the organizations facing a transformation journey.

Strategy content

There is an increasing focus on the importance of digital platforms and ecosystems, and on changes in the nature of collaboration and competition in these emerging ecosystems. Due to increasing industry convergence, organizations need to redefine their collaborative and competitive behavior as they take part in digital ecosystems comprising unconventional actors from previously unrelated industries.

A significant development that has challenged many incumbents is the trend towards using digital platforms. Platforms range from social media (e.g., Facebook) to firm-specific platforms (e.g., Windows) and industry platforms with multi-firm ownership (e.g., 5G) (Thomas, Autio, and Gann 2014), where several companies, consortia and users coalesce to develop multi-product platforms (Tiwana, Konsynski, and Bush 2010). How incumbents can respond to the growing dominance of platforms, especially if they have fallen behind and may struggle to replace, leapfrog, or outcompete the prevalent platform (Ansari and Krop 2012; Henderson and Clark 1990), is a key puzzle for strategy scholars. Disney, for example, has recently responded to the growing dominance of Netflix by launching its own platform, Disney+, even though this partly cannibalizes the revenue streams it earns from being on Netflix. Once platforms have become widespread, they tend to persist, because of the strong network effects, dominant technological standards and high switching costs that characterize platform-mediated markets (Katz and Shapiro 1985; Klemperer 1987). This makes it difficult for both established firms and new entrants to offer alternatives or to create a new platform. However, unlike new entrants, established firms are constrained by legacy systems, making it difficult for a traditional bank, for example, to create platforms that outcompete fintechs.

While scholars have explored the competitive dynamics of platform ecosystems (e.g., Evans, Hagiu, and Schmalensee 2006; Hannah and Eisenhardt 2018) less attention has been given to the de novo creation and expansion of platform ecosystems (e.g., DattÈe, Alexy, and Autio 2018; Khanagha et al. 2020). As in any new initiative, a key challenge in new platform creation is not just contending with existing, widely used platforms but also establishing legitimacy for the new platform (e.g., Vasudeva, Spencer, and Teegen 2013). A platform owner cannot create an ecosystem unless it establishes credibility that extends beyond its technical capabilities (Ozalp and Kretschmer 2019). Legitimacy matters, as the new technology may be rejected by targeted adopters, especially if it clashes with their technological architectures (Henderson and Clark 1990) or threatens their dominance (Garud, Jain, and Kumaraswamy 2002). In addition, the established firm may have stakes in the prevalent platform and benefit to some extent from being on it, even if it is not a keystone or hub player (Iansiti and Levien 2004). When seeking to establish legitimacy for a new industry platform and to win stakeholder support (Hagiu and Eisenmann 2007) in both the new and existing platform ecosystems, a firm needs to be aware that its objective of offering distinctiveness and novelty may conflict with the need to demonstrate conformance and compatibility (Sheremata 2004).

While many of the tensions in platform creation (e.g., start-up problems) hold in the context of industry platforms, they manifest differently because prevalent business-to-business (B2B) relationships in such contexts are often characterized by contestation over who owns data and customers, co-opetition, switching costs, and concerns about security and interoperability. First, to encourage others to join the platform, a firm needs to offer distinctive value propositions for users that differentiate the new platform clearly from other existing platforms in terms of its identity and positioning (Cennamo and Santalo 2013). This is crucial for overcoming the start-up problem (Rochet and Tirole 2006) and creating momentum for the new industry platform. However, innovations may never be adopted in the first place without building cognitive legitimacy and ensuring alignment with the dominant value-creation logic. If an innovation is too close in concept to other existing solutions (in this case, platforms), potential users will find it hard to see where its novelty lies (Hargadon and Douglas 2001), but if it departs too far from those solutions, they may reject it or react negatively to it. While unfamiliar concepts may be appealing to pioneering users in business-to-consumer (B2C) markets, in B2B markets users tend to be less open to novel initiatives that go against a widely shared paradigm (Capon et al. 1988). Consequently, depending on the type of market being served, novelty may be both vital and detrimental to creating a new platform.

Second, securing legitimacy for a new platform requires a balance to be achieved between openness and control (Boudreau 2010; Toh and Miller 2017). Second-movers may opportunistically harness the efforts of the aspiring platform creator and outcompete it. Additionally, powerful players may 'envelop' the emerging platform by adding similar functionalities to their own platforms (Eisenmann, Parker, and Van Alstyne 2011). To avoid such risks, the platform sponsor needs to develop exclusivity by embedding its own unique capabilities into the new platform's design. Attempts to develop control, however, imply potential lock-in (Schilling 2002), with the risk that the platform will be rejected by users and complementors averse to committing to a company-specific platform that may generate incompatibilities (Teece 2017). However, exerting too much control by embedding one's design into the platform may also deter potential allies, who in B2B relationships may also be direct competitors (Hoffmann et al. 2018). While control and value capture are key objectives for aspiring platform creators, relinquishing control is often crucial to building momentum and gaining wider acceptance for the platform (Schilling 2009). To navigate shifting strategic tensions and manage legitimacy challenges over time, a platform sponsor needs to deploy not only material actions such as monetary incentives and technological design. The sponsor should also include framing and signaling credible commitment to the new platform (Schilling 2003) to favorably shape viewpoints and resource access in the market (Santos and Eisenhardt 2009).

Although creating an alternative platform may seem like an appealing strategic choice for an established yet disadvantaged firm trying to sustain its business model, technological architectures, and capabilities (Gawer and Cusumano 2002; Iansiti and Levien 2004;

Nambisan and Sawhney 2011), it is far from straightforward to compete against dominant platforms protected by strong barriers created by network effects, technological standards, and switching costs (Katz and Shapiro 1985; Klemperer 1987). Moreover, in many business environments, creating a new platform requires not just developing capabilities and a distinctive and novel value proposition, but also ensuring that the platform is perceived as legitimate by powerful actors, who may resist or reject a new platform unless it aligns with the prevalent platform (Adner and Kapoor 2010; Ozalp and Kretschmer 2019). Such resistance was seen, for example, in Microsoft's initial refusal to endorse Sun's Java platform (Garud, Jain and Kumaraswamy 2002). Gaining such legitimacy may be even more critical in platforms in which there are many B2B interdependencies (Wareham, Fox, and Cano Giner 2014), as otherwise influential users and complementors may resist the new technology. Firms are typically averse to being locked into a sponsor's technology (Schilling 2002), or may struggle to integrate the new technology into their existing systems, especially when it is based on a clashing architecture (Henderson and Clark 1990). For example, despite its technological strengths, EMC's WideSky proprietary storage platform failed because EMC could not convince major players such as IBM, HP and Sun Microsystems to get on board, as they favored an open-standards platform (Gawer and Cusumano 2008).

Strategy context

With the development of digital technologies, many traditional products and services have become commoditized, and value creation for customers often now rests on delivering digital offerings in fundamentally new ways through business model innovation (cf. Foss and Saebi 2017; Volberda, Van den Bosch, and Heij 2018). Digital technologies can also be used to help improve or develop internal processes of value creation (Baden-Fuller and Haefliger 2013). This leaves us with many unanswered questions, including: how do industry incumbents identify and implement management innovations (i.e., new systems, structures, processes, and practices) that are essential in enabling organizations to make use of digital technologies in their products and services as well as in their internal activities (Khanagha et al. 2013); what alternative digital models are available and how can established organizations adopt and implement digital business models; how can organizations deal with the strategic contradictions that come with digital transformation and what are the managerial levers for managing paradoxes; how do the dynamic organizational capabilities required in this digital era differ from those needed in the past and what is needed to develop such capabilities; what are the implications of digital technologies for innovation processes and practices; how can organizations utilize digital technologies to pursue open innovation and open strategies within and across organizational boundaries; and in what ways do organizations need to reconfigure their resources and capabilities to cope with the requirements of the digital era?

Although the managerial initiatives needed to stimulate and foster exploration point toward the common goal (i.e., enabling the search for and identification, assimilation and use of knowledge of the emerging technology), the required adaptations are diverse in nature. Prior research highlights instances of new structures, processes, and practices that are crucial precursors to exploration in emerging fields. These can be brought about by managerial initiatives or management innovation defined as the introduction of new systems, structures,

Box 5.1 Ericsson update: transition to digital business model

Ericsson's transition to digital business model is characterized by specific requirements that are very different than what they had to fulfill in the past. These factors are the ones that influence and drive a major shift in managers' jobs at Ericsson. Three main categories emerged in our analyses of the key drivers of change:

i. ***Scale of business.*** Similar to many traditional companies, Ericsson's scale is being measured in traditional metrics specific to telecommunication industry, such as market share, subscribers, and mobile traffic. While these have been valid metrics their relevance in a digital era is questionable. The prevalent focus on the number of subscribers or mobile data traffic as indicators of business scope increasingly proves to be problematic. In the digital context, it is more about how many connections Ericsson has to customers, partners, consumers, talent, ecosystems, alliances, and other companies' products and services. These connections are expected to enable Ericsson to influence, explore, and evaluate alternative ways to monetize new business models that emerge with digital transformation.
ii. ***Scope of business.*** Ericsson traditionally has a clear focus on the telecommunication industry and a small selection of other markets that are in keeping with existing competences and resources. As a result of convergence in the ICT industry, scoping based on industry segments becomes less relevant. Instead, Ericsson has to provide technology, infrastructure, processes, and services across industries. Beyond traditional industrial sectors, it is believed that there is an ample opportunity to engage with various industries, cities, and markets that are all becoming digital.
iii. **Speed of change.** Ericsson operates in the telecommunication industry, which has traditionally been characterized by low speed of change. With digital transformation, the rate of the change has significantly amplified in a number of industries. The entry of new and nimble players puts pressure on incumbents that are attuned to a relatively slow pace of the change while they scramble to protect their core businesses from eroding. With the core businesses exposed to disruption, Ericsson (and other incumbent firms) face the need to respond to changing market conditions quickly through adaptation, reallocating resources, and pursue innovative mechanisms to seek new opportunities.

and processes to further organizational goals (Birkinshaw, Hamel, and Mol 2008; Volberda, Van den Bosch and Mihalache 2014). The novelty of such initiatives may be relative to the world, to the specific market, or to the firm (Vaccaro et al. 2012).

Tensions of organizing for digital transformation

There are two important tensions that firms need to consider for digital transformation: the centralization-decentralization dilemma and the integration-separation tensions.

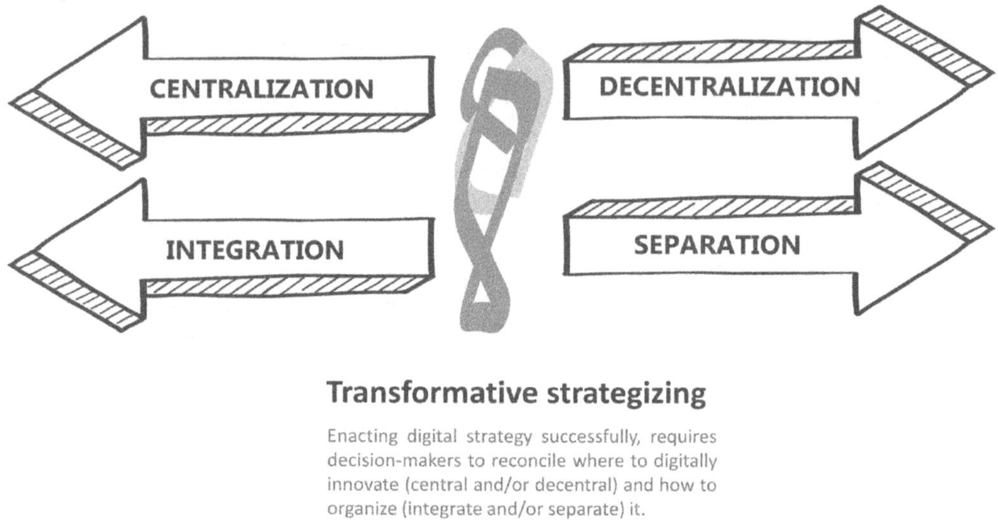

Figure 5.1 Centralization-decentralization and integration-separation tensions

Centralization-decentralization tension. When making key decision about transformation, for example the timing and intensity of investments, collaborations and alliances, and so forth, managers have to decide how much of the decisions must be made by the executive teams and how much authority they should delegate to the lower level units and teams. At one extreme, the CEO and executive retains the authority and creates a unified strategy that cascades throughout the organization. The executive team is responsible for identification of the change, understanding its implications, and planning for the optimum response. The strategy will be communicated with different units and closely monitored for execution. Such top-down approaches are effective for creating alignment and coordination without wasting time for getting different stakeholders on board. Moreover, the change initiative will receive sufficient resources and attention due to direct role of the senior managers. On the negative side, such approaches face resistance or lack of motivation from the subordinates who are responsible for execution of the strategy. Hence, no matter how great the change strategy is formulated, it may fail during the execution phase. Another issue is that senior management teams have limited information and processing capacity and organizations will deprive themselves from the insights and information at dispersed organizational nodes if they focus on top-down approaches.

At the other extreme, the responsibility of change is being delegated to autonomous teams at different levels of the organization. Such decentralized approaches enable organizations to utilize the knowledge and expertise from different units and at the same time give rise to engagement and motivation across the organization. However, delegating the authority will reduce the alignment and coordination in the organization and create confusion about what needs to be done and how. This situation will potentially give rise to politics and reduce the effectiveness of the change initiative. Different teams will compete over the organizational resources and most probably some key activities will remain under-resourced.

Table 5.1 Centralization-decentralization tension

	Strategy making	*Strategy execution*	*Pros*	*Cons*
Top-down, centralized approach	CEO and executive team identify the change, its implications, and optimum response.	Corporate level strategy cascades throughout the organization in the form of functional and unit level strategies.	Unity of direction and coordination of goals Fast and efficient decision-making Mobilization of complementary resources	Difficulty in execution at lower levels of the organization Limitation in utilization of internal and external knowledge
Decentralized, through self-organizing teams	Autonomous teams across the organization identify the change, its implications, and optimum response	Self-organizing teams leverage organizational resources to implement the change	Engagement and excitement at lower levels of the organization Access to wider array of internal and external information in strategy making	Lack of coordination and losing sight of the big picture Inefficiencies and lack of speed in strategy making Difficulty in mobilizing complementary resources

In practice, organizations act somewhere in between these two extremes of decentralization and centralization. This will enable them to benefit from some of the advantages of each extreme, but then this gain comes at the cost of having the problems of both. Organizations end up with strategic change efforts which are neither effective in formulation and alignment, nor successful in energizing individuals to execute the change across different levels of the organization.

Integration-separation tension. Given the difference in requirements of addressing the ongoing businesses and those of accommodating a major change, it seems to be beneficial to separate the units who are dealing with continuation of the existing operations from those groups focused on driving the change. Creating a separated savior organization enables developing new ways of working and supporting systems in line with the mandates of the changes in the business environment. Moreover, it allows for allocation of sufficient financial resources and attention without having to take into account the issues of day-to-day operations and short-term targets. The problem is that creating a separated structure is costly and requires heavy investment that is often beyond the capacity of an organization that is already struggling to sustain its profitability in the face of a major transformation in the industry. Additionally, a separated organization will result in a failure to transfer existing competences and knowledge to the savior organization, depriving the organization from their sources of competitive advantage.

Attempting to integrate the change effort within the same unit is efficient and maximizes the transfer of knowledge and competences. Nevertheless, in the conditions of resource constraints and short term profitability issues, this approach results in lack of attention and resource allocation to change initiatives. Moreover, employees find it difficult to navigate between the

Table 5.2 Separation-integration tension

	Strategy making	*Strategy execution*	*Pros*	*Cons*
Delegating the transformation task to existing units	Concurrent consideration of present and future in making strategic decisions.	Allocating a pool of resources to address present and future.	Retaining existing capabilities Cost efficient	Prioritizing the present over the future Confusion and lack of focus among employees.
Creating a separate savior organization	Separate consideration of the past and the future in making strategic decisions.	Dividing resources between the present and the future.	Sufficient attention to the future Creating focus in the organization	Costly, needs duplicating the organization Failure to utilize existing resources.

activities that are focused on ongoing businesses and those that are aiming at transformation. In practice, organizations utilize a combination of separated and integrated structures at the same time or alternate between different modes over time. Nevertheless, the downsides of separated and integrated approaches remain a major problem throughout the process.

Strategizing digital platforms

Advances in digital technologies give rise to the digital technology platform (see Box 5.2) as an instrument to organize innovations and to realize complex value propositions (Gawer and Cusumano 2014). With the promises to achieve economies of scale and network effects, many traditional industry leaders embrace the platform business model and try to create one. In response to this burgeoning phenomenon, the academic community has started to investigate strategies for firms to create a platform and to build an ecosystem surrounding it

Box 5.2 Sharing economy

The sharing economy, the collaborative economy, the digital economy, the circular economy, the peer-to-peer economy, and the gig economy are all labels to denote a new way of organizing economic activity. Though differences exist there are some commonalities. Individuals share or exchange goods, services, resources, or skills which were previously unused or under-used. Demand and supply are facilitated by a digital platform, often operated by a third party (who typically receives an intermediary fee) who ensures transaction speed, flexibility, efficiency, and scalability. In fact, consumers simply become producers, though in most instances ownership is not changed. The sharing economy is taking-off in all sort of economic sectors, including car/ride-sharing (e.g. Lyft, Uber, Cargo, RelayRides), apartment/home lending (e.g. Airbnb), peer-to-peer lending (e.g. Lending Club), and co-working (e.g. WeWork).

Source: Marr (2016)

(e.g., Eisenmann, Parker and Van Alstyne 2011; Gawer and Cusumano 2008). Prior research generally suggests two strategies for competing in platform markets: winner-takes-all (WTA) or differentiation strategy. While the former strategy suggests for domination in the ecosystem based on the enormous number acquisition of users and complementors, the latter suggests a competition based on distinctive positioning in the ecosystem (Eisenmann, Parker and Van Alstyne 2006; Cennamo and Santalo 2013). These studies generally assume that platform development activity follows a linear trajectory based on the firm's platform strategy (i.e., WTA or differentiation). However, in the context of an emerging ecosystem, it is not possible for the firms to come up with a definite platform strategy ex ante and be consistent with it. Scholars have recently called into more a processual view to illuminate the dynamic creation and evolution process of a platform ecosystem (McIntyre and Srinivasan 2017).

Strategy-process literature suggests that firms need to devise strategies that are dynamically in line with the firm's context, capabilities, and objectives that change over time (see Burgelman et al. 2018 for summaries). In similar notes, firms attempting to create a platform-based business may need to devise different strategies over time to address temporal challenges faced by the firm. Therefore, understanding the dynamic of platform strategy is essential to illuminate the process of creating a platform-based ecosystem. In addition, compared to new entrants or start-ups (e.g. Ansari, Garud, and Kumaraswamy 2016; Hannah and Eisenhardt 2018), large-established and not-digitally born firms face organizational challenges that prompt the firms to redefine and transform its existing organization identity and value logic (Gawer and Phillips 2013). For instance, platform leadership requires new business models that potentially contradict with the firm's existing one (Gawer and Cusumano 2014). Platform leadership ambitions may also be contested by the key resource providers in the existing ecosystem, which may hurt existing businesses of the firm (Christensen and Bower 1996; Gilbert 2005), especially in B2B settings where strong resource dependencies are prevalent (Wareham et al. 2014). In addition, established firms need to consider their existing networks of customers, suppliers, and partners when introducing a platform-based ecosystem (Nambisan and Sawhney 2011). This condition will increase the complexity of platform creation as the firms may deal with the same partners or customers with varying roles in different ecosystems (Pierce 2009). Thus, established firms need to devise a complex repertoire of strategies that correspond with certain organizational challenges during the creation of a platform-based business. As such, we need to understand how platform strategy coevolves and how established firms navigate tensions of the platform creation.

Addressing these shifting tensions to secure legitimacy requires consideration of temporal dynamics. Because expectations about the new technology may evolve (Schilling 1998), to gain legitimacy a platform creator needs to dynamically balance distinctiveness and conformance with openness and control (Claussen, Essling, and Kretschmer 2015). However, relatively few studies take a temporal approach when studying platforms (e.g., Claussen et al. 2015; Eisenmann et al. 2011) or examine how platforms and ecosystems coevolve (Cennamo 2018; Dattée et al. 2018; Teece 2017). Indeed, there have been calls for more attention to be given to the temporal aspects of platform strategies (e.g., McIntyre and Srinivasan 2017).

Prior research discusses organizational antecedents of engaging with new emerging technologies (see Lavie, Stettner and Tushman, 2010, for a comprehensive review), but those discussions are often limited to moderate levels of dynamicity and do not address the fundamental changes that come with digital transformation. However, understanding the determinants of competitiveness in highly dynamic environments mandates that one should go beyond such static views and gain a deeper understanding of the dynamic nature of strategic change process (Ansari et al. 2010). A dynamic approach implies the need for implementation of new managerial practices, processes, and structures through a process of domestication, reconfiguration and reconstitution to contextualize them within specific organizational environments (Ansari, Reinecke and Spaan, 2014). Such a need is more relevant for exploring an unfamiliar and fundamentally different technology area that requires an organization to break free from persistent and inflexible organizational routines that are tightly aligned with existing technologies and markets (Gilbert 2005; Schreyögg and Sydow 2011) while maintaining the efficiency of the ongoing businesses. Overturning these routines or introducing new ones with sufficient pace and scope to match the major changes taking place within the environment is a challenging task for managers, and requires considerable effort (Siggelkow 2001). In such conditions, managerial initiatives become crucial in order to enable exploratory behavior and to align the internal organization with the external changes (Lavie 2006).

A common theme among these studies is the focus on the more mature technologies and established business models that pose the question to the incumbents on whether and when to adapt. 'The theoretical insights are premised on the assumption that the existing model [and underlying technology] is successfully displaced by the new model [and underlying technology], and that the challenges of incumbency stem from the obsolescence of incumbents' competencies and the organizational inertia associated with the old model' (Eklund and Kapoor 2019: 1).

Hence, 'what is typically absent is engagement with the era of ferment, defined as the period after the new technology emerges, but before standardization and commercialization' (Eggers 2016: 1578). This nascent period of change is specifically interesting because it is the period when the firms are most likely to err in the form of overinvestment (Ahuja and Novelli 2017) or by committing to the wrong technology (Eggers 2012). Our received wisdom from the extant literature may not fully explain how firms navigate this journey.

A practical illustration

Collaboration with competitors is another aspect of strategies in digital ecosystems. In the following example, we illustrate how an established firm may find the need to collaborate with their rival, fintech start-ups and how they reconcile related tensions. By using technologies such as blockchain, fintech start-ups offer the promise of reduced dependency on traditional banks by creating a decentralized financial ecosystem (Gomber et al. 2018). In response, banks have begun to develop a symbiotic relationship with the fintech ecosystem to gain momentum and then try to establish their own distinctive platforms and ecosystem. The ecosystem strategy taken by banks and its boundary conditions and temporal components are relevant to understanding how banks aspire to achieve a leading position in the digital financial ecosystem.

Banks and other traditional financial institutions operate on notions of reliability, trust, and security, while maintaining centralized control of all kinds of services. Fintech start-ups, on the other hand, have the agility and technological know-how to provide innovative services that are not viable for banks (Sia *et al.* 2016), who struggle to compete with fintech on these services. In the early years of the fintech phenomenon, the trend was perceived to be highly disruptive to banks (The Economist 2015), because the vision for this new digital ecosystem was one that would potentially eliminate the role of banks in many financial services. To counter the threat of losing their leadership position in the financial ecosystem, banks could consider developing an alternative ecosystem that is more aligned with their core capabilities and central role in the financial sector.

In addition to the capability issues, traditional banks face legitimacy challenges. Many sections of society had lost confidence in traditional financial institutions and considered fintechs to provide an alternative:

> In the aftermath of the 2008 financial crisis, it became clear that the field of finance could no longer carry on as it had. Instead, both consumers and governments began to question financial actors' activities – a classic instance in which powerful actors call legitimacy into question. Trust in banking institutions fell to new lows, with financial institutions 'consistently at or near the bottom of any survey of public trust' (Flint 2014: 1), thereby opening the door for new actors to emerge.
>
> (Teigland *et al.* 2018: 6)

Hence, banks need to regain the trust of users in the existing and still dominant financial ecosystem. At the same time, many banks aspire to create a new digital ecosystem that enables them to provide innovative financial services in a way that is attuned to their core capabilities and business models. Such initiatives face legitimacy challenges. For example, JP Morgan recently introduced a cryptocurrency in a way that was aligned with the bank's operations, but this has not been well received by industry analysts and the cryptocurrency community: 'There's a lot of confusion, I see folks referring to it [JP Morgan's] initiative as a cryptocurrency. It's not a cryptocurrency. A cryptocurrency is one that is open and permissionless, if you want to download it, you don't need permission; you just need some software' (Jerry Brito, executive director at Coin Center, in Hankin 2019).

Despite the initial perception of threats, many banks realized that, to be active in the emergent digital ecosystem, they could not fight the fintech wave. Instead, they started to highlight the complementarity between fintechs and banks. For example, Kevin Tweddle, COO of ICBA, declared that '...the banking industry is at the dawn of a great new era of fintech partnerships that will change banking as we know it for the foreseeable future' (Tweddle 2018).

Leading banks in different countries utilized such symbolic actions to indicate compliance with the expectations of the various emergent Fintech ecosystems:

> ...established actors need to adjust to fit this emerging narrative, and one means is to mimic successful organizations (or elements of their strategies and managerial actions). This is not only how institutions change, but how organizations ensure their survival – at least until the next shift comes along. Thus, one means to gain back legitimacy that Sweden's established banks employed was to mimic the FinTech startups and develop their own innovative FinTech solutions.
>
> (Teigland et al. 2018: 7)

Banks also link their new initiatives to the fintech world. ING, for example, calls its innovation hub 'ING Fintech Village'. In doing so, they tend to put their own stamp on their initiatives to cultivate perceptions of exclusivity, and to be perceived as a leader in the digital ecosystem. After building momentum through symbiotic actions, banks start to adapt their strategies. Creating a perception that the relationship between the banks and fintechs is complementary provides an opportunity for banks to develop capabilities and gain legitimacy. However, the process is fraught with challenges and the outcomes are far from clear, as indicated by one industry expert:

> For banks, these partnerships won't generate the quantum leap they need to move beyond a decades-old, product-centric mentality to deliver next-generation financial services that consumers deserve. At best, financial institutions may gain a workable solution that squats awkwardly in the existing infrastructure and brand. At worst, after a lot of time and effort – and increasing their infrastructure costs – banks will fail to deliver any noticeable difference to customers beyond a flurry of press releases.
>
> (Beaumont, 2018)

Hence, despite showing initial symbolic commitment, banks with an ambitious digital agenda focused heavily on developing innovative digital services that were attuned to their core capabilities. After gaining initial momentum, banks' strategies gradually shifted from symbiotic to competitive, from exclusive to inclusive, and from internal investment and resource focus to standardization and ecosystem development. At this stage, banks used strategies ranging from acquisition of fintechs, diversification, providing service platforms, and modifying their business models to outcompete fintechs. Thus, the path to overcoming legitimacy and capability challenges starts with symbolic commitment but may turn to more competitive positioning and reduced symbolic commitment to the fintech ecosystem and its vision. In an interview with our research team, a senior manager from ING clearly stated that the bank was quite selective in its investments in fintechs: 'A bank will have like an innovation portfolio, an investment portfolio which allows it to invest in the development of FinTechs that should connect with that bank and it will have a possibility to "up the stakes" in the FinTech' (Interview with senior manager, ING).

Accordingly, banks' symbiotic relationship with fintechs may change or even end when they find that their investment in the fintech is misaligned with their own vision or capabilities. Another senior manager at ING explained this as follows:

> And we had many instances of failing FinTechs who probably had a good solution, but without receiving the adequate support, but also not getting the right stakeholders to take it forward within ING. And in the meantime, either they have given up or we have not enough trust for them to work with us anymore.
>
> (Interview with senior manager, ING).

While banks initially focused on their own exclusive innovation activities, they have increasingly started to join forces with *other* banks to scale up their solutions and place less emphasis on their own specific cultural and technological resources. For example, ING had invested heavily in developing blockchain technologies in collaboration with fintech start-ups, but

Box 5.3 Data and analytics strategy

According to the International Institute for Analytics, by 2020, businesses using data will see US$430 billion in productivity benefits compared to competitors that are not using data. Having a clear data strategy is vital when you consider the sheer volume of data that is available these days. A good data strategy is not about what data is readily or potentially available; it's about what your business wants to achieve, and how data can help you get there. As Justin de Graaf (director of data strategy and precision marketing, The Coca-Cola Company) stated:

> Data plays an increasingly important role in marketing and product development. Consumers do a great job of sharing their opinions with us - either by phone, email or social networks - that allow us to hear their voice and adjust our approach. [...]. Data is also helping us create more relevant content for different audiences. We want to focus on creating advertising content that speaks differently to different audiences. Some people love music. Other people watch every sport no matter what time of year. Our brands are already visible in those spaces, and we're working hard to use data to bring branded content that aligns with people's passions.

To enact a data and analytics strategy, business and digital leaders may consider the following to effectuate a data analytics strategy.

Assess	How are data related to business goals? How will data used? What data are needed?
Sources	What are appropriate internal and external data sources? How can you collect new data? Are the right things being measured? Who are the key informants/stakeholders? What is the context?
Storage	How is data integrated and stored, protected, and made accessible?
Analytics	What is the guiding hypothesis? What are appropriate analytical techniques? How can valuable business insights be extracted to improve decision-making and generate value? Can meaningful segments be used? How can insights be reported and visualized?
Technology	What hardware and software is required to turn data into insights?
Skills	Are the competences available within the organization, or do they need to be sourced externally?
Governance	Collecting and storing data, especially personal data, brings serious legal and regulatory obligations. Ignoring ownership, erroneous use of data, misleading data-providers (e.g., customers) privacy, and security issues could see data analytics move from being a huge asset to a huge liability.

Source: Kopanakis (2018)

in May 2019 it announced a collaboration with several competing banks to develop a joint 'private' blockchain trading platform (International Finance Corporation 2019), which would enable them to grow a platform ecosystem in which they could become central.

Reflection

In the digital era, new technological advances create a constant threat of obsolescence to incumbent firms. Technology is changing the process, content, and context of strategy. As discussed in this chapter, organizations are faced with new ways to develop strategies such as involving employees at lower hierarchical levels and even customers, new ways to compete such as the development of platforms and ecosystems, and new business models that allow them to create and capture value in new ways. However, adopting new ways of strategizing in the digital era does not come without its challenges, as organizations need to manage two central strategic tensions: centralization-decentralization and integration-separation.

Organizations may address these tensions by taking innovative approaches and management practices. An interesting illustration is how Ericsson reconciled transformation tensions when developing a new strategy process. Ericsson, with more than 100,000 employees, created a strategy platform, called Strategy Perspectives, to assist the organization in strategy making. The community attracted more than 1,000 individuals from different units of the company. The community demonstrated the capacity to support the strategy-making process in ways that were effective in addressing the two dilemmas that we discussed.

Utilizing such communities as complements to formal structures has several advantages. First, it allows a diverse and large organization to collect ideas from individuals in various geographical locations and with heterogeneous functional roles in an efficient way. Creating a formal unit of 1,000 employees with a diverse set of backgrounds is costly and comes with a lot of administrative issues. In contrast, an online strategy community had virtually no cost for the organization beyond the time of a few persons who were running the platform and those who took care of IT infrastructure. Second, it allows for alignment and coordination. Despite the bottom-up nature of the community-based strategy making, digital tools enable effective exchange of information. Hence, community members at Ericsson would be able to know more about different perspectives and to be able to act in a coordinated way in their formal roles. Third, using online communities for strategy making provides the possibility to orchestrate bottom-up activities. The strategy community can be aligned with the overall objectives and concerns of the executive management of the organization. Management can steer individuals towards what matters more for the organization by participating in the community and by communication and collaboration with community leaders. Fourth, it can help to energize organizational members and overcome resistance. When individuals are involved in the process of strategy making, they tend to become more committed to the change initiative. This is instrumental in executing the strategies across the organizational units.

Despite the benefits, there are several challenges associated with the creation of a strategy community. Several questions need to be addressed about who should be part of such communities and how large the community can be. How to synthesize the outcome and incorporate it into the formal strategy-making process is another major point for consideration. Several issues are revolving around orchestration activities, which include the appropriation of the contents when it is vital for legitimacy and continuity of the strategy community. However, despite these challenges, such communities can allow for inclusivity and openness in strategy making.

This chapter highlights that the digital era has brought new ways to compete, as companies can employ new strategy-making processes, compete based on new strategies (e.g., platform and ecosystem strategies), and implement new business models. We illuminated several strategic tensions and their prevalence during and after digital transformation. We also discussed new topics such as ecosystem strategies, platform dynamics, and coopetitive relationships, which are puzzling issues not fully understood or discussed in traditional textbooks. Lastly, we discussed the scale, scope, and speed of business as dimensions of strategic change that may call for the reconsideration of our assumptions and best practices of strategy formulation and implementation. The combination of these insights helps the next generation of managers to be more prepared for tackling digital strategy issues.

Learning and discussion questions

1 What are digital platforms and what characteristics make them successful in the digital era?
2 In what ways are the three dimensions of change (i.e., strategy context, content, and process) interrelated?
3 Explain the relationship between strategy and structure and discuss which one needs to be adjusted first to enable organizations to successfully embrace digital transformation?
4 While the chapter focused primarily on established firms, most of the topics are relevant for entrepreneurial firms as well. Which of the recommendations of the chapter are relevant for new ventures and which ones need reassessment?

Exercise: Signify and Li-Fi technology

Li-Fi is an initiative by producers of light bulbs (e.g., Philips Hue) to enter the communication sector using Li-Fi technology and to establish an ecosystem to compete with the pervasive Wi-Fi technology ecosystem. Li-Fi (short for light fidelity) is a relatively new wireless communication technology, which uses light to transmit data between devices. As the visible light spectrum is 10,000 times larger than the radio frequency spectrum that Wi-Fi uses, Li-Fi offers more space for data transmission without interfering with radio waves and provides internet access in places where wireless radio waves are not allowed, such as hospitals and airplanes. Light bulb producers such as Philips Hue hardly had any competence in the wireless communication ecosystem. Moreover, they had little know-how about the relationships and business models of the target sector. Being focused primarily on B2C markets, these producers did not have expertise in the B2B relationships that are dominant in the communication sector.

Light bulb producers such as Signify hardly have any competence in the wireless communication ecosystem. Moreover, they had little know-how about the relationships and business model of the target sector. Being focused primarily on B2C markets, these producers did not have expertise in the B2B relationships that are dominant in the communication sector. Because of these limitations, they did not have an option to enter this new sector outright, let alone to assume a leadership position. To run the trials and show some progress, Philips and its rivals in Li-Fi technology needed support from companies ranging from Intel to service providers such as O2 to standardization bodies such as IEEE. These actors would either benefit directly from Wi-Fi or had heavily invested in it. They could thus be expected to resist a potential contender entering their domain, unless they saw a substantial advantage in using the alternative technology. Jack Gold, president of mobility consultancy explains this challenge: 'there's the fact that Wi-Fi works well and is nearly ubiquitous. If you've got a technology that's in use that works fairly reliably and you come up with a new technology to replace or supplement it, it's got to be better'.

Case questions

1. Explain the importance of the Li-Fi initiative for Signify's ability to compete successfully?
2. How should Signify reconsider their strategy process, content, and context for succeeding in the Li-Fi initiative?
3. How should Signify deal with the other parties in this initiative?

References

Adner, R. and Kapoor, R. (2010) 'Value creation in innovation ecosystems: how the structure of technological interdependence affects firm performance in new technology generations'. *Strategic Management Journal*, 31(3): 306-333.

Ahuja, G. and Novelli, E. (2017) 'Redirecting research efforts on the diversification-performance linkage: The search for synergy'. *Academy of Management Annals*, 11(1): 342-390.

Ansari, S. and Krop, P. (2012) 'Incumbent performance in the face of a radical innovation: towards a framework for incumbent challenger dynamics'. *Research Policy*, 41: 1357-1374.

Ansari, S., Reinecke, J., and Spaan, A. (2014) 'How are practices made to vary? Managing practice adaptation in a multinational corporation'. *Organization Studies*, 35(9): 1313-1341.

Ansari, S., Garud, R., and Kumaraswamy, A. (2016) 'The disruptor's dilemma: TiVo and the US television ecosystem'. *Strategic Management Journal*, 37(9): 1829-1853.

Baden-Fuller, C. and Haefliger, S. (2013) 'Business models and technological innovation'. *Long Range Planning*, 46(6): 419-426.

Beaumont, L. (2018) 'Banks can't partner themselves into digital relevancy'. Available online at: https://www.americanbanker.com/opinion/banks-cant-partner-themselves-into-digital-relevancy (accessed 18 December 2020).

Birkinshaw, J., Hamel, G., and Mol, M. J. (2008) 'Management innovation'. *Academy of Management Review*, 33(4): 825-845.

Boudreau, K. (2010) 'Open platform strategies and innovation: granting access vs. devolving control'. *Management Science*, 56(10): 1849-1872.

Burgelman, R. A., Floyd, S. W., Laamanen, T., Mantere, S., Vaara, E., and Whittington, R. (2018) 'Strategy processes and practices: Dialogues and intersections'. *Strategic Management Journal*, 39(3): 531-558.

Capon, N., Hulbert, J. M., Farley, J. U., and Martin, L. E. (1988) 'Corporate diversity and economic performance: The impact of market specialization'. *Strategic Management Journal*, 9(1): 61-74.

Cennamo, C. (2018) 'Building the value of next-generation platforms: the paradox of diminishing returns'. *Journal of Management*, 44(8): 3038-3069.

Cennamo, C. and Santalo, J. (2013) 'Platform competition: strategic trade-offs in platform markets'. *Strategic Management Journal*, 34(11): 1331-1350.

Christensen, C. M., and Bower, J. L. (1996) 'Customer power, strategic investment, and the failure of leading firms'. *Strategic Management Journal*, 17: 197-218.

Claussen, J., Essling, C., and Kretschmer, T. (2015) 'When less can be more - setting technology levels in complementary goods markets'. *Research Policy*, 44(2): 328-339.

DattÈe, B., Alexy, O., and Autio, E. (2018) 'Maneuvering in poor visibility: how firms play the ecosystem game when uncertainty is high'. *Academy of Management Journal* 61(2): 466-498.

Eggers, J. P. (2012) 'All experience is not created equal: Learning, adapting, and focusing in product portfolio management'. *Strategic Management Journal*, 33(3): 315-335.

Eggers, J. P. (2016) 'Reversing course: Competing technologies, mistakes, and renewal in flat panel displays'. *Strategic Management Journal*, 37(8): 1578-1596.

Eisenmann, T., Parker, G., and Van Alstyne, M. W. (2006) 'Strategies for two-sided markets'. *Harvard Business Review*, 84(10): 92.

Eisenmann T. R., Parker G, Van Alstyne M. (2011) 'Platform envelopment'. *Strategic Management Journal*, 32: 1270-1285.

Eklund, J. and Kapoor, R. (2019) 'Pursuing the new while sustaining the current: Incumbent strategies and firm value during the nascent period of industry change'. *Organization Science*, 30(2): 383-404.

Evans, D., Hagiu, A., and Schmalensee, R. (2006) *Invisible Engines: How Software Platforms Drive Innovation and Transform Industries*. Cambridge, MA: MIT Press.

Flint, D. (2014) 'Business ethics in banking: Time for a second chance?' [Online] as appeared in Teigland, R., Siri, S., Larsson, A., Puertas, A. M., and Bogusz, C. I. (2018) 'Introduction: FinTech and shifting financial system institutions' in *The rise and development of FinTech* (Open Access). London and New York: Routledge, (1-18).

Foss, N. J., and Saebi, T. (2017) 'Fifteen years of research on business model innovation: How far have we come, and where should we go?'. *Journal of Management*, 43(1): 200-227.

Garud, R., Jain, S., and Kumaraswamy A. (2002) 'Institutional entrepreneurship in the sponsorship of common technological standards: the case of Sun Microsystems and Java'. *Academy of Management Journal*, 45(1): 196-214.

Gawer, A., and Cusumano, M. A. (2002) *Platform Leadership: How Intel, Microsoft, and Cisco Drive Industry Innovation*. Boston, MA: Harvard Business School Press.

Gawer, A., and Cusumano, M. A. (2008) 'How companies become platform leaders'. *MIT Sloan Management Review*, 49(2): 28-35.

Gawer, A., and Cusumano, M. A. (2014) 'Industry platforms and ecosystem innovation'. *Journal of Product Innovation Management*, 31(3): 417-433.

Gawer, A., and Phillips, N. (2013) 'Institutional work as logics shift: The case of Intel's transformation to platform leader'. *Organization Studies*, 34(8): 1035-1071.

George, G., Haas, M. R., and Pentland, A. (2014) 'Big data and management'. *Academy of Management Journal*, 57(2): 321-326.

Gilbert, C. G. (2005) 'Unbundling the structure of inertia: Resource versus routine rigidity'. *Academy of Management Journal*, 48(5): 741-763.

Gomber, P., Kauffman, R. J., Parker, C., and Weber, B. W. (2018) 'On the fintech revolution: interpreting the forces of innovation, disruption, and transformation in financial services'. *Journal of Management Information Systems*, 35(1): 220-265.

Hagiu, A., and Eisenmann, T. (2007) 'A staged solution to the Catch-22'. *Harvard Business Review*, 85(11): 25-26.

Hankin, A. (2019) 'JPM Coin is not a cryptocurrency, says crypto advocacy group'. Available online at: https://www.marketwatch.com/story/jpm-coin-is-not-a-cryptocurrency-says-crypto-advocacy-group-2019-02-14 (accessed 18 December 2020).

Hannah, D. P. and Eisenhardt, K. M. (2018) 'How firms navigate cooperation and competition in nascent ecosystems'. *Strategic Management Journal*, 39(12): 3163-3192.

Hargadon, A. B., and Douglas, Y. (2001) 'When innovations meet institutions: Edison and the design of the electric light'. *Administrative Science Quarterly*, 46(3): 476-501.

Hautz, J., Seidl, D., and Whittington, R. (2017) 'Open strategy: Dimensions, dilemmas, dynamics'. *Long Range Planning*, 50(3): 298-309.

Henderson, R. and Clark, B. (1990) 'Architectural innovation: the reconfiguration of existing product technologies and the failure of established firms'. *Administrative Science Quarterly*, 35(1): 9-30.

Hoffmann, W., Lavie, D., Reuer, J. J., and Shipilov, A. (2018). 'The interplay of competition and cooperation'. *Strategic Management Journal*, 39(12): 3033-3052.

Iansiti, M. and Levien, R. (2004) *The keystone advantage: what the new dynamics of business ecosystems mean for strategy, innovation, and sustainability*. Brighton, MA: Harvard Business Press.

International Finance Corporation (2019) 'Blockchain: Opportunities for Private Enterprises in Emerging Markets'. Available online at: https://hollandfintech.com/wp-content/uploads/2019/02/201901-IFC-EMCompass-Blockchain-Report.pdf (accessed 18 December 2020).

Katz, M. and Shapiro, C. (1985) 'Network externalities, competition and compatibility'. *American Economic Review*, 75: 424-440.

Khanagha, S., Ansari, S. S., Paroutis, S., and Oviedo, L. (2020) 'Mutualism and the Dynamics of New Platform Creation: A Study of Cisco and Fog computing'. *Strategic Management Journal*, (forthcoming).

Khanagha, S., Volberda, H., and Oshri, I. (2014) 'Business model renewal and ambidexterity: Structural alteration and strategy formation process during transition to a Cloud business model'. *R&D Management*, 44(3): 322-340.

Khanagha, S., Volberda, H., and Oshri, I. (2017) 'Customer co-creation and exploration of emerging technologies: the mediating role of managerial attention and initiatives'. *Long Range Planning*, 50(2): 221-242.

Khanagha, S., Volberda, H., Sidhu, J., and Oshri, I. (2013) 'Management innovation and adoption of emerging technologies: The case of cloud computing'. *European Management Review*, 10(1): 51-67.

Klemperer, P. (1987) 'Markets with consumer switching costs'. *Quarterly Journal of Economics*, 102: 375-394.

Kopanakis, J. (2018) '5 real world examples of how brands are using big data analytics'. Available online at https://www.mentionlytics.com/blog/5-real-world-examples-of-how-brands-are-using-big-data-analytics/#disqus_thread (accessed 25 May 2020).

Lavie, D. (2006) 'Capability reconfiguration: An analysis of incumbent responses to technological change'. *Academy of Management Review*, 31(1): 153-174.

Lavie, D., Stettner, U., and Tushman, M. L. (2010) 'Exploration and exploitation within and across organizations'. *Academy of Management Annals*, 4(1): 109-155.

Marr, B. (2016) 'The Sharing Economy - What It Is, Examples, And How Big Data, Platforms And Algorithms Fuel It'. Available online at https://www.forbes.com/sites/bernardmarr/2016/10/21/the-sharing-economy-what-it-is-examples-and-how-big-data-platforms-and-algorithms-fuel/#64affd787c5a (accessed 25 June 2020).

McIntyre, D. P. and Srinivasan, A. (2017) 'Networks, platforms, and strategy: Emerging views and next steps'. *Strategic Management Journal*, 38(1): 141-160.

Nambisan, S. and Sawhney, M. (2011) 'Orchestration processes in network-centric innovation: evidence from the field'. *Academy of Management Perspectives*, 25(3): 40-57.

Ozalp, H. and Kretschmer, T. (2019) 'Follow the crowd or follow the trailblazer? The differential role of firm experience in product entry decisions in the US video game industry'. *Journal of Management Studies*, 56: 1452-1481

Pierce, L. (2009) 'Big losses in ecosystem niches: How core firm decisions drive complementary product shakeouts'. *Strategic Management Journal*, 30(3): 323-347.

Rochet, J. C., and Tirole, J. (2006) 'Two-sided markets: a progress report'. *The RAND Journal of Economics*, 37(3): 645-667.

Santos, F. M., and Eisenhardt, K. M. (2009) 'Constructing markets and shaping boundaries: Entrepreneurial power in nascent fields'. *Academy of Management Journal*, 52(4): 643-671.

Schilling, M. A. (1998) 'Technological lockout: An integrative model of the economic and strategic factors driving technology success and failure'. *Academy of Management Review*, 23(2): 267-284.

Schilling, M. A. (2002) 'Technology success and failure in winner-take-all markets: The impact of learning orientation, timing, and network externalities'. *Academy of Management Journal*, 45(2): 387-398.

Schilling, M. A. (2003) 'Technological leapfrogging: lessons from the US video game console industry'. *California Management Review*, 45(3): 6-32.

Schilling, M. A. (2009) 'Protecting or diffusing a technology platform: Tradeoffs in appropriability, network externalities, and architectural control'. In A. Gawer (ed.), *Platforms, markets and innovation*. Cheltenham: Edward Elgar, (192-218).

Schrey^gg, G., and Sydow, J. (2011) 'Organizational path dependence: A process view'. *Organization Studies*, 32(3): 321-335.

Sheremata, W. A. (2004) 'Competing through innovation in network markets: Strategies for challengers'. *Academy of Management Review*, 29(3): 359-377.

Sia, S. K., Soh, C., and Weill, P. (2016) 'How DBS Bank pursued a digital business strategy'. *MIS Quarterly Executive*, 15(2): 105-121.

Siggelkow, N. (2001) 'Change in the presence of fit: The rise, the fall, and the renaissance of Liz Claiborne'. *Academy of Management Journal*, 44(4): 838–857.

Teece, D. J. (2017) 'Profiting from innovation in the digital economy: standards, complementary assets, and business models in the wireless world'. *Research Policy*, 47(8): 1367–1387.

Teigland, R., Siri, S., Larsson, A., Puertas, A., and Bogusz, C. (2018) *The rise and development of FinTech: Accounts of disruption from Sweden and beyond*. Abingdon: Routledge.

The Economist (2015) 'The disruption of banking' Available online at https://eiuperspectives.economist.com/sites/default/files/EIU-The%20disruption%20of%20banking_PDF_1.pdf (accessed 25 July 2020).

Thomas L. D., Autio E., and Gann, D. M. (2014) 'Architectural leverage: putting platforms in context'. *Academy of Management Perspectives*, 28(2): 198–219.

Tiwana, A., Konsynski, B., and Bush, A. A. (2010) 'Research commentary – Platform evolution: Coevolution of platform architecture, governance, and environmental dynamics'. *Information Systems Research*, 21(4): 675–687.

Toh, P. K., and Miller, C. D. (2017) 'Pawn to save a chariot, or drawbridge into the fort? Firms' disclosure during standard setting and complementary technologies within ecosystems'. *Strategic Management Journal*, 38(11): 2213–2236.

Tweddle, K. (2018) 'BankThink 'Doomed'? Fintech partnerships are vital'. Available online at: https://www.americanbanker.com/opinion/doomed-fintech-partnerships-are-vital (accessed 18 December 2020).

Vaccaro, I. G., Jansen, J. J., Van Den Bosch, F. A., and Volberda, H. W. (2012) 'Management innovation and leadership: The moderating role of organizational size'. *Journal of Management Studies*, 49(1): 28–51.

Van Knippenberg, D., Dahlander, L., Haas, M. R., and George, G. (2015) 'Information, attention, and decision making'. *Academy of Management Journal*, 58(3): 649–657.

Vasudeva, G., Spencer, J., and Teegen, H. (2013) 'Bringing the institutional context back in: a cross-national comparison of alliance partner selection and knowledge acquisition'. *Organization Science*, 24(2): 319–338.

Volberda, H. W., Van den Bosch, F. A., and Mihalache, O. R. (2014) 'Advancing management innovation: Synthesizing processes, levels of analysis, and change agents'. *Organization Studies*, 35(9): 1245–1264.

Volberda, H., Van den Bosch, F. and Heij, K. (2018) *Reinventing Business Models: How firms cope with disruption*. Oxford: Oxford University Press.

Wareham, J., Fox, P. B., and Cano Giner, J. L. (2014) 'Technology ecosystem governance' *Organization Science*. 25(4): 1195–1215.

PART 3

Collaboration and responsibility

6 Collaborative transformation

Brian Tjemkes

Summary

This chapter explores issues around collaborative transformation; specifically what drives change and progress in collaborative arrangements. Collaboration between companies has become the cornerstone of corporate strategizing, though collaborative endeavors appear in many forms. After providing a definition of collaborative arrangements and detailing on their uniqueness, our focus shifts toward a tension inherently tied to inter-firm collaboration: the tension between cooperation and competition. How strategists frame and deal with this tension has a direct impact on whether collaborative arrangements progress towards success or failure. Focusing on collaborative transformation, this chapter provides details on four theoretical perspectives on change and discusses how each perspective is associated with four forms of collaborative arrangements: alliances, alliance portfolios, alliance networks, and business ecosystems. The chapter ends with an overview of learnings.

Case: Netflix Inc. - from competition to cooperation?

Ranked fifth in terms of the most innovative leaders on America's *Forbes* list are Reed Hasting, the man behind Netflix Inc. (Netflix), and co-founder Marc Randolph. In 1997, USA-based Netflix started as a website-based DVD rental company; by 2019 it had evolved into a company with revenue of US$20.156 million. Initially the company provided a website where customers could request to rent a DVD for a set fee, plus postage. With the advancement of technology, Netflix has evolved into an online streaming service where members can watch movies and shows.

In its early years, Netflix had 30 employees and 925 available titles, almost the entire catalogue of DVDs at the time. However, Netflix was able to leverage its technology to become a superior DVD rental service. Today, Netflix is a subscription-based streaming service, with approximately 150 million paid subscribers worldwide. Since its launch, Netflix has begun operating in almost every country in the world, except those sanctioned by the USA (such as North Korea) or shut out by the national government (China, for example). Netflix not only provides content from third parties, but also produces its own shows and films.

Except for the online aspect, in the early days the business was comparable to Blockbuster in that both offered a pay-per-rent model. In the 2000s, however, Netflix replaced its rental model with a monthly subscription service, basically offering unlimited rentals for an unlimited time. Despite their 300,000 subscription customers, Netflix initially operated at a loss. In response, in the late 2000s Netflix approached its competitor Blockbuster to acquire it for US$50 million; the offer was rejected. During these years Netflix embraced a competitive differentiation strategy, offering a new, more convenient, service with a different pricing model than that of regular video stores. In support, it invested in technology to enhance its algorithm, which also resulted in improvements in the infrastructure, its market position, and a reduced threat of substitution. After surviving the dot-com crisis, Netflix saw a strong increase in its business after the cost of DVD players reduced significantly. In 2002 Netflix was publicly listed and in 2005 was shipping approximately 1 million DVDs to customers every day.

The rise in internet speeds and reduction of bandwidth costs made it possible to download and stream movies faster than Netflix could ship their DVDs. Netflix realized the rising desire among customers to stream content directly from the internet after discovering the growing popularity of YouTube. In 2007, Netflix decided to move in a parallel direction, offering a small selection of movies on its homepage to see whether customers would enjoy it - and they did. In 2010, Netflix shifted its focuses from DVD rental to online streaming. The first Netflix production, *House of Cards*, was introduced in 2013, and became a huge success, attracting many new subscribers. Following this success, Netflix expanded internationally, continuously seeking a balance between producing original content and maintaining market leadership as a content distribution platform. Netflix's third-party offer was organized via licensing agreements, such as with the Walt Disney Company. By 2013, Netflix provided services to approximately 36 million subscribers. To support further growth, Netflix decided in 2008 to gradually outsource its hosting and streaming to Amazon Web Services (AWS) and completed this transition in 2016.

More recently, Netflix's leading market position has come under attack, as other parties have entered the video on demand (VOD) market. Companies such as Disney+ and Apple TV have entered the market and have occasionally collaborated to battle against Netflix. In response, Netflix has kept its investment levels high (e.g., US$8 billion via investors in 2018) to secure subscription growth and technological superiority. Netflix is able to invest in exclusive content while keeping prices low.

Overall, the success of Netflix can be attributed to multiple factors including timing, first-mover advantage, technological capabilities, branding, and perhaps luck. If we take a collaboration perspective, one could conclude that success may depend on Netflix's ability to forge collaborative arrangements with a variety of partners, including studios, consumers, investors, and platform providers. Whereas Netflix was focused on competition in its early days, growth may resulted from collaboration, and it is through collaboration that Netflix is able to withstand emerging competitive threats.

Questions:

1 How would you describe the constellation of Netflix's business partners?
2 How would Netflix manage this constellation of business partners?
3 How and to what extent did the Netflix business partners contribute to its growth strategy and success?

Sources: McFadden (2020); Pahwa, (2019); Sherman (2019); Wieringa (2019)

Learning objectives

The objectives of this chapter are to:

1 Provide readers with an introduction to collaborative arrangements
2 Acquaint readers with the cooperation-competition tension inherently tied to collaboration
3 Familiarize readers with the governance principles of four types of collaborative arrangements: alliances, alliance portfolios, alliance networks, and business ecosystems
4 Provide readers with (theoretical and practical) insights into how collaborative arrangements transform over time.

Introduction to collaborative arrangements

In today's competitive business landscape, firms rely heavily on collaborative arrangements to sustain a competitive advantage (Tjemkes, Vos, and Burgers 2017). Collaboration has become the cornerstone of the competitive strategy of many firms, enabling them to achieve objectives that would otherwise be difficult to realize. For example, collaboration provides firms with an opportunity to increase their innovative capacity, improve their market response, achieve efficiency and share investment risks with partner firms. This view encompasses a wide variety of collaborative arrangements, such as joint ventures, purchase partnerships, research and development partnerships, co-makerships, co-creation efforts, multi-partner alliances, public-private partnerships, and consortia, but it excludes arrangements such as market transactions and mergers and acquisitions.

Historically, the use of collaborative arrangements shifted from relatively simple, focused arrangements to more complex, multi-purpose constellations (Tjemkes et al. 2017). During the 1970s, for example, firms focused on product performance (that is, efficiency and quality) and engaged in collaboration to obtain access to technology and new domestic and international markets, as well as to realize market stability. During the 1980s, the focus shifted to obtaining flexible market positions, as continuing globalization, increasing competition, and more demanding customers required firms to become flexible. Their external partnerships provided flexibility, deployed to build industry stature, consolidate industry positions, and gain economies of scale and scope. Then, during the 1990s and 2000s, firms switched their attention to learning and capability development for innovation; they began using partnerships to ensure a constant stream of prospects for advancing technology, proactively maximize value, optimize their total cost for product or customer segments, and gain an ability to respond to changing internal and external conditions. More recently, firms embraced business ecosystems - value-proposition-driven constellations of firms - as a way to sustain a competitive advantage in increasingly dynamic and uncertain environments. Leading and/or participating in ecosystem has enabled these firms to accelerate innovation, offer integrated solutions to their customers, and explore and exploit new market opportunities.

Regardless of the rationale or form, the strategic value of collaborative arrangements is apparent, especially in a contemporary context of rapidly growing and changing markets, global competition, network organizations, and dynamic, complex, expensive technologies. However, as organizational entities, collaborative arrangements are inherently complex to manage and are continually under threat from external contingencies that originate either in the partners' own organization or in the external environment. Specifically, our view of collaboration is built on four important pillars:

1 A collaborative arrangement is an instrument that firms use to achieve their objectives, ultimately to develop and sustain their competitive advantage (Ireland, Hitt, and Vaidyanath 2002). Therefore, the management of collaborative arrangements constitutes a strategic activity within firms.
2 A firm remains an independent organizational entity (as opposed to mergers and acquisitions), but connects voluntarily to external parties through a collaborative arrangement. Therefore, collaborative arrangements offer speed and flexibility, but come with risk and reward sharing.
3 As critical resources get exchanged, firms engaged in collaborative arrangements grow increasingly dependent on each other. Therefore, firms must anticipate power dynamics that, if left unresolved, may adversely affect value creation and value appropriation (Dyer, Singh, and Kale 2008).
4 Collaborative arrangements are transitional entities because firms can withdraw or repair from them at any convenient time. Therefore, firms must prepare for (premature) termination to safeguard reputation and resources, but decision-makers should also understand how internal and external circumstances prompt change and adaptation.

Tension: cooperation versus competition

Collaborative arrangements involve tensions that, if left unresolved, may jeopardize their success. In general, decision-makers are confronted with a tension among rational, purposeful, and calculative approaches versus approaches focusing on social bonds - individual entanglements - to encourage managers to reciprocate cooperative behaviors. In this chapter, however, we proffer that the most prominent tension in collaborative arrangements pertains to the tension between cooperation and competition (Das and Teng 2000a; Niesten and Stefan 2019). This is because, throughout the development of any collaborative arrangement, any form of cooperation between partners is balanced against the competitive aspects of their partnership.

Cooperation consists of the parties' efforts to implement value-creating conditions and processes. As the alliance progresses, partners may contribute complementary resources, make alliance-specific investments, initiate reciprocal learning, or invest in relational capital to support the collaborative logic of the relationship (Ariño and de la Torre 1998; Das and Teng 2000b). By enacting knowledge sharing between partners, the partners together capitalize on the joint synergies created via the arrangement. In contrast, competition implies efforts to appropriate value from the alliance, if necessary, at the expense of the partner firm (Dyer et al. 2008). As the arrangement evolves, the partners' focus shifts to realizing a favorable pay-off structure, opportunism, unilateral knowledge acquisition, and the use of bargaining power to support their individual interests. Thus, value appropriation aims to divide resources (such as financial and knowledge resources) that are shared between the partners (Niesten and Stefan 2019).

Thus, cooperative and competitive forces are at odds, differing in both philosophy and spirit and, depending on context, they become manifest sequentially or concurrently. Consider the following example: to reap the benefits of economies of scale and scope and to seize market opportunities related to innovations, (rival) companies may collaborate to set new standards, and/or integrate existing businesses through complementary technologies. Value creation implies that partner firms reveal information and further co-coordinate to develop the technology. However, if partners reveal too much information, there is a risk that either one of them will gain a marketization advantage, whereas sharing too little information may result in an under-developed technology. Thus, value appropriation entails competition between the partners to capture benefits from the collaboration to ensure a smooth transition towards marketization of the technology. These examples show that value creation and appropriation are interrelated, such that prioritizing one over the other has adverse effects. Thus, collaborative arrangements are distinct from transactional arrangements, as the former associates with a positive-sum and the latter with a zero-sum situation. To realize high-performing, sustainable collaborative endeavors, cooperative and competitive forces are indispensable and must be reconciled.

Before resolving the tension, however, partners must recognize that the cooperation-competition tension is embedded in any collaborative arrangement. Typically, partners become aware of the tension when they are rivals (for example, coopetition), resources are scarce (for example, small versus large partners), or internal and external changes (such as new

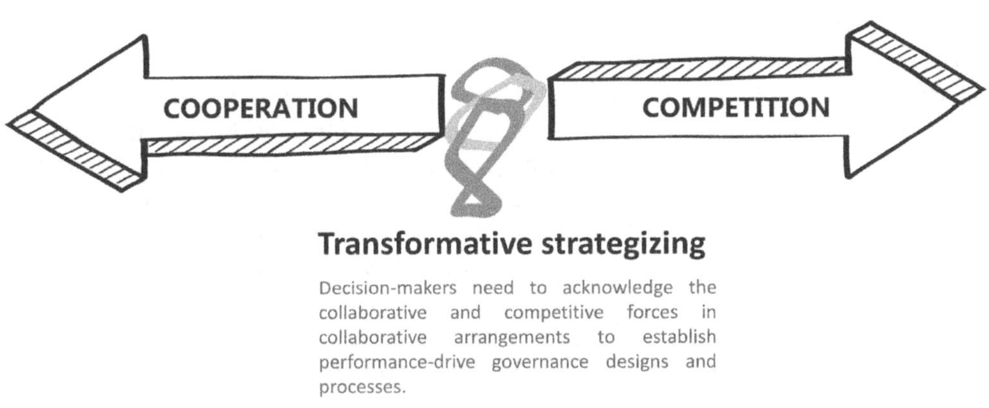

Figure 6.1 Cooperation-competition tension

technologies or new market entrants) occur. To reinforce a constructive interplay between cooperation and competition, decision-makers must establish balanced governance designs (such as contracts and trust), build and deploy collaboration capabilities (for instance, relative absorptive capacity), and opt for hybrid compensation schemes (residual sharing, for example). In contrast, distrust, learning races, and learning myopia may cause value appropriation to be prioritized over value creation, jeopardizing the health of the collaboration.

Collaborative arrangements and transformation logics

Different types of collaborative arrangements

We depart from the view that a focal firm seeks to deliver on a value proposition, and to this end purposively forges (formal) relationships with external parties to create and exchange resources to attain individual and common objectives. Building on this view, we next present four types of collaborative arrangements: (i) alliances; (ii) alliance portfolios; (iii) alliance networks; and (iv) business ecosystems.[1] Table 6.1 provides an overview.

Alliance

An alliance is a voluntary, long-term, contractual relationship between two or more autonomous and independent organizations (that is, firms) designed to achieve mutual and individual objectives by sharing and/or creating resources (Ariño, de la Torre, and Ring 2001: 110; Gulati 1995: 621). Compared with other organizational arrangements, such as stand-alone organizations, mergers, or market transactions, alliances have specific management challenges (Albers, Wohlgezogen, and Zajac 2016). In an alliance, interdependent parties must develop joint business propositions, share control and management, accept overlapping roles and responsibilities, engage in adaptation through mutual cooperation, install internal and proactive monitoring mechanisms, and develop long-term incentive systems. In turn, parallel to cooperation, competition between the partners exists because partners simultaneously compete with one another to attain individual objectives, occasionally at the expense of their counterparts. To steer alliances towards success, the partners involved establish governance design and enact management practices.

Alliance design. An alliance design consists of the configuration of an alliance's structural building blocks, which aim to organize the partners' coordination and contractual enforcement legally (Williamson 1985). With minimum cost, an appropriate governance form can ensure the control that parties need before they will come to believe that engaging in the alliance will be of benefit to them. Accordingly, an efficient governance design aligns parties' interests by imposing an incentive structure that stimulates the creation of long-term gains through cooperation, while reducing short-term gains from competition. In addition, partners need to safeguard themselves against exchange hazards (e.g. opportunistic behavior, free-riding), requiring them to install deterrents, which may include equity exchange, contractual stipulations, and a code of conduct (Das and Rahman 2001).

A first design decision relates to the type of governance form, which differs when alliance partners take actual ownership of the alliance structure (for example, joint venture), versus when they rely on non-equity-based arrangements (Hennart 1988). A non-equity

Table 6.1 Alliance, alliance portfolio, alliance network, business ecosystem

	Alliance	*Alliance portfolio*	*Alliance network*	*Business ecosystem*
Description	Arrangement between two or more organizations	Firm-centered constellation of multiple alliance arrangements	Firm-centered constellation of multiple direct and indirect inter-firm relationships	Dynamic constellation of organizations, collaborating to deliver a core product/service and complements
	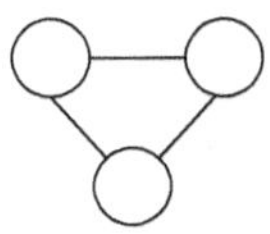	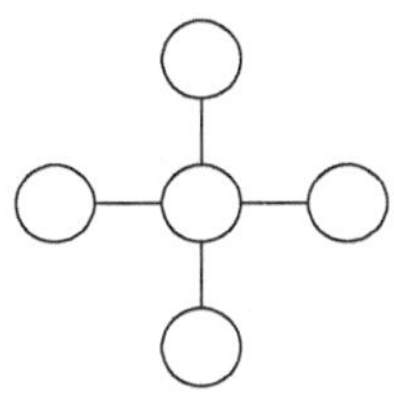	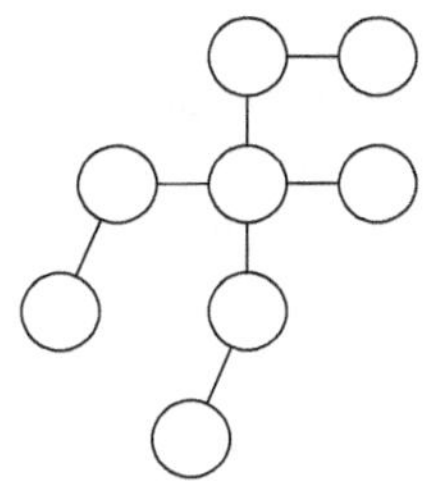	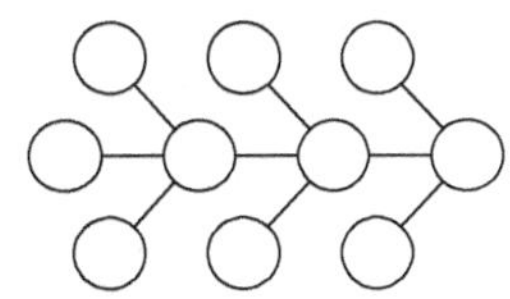
Main motive	Creation and exploitation of shared resources	Creation and exploitation of synergies across alliance partners	Access and exploitation of second- and third-party resources and information	Creation and exploitation of existing and emerging market opportunities
Structural focus	Design:	Configuration:	Position:	Form:
Goal	- Effectuate coordination, secure protection, and enable appropriation	- Maximize facilitating and minimize constraining interdependencies	- Optimize resource and information flows and mitigate lock-in effects	- Formulate a value proposition encompassing ecosystem and members' interests
How	- Legal entity, contracts, and control mechanisms	- Number of partners, selection, termination, and partner attributes	- Number of direct/indirect partners, selection, termination, and relationship attributes	- Type of ecosystem, nature of ecosystem governance, co-investments, standardization, and incentives
Process focus	Management:	Coordination:	Influence:	Orchestration:
Goal	- Effectuate coordination, enact enhancements and relationship repair	- Effectuate cross-partner coordination, enact enhancements and portfolio repair	- Enact network role, build social capital, and promote information flows	- Promote learning and adaptation, embrace self-organizing and ecosystem renewal
How	- Relational governance, conflict resolutions, and learning	- Relational governance, conflict resolutions, and learning	- Framing, activating, mobilizing, and synthesizing	- Information exchange, innovation efforts, self-selection, and role allocation

arrangement implies that the alliance agreement is organized through an alliance contract, without any transfer of equity between the partners. This type of arrangement is relatively easily to establish because it relies solely on a relatively simple contractual agreement. In an equity-based arrangement, by contrast, the partners transfer equity or establish a new organizational entity, called a joint venture, in which they both participate with equity. Thus, the exchange of equity provides an additional protection against exchange hazards because partners become dependent on each other to achieve their objectives. Equity-based arrangements usually reflect a long-term commitment and a sense of mutual cooperation, shared risks, and benefits.

The second design decision relates to the contract. An alliance contract provides a legally binding, institutional framework that codifies each party's rights, duties and responsibilities, and specifies the goals, policies, and strategies that underlie the anticipated cooperation (Mayer and Argyres 2004). An alliance contract safeguards investments and property against misappropriation by a partner, and codifies the penalties a firm can impose on a counterpart if the latter violates the alliance agreement. An alliance contract also provides a clear overview of the tasks and responsibilities of each party, such that it also functions as a coordination mechanism. In order to cope with additional internal and external challenges that may emerge unexpectedly as the partnership unfolds, alliance contracts can enable adaptation. This so-called contingency adaptability refers to the specification of principles or guidelines that describe how to handle changing situations.

A third design decision is related to management control. In alliances, the primary purpose of control mechanisms is to encourage coordination and ensure that the partners achieve their predetermined objectives (Dekker 2004). Control mechanisms organize the coordination of interdependent tasks; e.g., firms might put command and authority systems in place to force their partner to comply with the tasks required to achieve alliance objectives or allocate resources even if the partner is unwilling to do so. Management control also enables a firm to acquire influence over alliance development and outcomes by installing incentive systems, standard operating procedures, and conflict resolution procedures, which provide incentives to collaborate. Therefore, reducing appropriation concerns and fulfilling coordination requirements are critical rationales for management control. Management control may also be embodied in alliance contracts, but it extends beyond governance form; for example, control is not a strict consequence of ownership and instead results from a variety of control mechanisms. The mechanisms that partners use to exercise control can vary, including power, authority, or a wide range of bureaucratic, cultural, and informal mechanisms.

Alliance management. The alliance management stage confronts alliance partners with the next challenge - monitoring and coordinating alliance activities - and, if required, impose changes, with the purpose of creating value-creating conditions and mitigating the potential threat of exchange hazards. Alliance managers must oversee whether the partners deploy their resource contributions, adhere to coordination mechanisms, act on expressed commitments, and complete the tasks assigned to them. The task of alliance managers is to respond to these contingencies and steer the relationship towards its objectives. To inform their alliance management, managers need to recognize how to deploy a range of soft approaches.

Classical contract law relies primarily on the legal framework as a mechanism to plan exchanges, (re)negotiate contracts, and resolve contractual conflict. Alternatively, relational governance governs and guides parties such that they behave in a mutually beneficial manner because of their common understanding of relational norms and relational capital (Das and Teng 2001). Relational governance emerges in alliances that include socialization between the partners, which itself results in shared beliefs and values, and influences partners' behavior as to increase commitment to the alliance. Relational governance rests on the premise that, for alliance contracts to function, a set of common unwritten social rules must exist to describe the unwritten social rules that guide partner firms' behaviors. For example, rules may pertain to notions of flexibility, solidarity, and information exchange. An alliance arrangement exhibiting relational governance is characterized by partners who feel comfortable, rely on trust, and commit to the relationship. Relational governance contributes to a freer, greater exchange of information and know-how because decision-makers do not worry about protecting themselves from opportunistic behavior (Ariño et al. 2001).

Conflicts in alliances pertain to a perceived divergence of interests, or the belief that partners' current aspirations cannot be achieved simultaneously (White, Joplin, and Salama 2007). Conflict is generally imagined as destructive because it creates negative reactions that can intensify partner tensions. Moreover, conflicts, tensions, or disagreements induce heightened competitive processes, create misperceptions of alliance progress, and stimulate a sense of the inequitable distribution of alliance outcomes. They also can give rise to distrust and anxiety, reduce the level of cooperation and efficient integration of activities, and hamper alliance performance. To resolve conflicts (before they escalate) proactive conflict management is necessitated. Conflict resolution forces alliance members to disagree and debate the merits of their alternative solutions, which can mitigate the negative effects of conflicts and exploit their beneficial aspects. However, if conflicts cannot be resolved, tensions escalate and the dissolution of the partnership becomes inevitable.

In the context of alliance management, inter-partner learning refers the extent to which partner firms create a regular and repeatable pattern of routines that support knowledge and information transfer (Simonin 1999). Such learning is distinct from the motive to form the alliance, as this type of learning involves the process rather than the content of learning (that is, inter-firm learning). One role of alliance management pertains to creating a climate in which partners can enact knowledge and information transfers. As firms learn about their alliance partners, they also learn how to interface and communicate with them, which allows partners to revisit and revise their expectations and to gain a deeper understanding of their counterparts. In removing information-processing barriers between parties, three factors support the claim that inter-partner learning fosters alliance success: (i) increased openness; (ii) transfer of tacit knowledge; and (iii) reduced risk of competitive behaviors.

Alliance portfolio

By adopting an alliance portfolio approach, a firm shifts its focus from single-alliance governance to systematic governance of its bundle of alliances (Hoffmann 2007). The argument is that firms can benefit from engaging in multiple simultaneous alliances that may not be available if the firm had only one alliance at a given point in time. In other words, the linkages and interdependencies between a firm's alliance partners provide additional opportunities for synergy (Wassmer 2008). The way in which a focal firm organizes these intertwined relationships has a notable influence on its competitiveness, which means that a goal-oriented alliance portfolio approach could play a decisive role in firm performance. The core value of an alliance portfolio lies in the notion that it allows the focal firm to focus on its core competences while benefiting from alliance partners' resources and market positions on the one hand, and dealing with strategic uncertainty on the other. Apart from gaining access to a wide variety of resources and knowledge, an alliance portfolio also allows for risk mitigation and sharing of costs. Overall, a firm's alliance portfolio can be considered a crucial tool in its quest to reach strategic goals and related performance outcomes.

Portfolio configuration. The challenge of portfolio design is to configure a set of intertwined alliances in such a way that maximizes portfolio synergies (that is, exploits facilitating interdependencies) and minimizes coordination costs (that is, controls constraining interdependencies). An efficient portfolio design determines: the quality, quantity, and diversity of information and resources to which the focal company has access; the efficiency of getting access to these resources; and the flexibility or stability of the firm's position in the industry (Wassmer 2008). Prior research on alliance portfolios has generated valuable insight in its properties and related consequences for firm performance, suggesting that firms may proactively design their alliance portfolio in accordance with specific strategic goals. For instance, with respect to alliance portfolio configuration, it pays to approach prominent partners simultaneously when seeking to establish high-performing portfolios. Also, it makes sense to balance cohesive ties with bridging ties, especially in view of innovation performance, and allow for certain levels of functional and industry diversity when aiming to impact firm performance (Jiang, Tao, and Santoro 2010). Prior studies on alliance portfolio design have identified various relevant design parameters, including: (i) a structural dimension; (ii) a governance dimension; and (iii) a partner dimension (Wassmer 2008).

The structural dimension pertains to the level of redundancy across alliances within the portfolio. Redundancy within an alliance portfolio is the result of a firm collaborating with multiple partners that make similar resource contributions. The main advantage is that redundancy provides a firm with multiple access points to critical resources, valuable knowledge, and information about existing and potential partners. In contrast, an alliance portfolio characterized by non-redundant relationships (that is, where each alliance makes a unique contribution) enables firms to enhance portfolio performance by leveraging and exploiting resources obtained through the few specialized alliances they have.

The governance dimension pertains to the level of commitment, degree of integration, and learning of alliances in the portfolio; this is also referred to as tie strength. Strong ties, such as equity-based arrangements, serve as vehicles for learning and information exchange, as partners are highly interconnected through reciprocal financial and organizational relationships. An alliance portfolio comprised of primarily strong ties has a positive effect on a focal firm's innovative capabilities, especially if they are trust-based, knowledge-intensive, and reinforced through relationship-specific investments. Alternatively, an alliance portfolio comprised of primarily weak ties, such as non-equity-based arrangements, provides firms with strategic flexibility, as these relationships are more easily established and terminated. Firms that build a homogeneous portfolio of governance forms tend to experience higher performance, as repeated experience with a specific governance form often translates into institutionalized knowledge that can be readily applied to future alliances, thereby reducing managerial costs.

The partner dimension refers to partner-related characteristics, including partner industry, organizational characteristics, nationality, and functional orientation. Because no single firm can possess all of the critical resources required for long-term success, an effective means of achieving a firm's objectives is to ally with partners operating in different industries. Partners from the same industry are often competitors, whose overlapping backgrounds, experiences, knowledge, and technological bases may provide learning in the form of imitation and greater absorptive capacity. However, conflicts of interest do exist and learning races can occur, which increases monitoring and safeguarding costs. In contrast, although collaboration with partners from different industries tends to increase coordination costs, owing to different routines and processes that can make collaboration difficult, it also leads to novel resources, knowledge, and information. As is the case with partner diversity within an alliance portfolio, organizational characteristics, nationality, and functional orientation all have positive and negative performance implications. Consider functional orientation, for example: firms employ a mixture of marketing, manufacturing, and distribution alliances to broaden their market reach and enhance value creation, and for further exploitation of core competences; a primary focus on R&D alliances, on the other hand, enables firms to build new capabilities and competences.

The portfolio design dimensions combined constitute an alliance portfolio configuration and a configuration is 'high-performing' when it supports an alliance portfolio strategy. In designing an alliance portfolio configuration, decision-makers should not only consider individual alliance motives, but also extend their partner selection (termination) with portfolio considerations. The goal is to forge alliance arrangements supportive of facilitative and mitigating constraining interdependencies. For example, a new alliance partner may reinforce existing partners (as it is part of the same collaborative network), provide complementary offerings, promote similar standards or infrastructure, or view the presence of other partners in the portfolio as a way to mitigate risks. In contrast, constraining interdependencies emerge if a new portfolio partner is, for example, a member of a competing collaborative network, depicts a strong rival of existing partners, or promotes competing technologies.

Portfolio coordination. Portfolio coordination pertains to governance of the set of alliances and the linkages between partners. Whereas prior studies have indicated that firms differ in the extent to which they exhibit coordination capabilities, other literature suggests that it is worthwhile investing in the development of alliance portfolio capabilities. The design and management of single-alliance relationships are critical; however, to secure a competitive advantage, firms must extend single-alliance governance with portfolio coordination. The two factors that allow firms to maximize their return on their alliance portfolio are knowledge management and internal coordination (Parise and Casher 2003).

When managing an alliance portfolio, it is critical to initiate some form of knowledge management, targeted at knowledge creation and exchange between partners. The degree to which a firm captures, shares, and leverages information and knowledge across its alliance portfolio, as well as the mechanisms it has in place to promote communication among its partners' alliance managers, has a direct effect on its performance. Examples of knowledge practices include designated project teams, a secure extranet, a directory that contains contact details, a virtual team room, joint training and education, and a repository with important alliance documents. For example, Dyer and Nobeoka (2000) showed that intentionally facilitating knowledge transfer between Toyota's suppliers increased those companies' commitment to share valuable knowledge, prevented free-riding, and reduced the costs associating with finding and accessing knowledge. Thus, knowledge management targeted at knowledge exchange between partners in an alliance portfolio increases awareness of partners' abilities, enables inter-firm knowledge creation, and stimulates partner referral.

Managing an alliance portfolio requires the internal coordination of alliance activities, which will enable a firm to orchestrate the linkages between alliance partners. Internal coordination provides a holistic approach to a firm's set of alliances, which enables the firm to identify and resolve opportunities and threats within the alliance portfolio. Internal coordination helps firms to align the alliance portfolio strategy with the separate parts of the organization (such as corporate and business units). Communication structures and information exchange between managers operating at different levels and businesses allows managers to keep up to date with latest developments in strategy and adapt their alliances accordingly. Managers become informed about alliance initiatives outside their responsibility, which reduces the risk of forging alliances that undermine portfolio performance. Internal coordination also involves a systematic approach to defining and measuring portfolio performance. In addition to metrics that capture the performance of single alliances, a performance metric system should include measures of the entire portfolio's performance.

Alliance networks

The network view on alliances states that firms are embedded in a set of inter-firm linkages between multiple parties. Whereas alliance portfolios only consider the set of direct relationships between a firm and its partners, alliance networks also involve indirect relationships: the set of relationships between a firm and third parties intermediated by the firm's alliance partners (Gulati and Gargiulo 1999). An alliance network functions as a repository of knowledge, resources, and information, and can potentially enhance a firm's competitive advantage. The extent to which network benefits outweigh costs depends on a firm's strategic intent, its position in the alliance network and its ability to influence network processes and outcomes. Whereas a direct relationship entails a single alliance between partners, an indirect relationship connects two parties (such as firms) through a third party. For example, a supplier alliance directly connects a manufacturer to a supplier, but the supplier can also be indirectly connected to a manufacturer's wholesaler if the manufacturer and the wholesaler are connected through an alliance of their own. According to alliance network logic, despite the lack of a formal partnership between the supplier and the wholesaler, all three firms may possess relevant technologies, knowledge, and/or expertise that could be beneficial to all of them. Essentially, these relationships could take multiple forms, such as informal relationships (for example, regular meetings at professional associations) and formal relationships (such as supplier alliances). An alliance network can enhance a firm's competitive advantage, as its set of direct relationships provides access to a pool of resources that might not otherwise be easily available, including financial capital, R&D facilities, and human resources. The network also functions as a source of valuable information through its indirect relationships, by means of referrals, contacts, and knowledge and reputational spillovers (Baum, Calabrese, and Silverman 2000).

Network position. A firm's network position refers to the number and pattern of structural linkages between a firm and other parties in a network (Gulati and Gargiulo 1999). Prior studies have assessed a firm's network position by focusing on the structural configuration of an alliance network; their key argument was that a firm's position influences its resources and information availability, as well as how much control a firm has over resource flows in the network. An alliance network view extends beyond an alliance portfolio view (also referred to as an egocentric alliance network) by encompassing indirect relationships. As such, a network view introduces concepts and measures to capture inter-firm linkages. Network density (or closure) refers to the extent to which firms in an alliance network are directly connected, as opposed to being connected through a series of indirect relationships (Coleman 1990). Density tends to make inter-party interactions observable to others because those parties have known and common contacts, which increases their willingness to share information freely amongst each other. Network centrality is the relative proximity of firms to the core of the alliance network's inter-firm linkages and is regarded as a measure of network power. A central position in a network is a strategic location because it enables a firm to exercise influence over resource flows and the diffusion of information. For example, obtaining some control over network processes and outcomes provides a firm with preferential access to resources, such as market information, customer information, and technological developments.

When the network dimensions are considered together, it follows that a firm can occupy different network positions, each of which enables the firm to acquire different types of network benefits (Ahuja 2000). This heterogeneity in various network positions also indicates that a network position is only beneficial to a firm when it is aligned with the firm's strategy. In terms of a firm's exploitation intent, favorable outcomes (that is, performance) stem from occupying a structural hole position (Burt 1982) in an alliance network that is characterized by centrality, relatively few strong direct and indirect relationships, non-redundant relationships, and partner homogeneity. A structural hole position suggests that a firm functions as a broker between two otherwise disconnected groups of intertwined parties. Although the two disconnected groups are not necessarily unaware of one another, information, resources, and knowledge are exchanged through the intermediate firm. In terms of a firm's exploration intent, favorable outcomes (that is, innovation) stem from the firm's closure position (Coleman 1990) in an alliance network that is characterized by density, multiple weak direct and indirect relationships, redundant relationships, and a high diversity of partners. Closure suggests that a firm is embedded in a network of highly but loosely coupled, interconnected parties. Closure provides a firm with informational advantages, as it possesses access to multiple sources increasing reliability, timing, and early acquisition of information.

Network influence. Firms engage in network management in order to attain and support their position in an alliance network (Jarvensivu and Moller 2009). Network influence involves restructuring the existing network and improving the conditions of cooperation within the existing structure. Whereas restructuring involves adding or removing alliances, improving the conditions of cooperation involves various network activities to facilitate cooperation between network partners. We intentionally refer to network influence, as a focal firm may exercise influence on its position, but its definitive position results from the collaborative actions by other network members. As such, network management as a label would convey an instrumental view, which does not fit with reality.

To attain a degree of network influence, we suggest that a firm can fulfil the four functions described below and take on associated network roles (Knight and Harland 2005). First, framing entails a firm's attempts to influence the roles that each participant may play at any given time, as well as perceptions about the common purpose of the alliance network. Second, activating involves identifying potential network participants and assessing the extent to which their skills, knowledge, and resources improve network performance. Third, mobilizing involves building commitment among parties in an alliance network to carry out the necessary activities. This is a common and ongoing task for achieving network outcomes. Fourth, synthesizing relates to organizing and controlling, and involves creating conditions for productive interaction while preventing, minimizing, and removing obstacles to collaboration.

To conclude, an alliance network enriches a firm's repertoire of strategic actions, as it provides managers with greater access to industrial intelligence and other types of information than they would generate operating autonomously. An alliance network can provide a firm with substantial benefits, but it also brings a degree of managerial complexity that extends beyond the governance of single alliances and alliance portfolios. The challenge for a firm navigating an alliance network is to capture network benefits (resources, information, etc.) while curbing the negative implications of alliance networks (such as locked-in and locked-out effects).

Business ecosystems

The last few years have seen a surge of interest in the concept of 'business ecosystems' as a new way to organize in competitive environments. While different conceptions exist about what an ecosystem is (Adner 2017), here we define a business ecosystem as a constellation of organizations that co-evolve their capabilities and roles, align their investments so as to create additional value and/or improve efficiency, and share a set of dependencies as they produce the goods, technologies, and services that customers need (Moore 1996). Business ecosystem members come together to create and deliver a shared value proposition in a partially intentional, highly self-organizing, manner, such that members provide contributions that fill out and complement those of the others (Adner 2006; Moore 1998). Within this network of autonomous parties, which is loosely coupled, both horizontally and vertically, ecosystem members co-evolve through a complex system of interdependencies (Aarikka-Stenroos and Ritala 2017), which simultaneously enact cooperation (value creation) and competition (value appropriation). This is because business ecosystems create, scale, and serve markets and possess a collective ability to learn, adapt, and innovate (see Box 6.1).

Forms. In general, business ecosystems possess unique attributes - (i) core and complements; (ii) accelerated innovation; and (iii) continuous co-evolution - that make them different from other collaborative organizational arrangements. A business ecosystem is generally built around a core product/service and complements to increase value to the user (Moore 1996). The core product/service constitutes the basis for providing value to end customers, enabling a firm to obtain economies of scale and large volume sizes. Complementary

Box 6.1 The Apple and Amazon business ecosystems

With the introduction of the iPhone in 2007, ***Apple*** allowed third-party software developers to develop software for Apple devices. Third-party developers could download a software development kit for free to develop applications for the iPod and iPhone, and later the iPad. An application can only be published and put 'on sale' in the App Store after paying an Apple Developer Connection membership fee. The software developer can set its own price for the app, but Apple receives a 30 percent fee. The App Store set the standard in the smartphone market, which has been followed by Google's Play Store and Microsoft's Windows App store. In the business ecosystem that Apple has created, Apple is the dominant player and holds firm control over its ecosystem. Apple must first sell its devices, with high margins, before publishers in the App Store can sell their products. This latency in earning models requires publishers to be fully dependent on the ability of Apple to develop and market an attractive platform. Next, Apple has the final authority to decide what it will and will not publish on the App Store.

As ***Amazon*** grew from an online bookstore to an online retailer, it realized that it could benefit from other entrepreneurs selling products on the internet if it were able to cross-sell through the Amazon retail engine. By the end of 1996, Amazon had launched the Amazon Associates Program, whereby Amazon associates could place an Amazon banner or a link on their website or link directly to the Amazon homepage. If a visitor clicked on an associate's website and landed on the Amazon website and purchased a book, the associate would receive a commission fee. Through this program, Amazon enabled third-party website owners to build their business through the advertising of Amazon products. The website owners earn referral fees at the moment a purchase takes place. In the following years, Amazon began to increase its service offerings to affiliates by developing technology to support the start-up of web shops, thereby lowering the entry barriers and subsequently increasing traffic to Amazon websites. With the introduction of the eReader, Kindle Fire, Amazon sacrificed hardware profits in order to subsidize book publishers and movie studios to publish their content on the Amazon Kindle. Given that affiliate marketing is performance-based and financially motivated, Amazon adopted a balanced incentive system. Amazon and its partners benefit directly from an online purchase from the Amazon platform, and Amazon enables writers and booksellers to proactively participate in the ecosystem, as well as those that want to sell directly to the Amazon community.

Apple and Amazon have taken very different approaches to managing their respective business ecosystems. Apple has created an Apple community in which Apple is the cornerstone and has a dominant position. Amazon positions itself as a facilitator of retailing business using its retailing platform. Unlike in the Apple ecosystem, retailers have a high liberty of use and have an equitable stake in the ecosystem. Both models have been very successful. Apple has become the most valuable company in the world and has sold over 140 billion apps in its App Store. Amazon has attracted millions of affiliates and has become the biggest online retailer in the world.

Source: Adner (2012); Than (2020)

products and services ensure that the customer receives a 'total experience' (Adner 2006), which cannot be created by the core product/service alone. Thus, a business ecosystem combines a core product with a network of specialist niches, in which parties make unique contributions to enhance customer value and create critical mass. To be effective, the system's logic is based on an access and usage instead of transaction and ownership logic (Williamson and De Meyer 2012). Also, firms reinvest profits from the core products and services in further additions to capabilities, and in developing future generations on offers. Competition is not the sole driver of success; actors are incentivized by shared goals and values, as well as by the need to collaborate (Moore 1996). Thus, the key to a healthy ecosystem is a network of mutually rewarding relationships. Business ecosystems provide members with access to people and resources, whether they are located with suppliers, customers, or competitors. Innovation is the result of connecting and integrating knowledge across different fields and industries, and is therefore accelerated in the fluid, permeable, exchange-oriented, and co-creative communities that are forged by ecosystems. Thus, within ecosystems, innovation drives value creation and opens up niche markets. A key to a healthy business ecosystem is that members adopt these innovations, create critical mass to leverage resources, and bring them successfully to (niche) markets. Business ecosystems are the cause and consequence of adaptive processes among ecosystem members. Specifically, ecosystem communities co-evolve their capabilities (Moore 1998). Each member must enhance and transform itself while paying attention to, and actively relating to, other members of the community. Thus, companies must pay attention to their core business and ensure performance improvement, but also ally with others to ensure the required complementarity in contributions and offerings. Connectivity across specialized capabilities enables actors to co-create solutions and new business models (Moore 1996). These continuous processes of co-evolution and renewal ensure the viability of an ecosystem, but may also render an ecosystem obsolete as new business ecosystems emerge.

Business ecosystems tend to become increasingly omnipresent across industries. Originally, business ecosystems were high-tech-driven, as technological platforms functioned as a bonding mechanism between ecosystem members. For example, with a ***platform-based ecosystem*** (see also Chapter 5), a focal firm creates value by organizing suppliers and customers around a core technological platform (see Box 6.1). Value is co-created with various stakeholders, including complementary providers and customers, in an attempt to leverage network effects; that is, the value of a product/service increases in line with the number of customers that use the platform. The platform-owner serves a two-sided market: the focal firm earns more benefits if its platform is home to customers and suppliers. To this end, a platform-based ecosystem typically adopts an integrator business model, where the technology platform owner seeks to forge connections between suppliers and complementary firms in support of a joint value proposition (e.g. integrative customer offering).

Ecosystem members in an ***innovation ecosystem*** co-evolve around a new innovation to support new products and/or services to satisfy customer needs. This ecosystem form centers on a focal innovation and the set of components (upstream) and complements (downstream) to develop and market the innovation. The anchoring point is not the firm, but the system of innovations that allows customers to use the end product. The firm(s) producing the focal innovation may or may not be directly connected to complement providers. Regardless, the extent to which firms align through different arrangements will affect their capacity to create value for the end customer (Adner 2017). An example is digital innovation ecosystems that emphasize industry-spanning co-operative and competitive dynamics among firms related to innovations that combine physical and digital elements, such as 3D printing (Beltagui, Rosli, and Candi 2020). Science-based ecosystems are geared towards the front-end of the innovation-conversion cycle (that is, idea generation). In such an ecosystem, value is created and captured by building critical mass when pushing the scientific frontier in an applied field. Service-based ecosystems are oriented towards solution adoption. Their key role is to create and capture value through asset optimization around the services offered and to enhance customer experience.

Roles. Ecosystems come in many forms, but they share a set of ecosystem characteristics (see Table 6.2). Creating a sustainable business ecosystem requires members to pinpoint why the ecosystem will create added value for the customer. Partners in an ecosystem will only co-invest if they see the prospect of building a profitable business. To systematize interactions between partners, members may develop and share a set of tools, protocols, and contracts. A sustainable ecosystem exhibits an architecture that can be changed and adapted in response to developments in the market and technological environment. Therefore, a healthy ecosystem is a highly malleable structure combined with specifications with regards to roles,

Table 6.2 Business ecosystems characteristics

Key to advantage	*Focus*	*Implication*
Pin point added value	Enhance customer value by improving functionality, innovative solutions, and offering higher levels of customization	Identify sources of value creation, target resource complementarities, select and invite potential ecosystem members
Structure member roles	Organize ecosystem members' roles to achieve benefits of specialization and provide focus	Decide on ecosystem role and reduce partner interaction to manageable levels
Stimulate co-investments	Enable ecosystem members to amplify the impact of their investments and create potential for increasing returns to scale	Develop (joint) value propositions, reduce uncertainty by making co-investments
Reduce transaction costs	Standardize exchange between ecosystem members to reduce bargaining, coordinating, and monitoring costs	Grant access to knowledge, resources, and tools; establish flexible exchanges with high degrees of transparency and standardization
Enable flexibility and co-learning	Enable a mix of formal and informal knowledge sharing, to flexibly promote knowledge creation and innovation	Stimulate interaction and learning between ecosystem members; they and the system as a whole then become adaptive and resilient
Engineer value capture	Creatively engineer value-capture mechanisms to monetize members' contributions and incentivize them	Leverage proprietary knowledge, reap economies of scale, acquire access to new members, and optimize value capture

Source: Adapted from Williamson and De Meyer (2012); Tjemkes, Vos, and Burgers (2017)

contributions, and performance. The members (or lead member) need(s) to engineer mechanisms to monetize the value of this contribution, which may include license fees, royalties, expanded margins, or profits on higher sales volumes. One mechanism for capturing value entails that a member contributes a unique component or activity to the ecosystem, one that cannot be easily replaced with an alternative, procured through an open market, or imitated. The emphasis is on understanding how interdependent ecosystem members interact to create and commercialize products and/or services that benefit the end customer. Ecosystems are not hierarchically managed, ecosystem membership is 'open', and future members can participated based on self-selection. The management of standards and interfaces, platform governance, or intellectual property rights and other contractual forums are key tools that ecosystem leaders use to discipline and motivate ecosystem members. As such, members may fulfil different roles in an ecosystem.

Adner and Kapoor (2010) provided a schema of an ecosystem that identifies four different types of actors: (i) focal firm (i.e. providing core technology); (ii) suppliers (i.e. offering technology enhancements); (iii) complementors (i.e. providing add-on offerings); and (iv) customers (i.e. procuring integrated solutions). In addition, other actors may be part of an ecosystem, including governmental entities, media, and non-profit organizations. These ecosystem members fulfil roles, and to orchestrate business ecosystems it is important to understand which roles exists.

Established firms may initiate the building of business ecosystem and take on a leadership role (Williamson and De Meyer 2012). They exhibit a deliberate intention to establish and develop the ecosystem, and are referred to as lead firms, keystone organizations, or ecosystem captains. Ecosystem leaders enable members to offer integrated solutions to customers, reduce the need to own complementary resources, offer flexibility, access a repository of knowledge, and leverage entry barriers (that is, entrants have to duplicate the core product and compete against the whole system). In a broad sense, lead firms may take on the role of ecosystem frontrunner, either as keystone or dominant leader. An effective keystone leader ensures the survival and prosperity of the ecosystem by improving the health of the ecosystem as a whole, and creates and shares value with ecosystem members. That is, keystone leaders exercise a system-wide regulator role despite their small part in their ecosystem's mass. In contrast to this open approach, a dominant leader favors a closed approach and aims to integrate horizontally or vertically to exercise control, or even directly own, a large proportion of the ecosystem. It attempts to dominate all niche markets, by means such as leveraging and controlling access to the technological platform. Even if a dominant firm relinquishes direct control over the ecosystem, its main goal remains to extract as much value as possible.

Niche players represent the bulk of the ecosystem and play a critical role in value creation and innovation. Niche players develop specialized capabilities that differentiate them from other members; they are referred to as complementors (Brandenburger and Nalebuff 1995). They focus on a narrow domain and seek to improve their position while leveraging complementary resources. New entrants and corporate ventures create new products and services that complement the core technology or become part of an integral solution when combined with the core technology. In addition, other members such as research centers and governments partake in the ecosystem as they envision and develop an innovation in an emerging or radically new field. The objectives and the direction of the innovation organically emerges from interactions without a central coordinative and directive leading member. New ventures are critical for generating and exploiting knowledge, and knowledge generation may drive the creation of new business ecosystems (rendering the old one obsolete). Other roles pertain to suppliers and assemblers who support value creation by providing critical resources and knowledge to advance, for example, the platform technology. Regulators provide favorable conditions for the ecosystem to thrive.

Transformation logics

Above, we outlined four ways to look at collaborative arrangements. As evident from this introduction, transformation constitutes an integral part of how these arrangements transition from birth to dissolution. A shift in corporate strategy, internal reorganizations, changing resource requirements, a shift in financial position, changes in required technology, and even a change in the board of directors may encourage decision-makers to modify collaborative governance. As a collaborative arrangement progresses, it may also cause changes within the partner firms' organizations. Reciprocal financial and organizational relationships facilitate the transfer of resources, information, and routines, prompting partner organizations to change. Environmental triggers also affect a firm's decisions to form and manage collaborative arrangements. In a stable environment, a firm may enhance its competitive position by establishing exploitation alliances to use existing capabilities with the aim of achieving cost reductions and economies of scale. In contrast, exploration alliances are more suitable in a dynamic environment, as a heterogeneous resource endowment contributes to a firm's ability to respond to new circumstances in an appropriate and timely manner. In this chapter, to organize and make sense of transformation in collaborative arrangements, we draw on the work by Van de Ven and Poole (1995) and present four generic transformation logics (also see De Rond and Bouchikie (2004)).

Life-cycle logic. A life-cycle logic focuses on how organizational entities develop over time and on their configurative evolution as a result of firm action and coordination. The life-cycle logic considers change as a process of organic growth in which organizations proceed through a unitary sequence of stages (Van de Ven and Poole 1995). This sequence is irreversible, cumulative, linear, and predictable, tracking organizational development from inception to termination as if predestined by a genetic code (De Rond and Bouchikie 2004). Change is imminent, in that entities 'grow up'; they develop from a formative period to one of maturity through a series of discernible but generic life-cycle phases, each of which contributes a piece to the final product (Van de Ven and Poole 1995). Every successive stage constitutes a logical progression from a previous one and calls for identifiable managerial tasks or programs suited to it.

Drawing on a life-cycle logic, extant studies of collaboration development have adopted the (implicit) assumption of a linear process of collaborative transformation. For example, alliance research adopted a life-cycle logic to understand how alliances transition from formation to termination. Based on a review of alliance development approaches, Tjemkes and colleagues (2017) suggested that alliances progress through eight stages: (i) strategy formulation; (ii) partner selection; (iii) negotiation; (iv) design; (v) launch; (vi) management;

(vii) evaluation; and (viii) termination. Each development stage depicts a specific decision-making situation that requires unique know-what and know-how. An alliance transforms and proceeds to the next stage only after it has achieved the objectives of the preceding stage. For example, once the alliance design stage is completed – that is, formalization of the arrangement via a signed contract – managerial attention shifts to the alliance launch stage, with a focus on executing the contractual agreement. Alliance portfolio studies drawing on a life-cycle logic indicate that alliance portfolios transition through a process of emergence, configuration, and management (Lavie and Singh 2011). Investigating Toyota's supplier portfolio, Dyer and Nobeoka (2000), for example, showed how the portfolio progressed from governing weak ties to governing strong ties, to finally governing inter-supplier relations. Alliance network studies also adopted linear approaches and assumed that the informational and resource value of an alliance network would remain constant over time or to evolve from carrying low value to progressively higher value; indicating a birth, transition, maturity path (Gilsing, Cloodt and Rooijakkers 2016). Business ecosystems also progress through sequential stages. For example, Moore (1993) indicated ecosystem progression through birth, expansion, authority, and renewal. In Stage 1 (birth), ecosystem members forge a value chain for creating value for customers; in Stage 2 (expansion), emerging business models capture value for a larger number of customers – members are able to scale up; in Stage 3 (authority), ecosystem leaders set the future direction to encourage partners to work together and secure stability within the ecosystem; and in Stage 4 (renewal), via learning and adaptation a new business ecosystem emerges from the incumbent business community by bringing new ideas and innovations. Alternatively, in the absence of self-renewal, the business ecosystem dissolves.

Teleological logic. In an attempt to overcome the limitations of lifecycle frameworks – primarily their linearity, determinism, and predictability – open-ended and teleological process models emerged; purpose is the cause of change (De Rond and Bouchikie 2004). Organizational entities are considered purposeful, but able to learn and adapt to changing circumstances. Process is viewed as "a repetitive sequence of goal formulation, implementation, evaluation, and modification of goals based on what was learned or intended by the entity" (Van de Ven and Poole 1995: 516). A teleological logic considers change as the result of a recurring sequence of negotiation, commitment, and execution. Each phase is governed by formal and informal processes and focused on attaining efficient and equitable (or fair) outcomes. Unlike life-cycle approaches, teleology does not necessitate a uniform and predictable sequence of predictable stages. Like life-cycle theory, it retains a sense of purpose, if only to facilitate assessments of progress and evaluations. A teleological logic recognizes that unforeseen circumstances, unexpected results, and conflicting interpretations can and do happen. Management can neither plan in advance nor control the sequence of events, but is supposed to play a central role in enabling learning and adaptation.

Alliance arrangements represent purposeful entities that can learn and adapt to changing circumstances, indicating that alliance development also entails a repetitive sequence of goal formulation, implementation, and modification, based on lessons learned or changed intentions among the partner firms (Büchel 2002). Ariño and de la Torre's (1998) account of the development of an international joint venture suggests that assessments of efficiency and equity conditions prompt partner firms to address dissatisfying situations in various manners, such as by improving relational governance, engaging in contractual renegotiations, doing nothing, or terminating the alliance. At the alliance level, outcome and process discrepancies may prompt adaptation in alliance conditions and processes, including changes in the governance, the alliance contract, the division of activities, decision-making and performance expectations. According to a teleological logic, firms consider alliance portfolios and alliance network as powerful tools to realize their strategic objectives (Hoffmann 2007; Lavie and Singh 2011). Current and past performance assessments guide a continuous process of portfolio and network transformation by forming and discontinuing alliance relationships (Dittrich, Duysters, and de Man 2007). For example, Kavusan and Frankfort (2019) showed that below-performance aspirations drive firms to establish alliances with novel partners within the scope of their existing alliance portfolio. According to a teleological perspective, business ecosystems progress through a repetitive sequence of continuous adaptions towards a desired goal. For example, based on a review of ecosystem literature, Adner (2017) proposed an ecosystem-as-structure approach, stipulating that an ecosystem represents an 'alignment structure of the multilateral set of partners that need to interact in order for a focal value proposition to materialize' (p. 40). That is, different actors may have different end states and end goals in mind and initiate action to attain these goals.

Dialectical logic. A dialectical logic of change stipulates that the collision of coexisting but contradictory social forces, which compete with each other for domination and control, produces a new social order (Van de Ven and Poole 1995). These contradictions may be internal to an organizational entity because they may have several conflicting goals or interest groups competing for priority. Within the context of organizations - comprised of conflicting goals and interest groups - dialectical forces compete for scarce resources and managerial attention and thus help account for conflict and, more relevantly, the emergence of new organizational arrangements (De Rond and Bouchikie (2004). Contradictory forces may also originate via interaction with the external environment, as an organization pursues directions that collide with the direction of other organizations. The dialectical logic stipulates that stability and change are explained by the (im)balance of power between opposing entities. Accommodations that maintain the status quo between oppositions produce stability, whereas change occurs when opposing values, forces, or events gain sufficient power to confront and upend the status quo. The relative power of an antithesis may mobilize an organizational entity to a sufficient degree to challenge the current thesis or state of affairs and set the stage for producing a synthesis (De Rond and Bouchikie (2004).

While there is consensus in the alliance literature that alliance arrangements are replete with tensions, only a few studies have used a dialectical logic to explain alliance development. Das and Teng (2000a) suggested that to understand alliance instability and failure, three pairs of internal tensions need to be accounted for: cooperation versus competition, rigidity versus flexibility, and short-term versus long-term orientation. De Rond and Bouchikie (2004) reported on a biotechnology based alliance and illustrated how change unfolds as the partners seek to reconcile tensions between design and emergence, cooperation and competition, trust and vigilance, expansion and contraction, and control and autonomy. Based on a literature review, Majchrzak and colleagues (2015) showed that alliance arrangements are inherently instable, that instability does not necessarily contribute to detrimental outcomes, and that positive or negative outcomes depend on the pattern of dynamics between contractual and relational governance exhibited as a relationship progresses. Alliance portfolios and alliance networks also exhibit tensions, including facilitating versus constraining interdependencies, openness versus disclosure, and formal versus relational governance. One prominent tension pertains to exploitation and exploration intents (Ahuja 2000). An exploration strategy is likely to be effected by heterogeneous portfolios and networks, as it increases the richness of information and resources, broadens search options, improves a firm's ability to develop new capabilities, and increase its visibility in the broader industry network, which enhances performance. An exploitation strategy is more likely to be effectuated by homogenous portfolios and networks as it enables a firm to build and leverage a specialized resource pool, exploit existing capabilities, and react flexibly and quickly to changing circumstances. When seeking to reconcile exploration and exploitation strategies, firms may opt for hybrid (integrated), parallel (separate), or temporal (sequenced) portfolio configurations and network positions (Tjemkes et al. 2017). Akin to the other collaborative arrangements, business ecosystems exhibit a tension between cooperation and competition. For example, Beltagui, Rosli and Candi (2020) investigated a digital innovation ecosystem and indicated that ecosystem members cooperate to develop and deliver a joint value proposition; within the ecosystem, however, members compete for market niches and the ecosystem as a whole competes with rival ecosystems offering a similar value proposition to end-customers.

Box 6.2 Update: Netflix's business ecosystem

As of 2018, Netflix spent up to US$8 billion on content annually, had a market capitalization of more than US$100 billion, with more than 118 million streaming subscribers globally and a customer base in 190 countries.

Netflix's value proposition centers on serving customers by offering on-demand video streaming with personalized recommendations and a large (locally tailored) content library. This value proposition sets Netflix apart from other streaming providers such as Apple TV and Disney+. Netflix was the first to offer video on demand, has the largest range of movies, supports a wide range of devices, provides high-quality connection, and has a simple subscription scheme. Compared to movie theatres, Netflix offers the comfort of home and provides access to Netflix originals; and compared to cable TV, Netflix offers on-demand movie watching, shows no advertisements, and allows binge-watching.

Netflix's ecosystem supports the value proposition. First, Netflix has several subsidiaries. Netflix can produce original content in its subsidiary ABQ studios. It acquired the comic book company MillarWorld to develop new content, and StoryBots to develop educational content for children. Second, to obtain access to content, Netflix has license agreements with other parties, such as DreamWorks and Sony Pictures. Third, original content for Netflix is produced by a large community of international and local producers, writers, and actors. Fourth, investment companies, such as Blackrock, Vanguard, and Capital Group, invest in Netflix, while BMG manages the intellectual property rights for Netflix outside the USA. Fifth, Netflix uses a number of platforms: AWS for storing content, internet service providers (ISPs) for streaming and for local content storage,

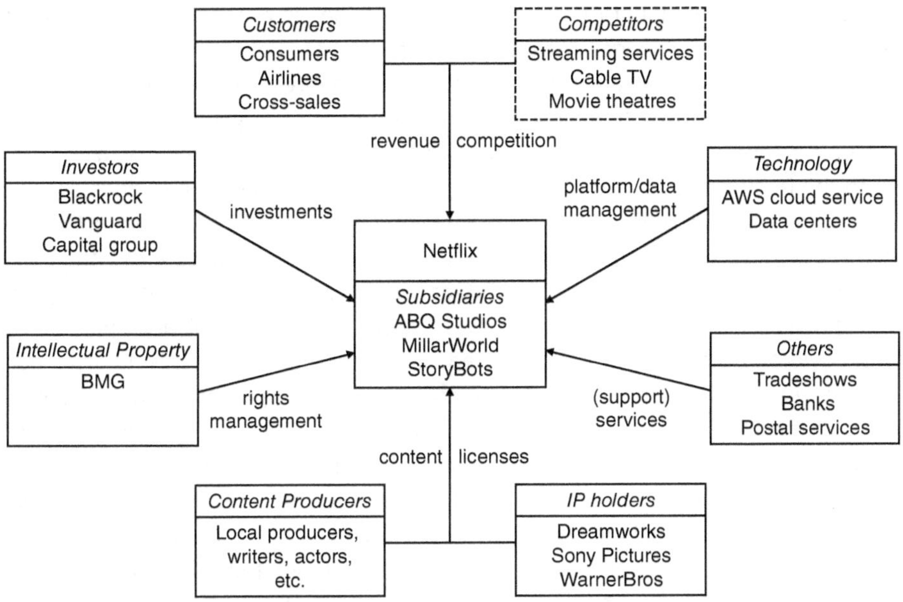

Figure 6.2 Netflix's business ecosystem
Disclaimer: the figure depicts a simplified overview and other parties are part of the business ecosystem

banks for payments, and trade shows to connect to stakeholders in the entertainment space. It even still uses postal services to send and receive DVDs (in the US market). Finally, it also uses customer collaboration. Gwyneth Paltrow's Goop uses Netflix as a platform to sell health advice to consumers. Netflix has partnered with airlines to offer its streaming technology and content in airplanes, which improves the service that an airline can provide its customers.

Source: Wieringa (2019)

(Co-)evolutionary logic. An evolutionary perspective entails that organizations must continuously compete for survival given a scarce resource base and a series of blind (or chance) variations (Volberda and Lewin 2003). In contrast to life-cycle and teleological approaches, the emphasis is on the environment as the principal motor of change, retaining only those entities that best fit its evolving nature. In other words, evolution is quite deterministic. Change proceeds through a continuous cycle of variation (the emergence of new forms), selection (competition between forms), and retention (persistence of new forms). One ramification of the evolutionary logic pertains to co-evolution and refers to the simultaneous development of organizations and their environment, both independently and interactively (Wilson and Hynes 2009). Co-evolution assumes that change may occur in all interacting populations of organizations, which allows changes to be driven by direct interaction and by feedback (Tjemkes et al. 2017). A co-evolutionary view captures multi-directional causalities over a long period of time, in which the outcomes of co-evolution are emergent and in which changes in any one variable may be caused endogenously by changes in the other (Das and Teng 2002).

Consequently, a co-evolutionary view is made up of dynamic trajectories evoked by drivers that enable and restrict change. Because firms are able to proactively change themselves, their collaborations, and their environment (to a certain degree), co-evolution occurs through a deliberate approach rather than via random chance-like processes.

Adopting a co-evolutionary lens, Wilson and Hynes (2009) showed that a firm seeking access to the fresh produce market in the UK through an international alliance experienced changes in its technical skills, new product development and networking opportunities as a result of the alliance. They also reported that the formation of alliances within the fresh produce industry in the UK changed the power dynamics across the value chain, which prompted other parties in the value chain to form new alliances. Focusing on alliance portfolio development, Lavie and Singh (2011) indicated that co-evolutionary mechanisms drive portfolio evolution. Lavie and Singh found four idiosyncratic interacting processes that influenced the evolution of the alliance portfolio of Unisys Corporation, a US-based technology company, over time. These processes were: (i) co-evolution, referring to the process of adjusting the alliance portfolio configuration as a result of changes in the focal firm's strategic orientation, while changes to its alliance portfolio would support or constrain the implementation of strategies; (ii) external stimuli, referring to external stimuli that instigate the (co-)evolutionary process referred to above, such as changes in the technological environment; (iii) inertial pressures, referring to internal crises and processes of resistance to change that would delay or alter the evolution of Unisys' alliance portfolio; and (iv) restructuring and realignment, referring to organizational structural changes that would promote changes in the alliance organization in order to realign Unisys' alliance portfolio configuration and strategy (Lavie and Singh 2011). Firms rely on information from their alliance network, and co-evolution would suggest that firms with equivalent network positions would evolve in similar directions. Adopting an intertemporal perspective, Jacob and Duysters (2017) showed that firms operating in shared alliance blocks tend to develop similar technology profiles over time. A key feature of contemporary business ecosystem conceptualizations is that they are, by nature, co-evolutionary (Moore 1996). Establishing and maintaining business ecosystems causes changes in partners' organizations and environments, which could force managers to modify their design and management in an effort to maintain a fit among the ecosystem, the ecosystem members, and the environment. Beltagui, Rosli, and Candi (2020) indicated that within digital innovation ecosystems, internal disruption, resulting from competition for niches within an ecosystem, and external disruption introduced by an actor external to an ecosystem, invoke learning and adaptation processes.

Reflection

Collaborative arrangements, such as alliances and business ecosystems, depict a form of organizing economic activities and constitute a powerful and – according to some – the only source of competitive advantage. The challenge to deliver more complex solutions to customers while simultaneously limiting capital expenditures and costs has extended beyond high-tech industries into other industries, promoting a plethora of collaborative activity. Activating, catalyzing, guiding, and promoting collaboration will enable the firms involved to innovate, reconfigure, and create added value to the customer base. Despite the advantages, a collaborative arrangement is not always the most optimal and viable strategy. Firms should avoid the inclination to hop on the bandwagon and, for example, participate or lead ecosystems without value potential. Moreover, depending on the extent to which a company has stakes in multiple collaboration, it should invest in building a collaborative competence. Although collaborative arrangements can improve a firm's competitive advantage, they are also inherently fragile, unstable, and difficult to manage. The drivers of collaborative transformation stem from the internal and external environment of the focal firm, materializing through processes of lifecycle stages, teleological purpose, dialectical tensions, and co-evolution, thereby showing an intricate interaction among external, organizational, and strategic stimuli that leads to collaborative transformation.

The drivers of collaborative transformation stem from the internal and external environment of the focal firm, materializing through processes of lifecycle stages, teleological purpose, dialectical tensions, and co-evolution, thereby showing an intricate interaction among external, organizational, and strategic stimuli leading to collaborative transformation.

A comparison between the four views of collaborative arrangements and the four transformation logics indicates that all logics have been directly and interactively applied to advance insight in collaborative transformation (see Table 6.3). The result of our (concise) analysis offers four key implications.

1. The ***life-cycle*** (start-up, maturity, and decline) determines the stages of collaborative transformation and governs progression through the stages. Although its deterministic focus negates learning and adaptation, the value of a life-cycle view originates in its analytical (that is, step-by-step) perspective; highlighting that decision-makers drive collaborative transformation by adhering to a pre-set sequence of development stages.
2. The ***teleological logic*** stipulates that collaborative arrangements change through purpose-driven learning and adaptation, such that reflexively monitored action guides transformation towards a common end-goal. While transformation can unfold via many (unknown) trajectories, the value of a teleological view originates in its learning and adaptation tenets; highlighting that decision-makers based on efficiency and equity considerations drive collaborative transformation.
3. The ***dialectical logic*** stipulates that collaborative arrangements change as conflicts emerge between opposing forces (thesis and antithesis) that collide to produce a new organizational form (synthesis). Resolutions may not always represent a (creative) reconciliation, but the value of a dialectical view originates in its logic of continuous progression through dialectical cycles; highlighting that decision-makers who are able to identify and reconcile tensions are also able to effectively drive collaborative transformation.
4. The ***co-evolutionary logic*** stipulates that collaborative arrangements (and their environments) change as they engage in continuous and interrelated self-renewal processes

in an attempt to seek and maintain fit. While (un)intentional adaptations may or may not contribute to ecosystem viability, the value of a co-evolutionary view originates in the concept that collaborative arrangements represent adaptive entities. This highlights the idea that decision-makers pro-actively drive collaborative transformation based on learning and experience.

Taken together, the four change logics separately offer a comprehensive picture of how collaborative transformation may unfold. Integration between the four change and transformation logics is desirable, but it must preserve the distinctiveness of alternative theories of organizational change and transformation (Van de Ven and Poole 1995). Integration is also possible if the four change logics are viewed as providing alternative pictures of the same collaborative change processes without nullifying each other. An integrative approach preserves the authenticity of each change logic and, at the same time, advances theory-building and application power. This is because it highlights circumstances, when interplays among the theories may provide a stronger and broader explanatory power of collaborative

Table 6.3 Collaborative transformation

	Life-cycle logic	*Teleological logic*	*Dialectical logic*	*Co-evolutionary logic*
Description	Change via a unitary sequence of irreversible stages	Change via purpose-driven learning and adaptation	Change via reconciling opposing forces	Change via interactive self- and co-renewal
Alliance	Formation Management Dissolution	Efficiency and equity considerations drive alliance adaptation	The interplay between value creation and value appropriation	Changes in alliance attributes and alliance partners interactively drive adaptation
Alliance portfolio	Emergence Configuration Management	Efficiency and learning considerations drive portfolio adaptation	The interplay between facilitative interdependencies and constraining interdependencies	Changes in the alliance portfolio and focal firm interactively drive adaptation
Alliance network	Activation Collectivity Institutionalization Reorientation or decline	Information and resource access considerations drive alliance forging or ending	The interplay between exploration and exploitation intents	Changes in the alliance network and network actors interactively drive adaptation
Business ecosystem	Birth Expansion Authority Renewal or Ending	Value creation opportunities drive ecosystem participation or withdrawal	The interplay between delivering a joint value proposition and internal/external disruptions	Changes in the business ecosystem, ecosystem members interactively drive adaptation

transformation. Integration would also make it possible to further explore within and between collaborative arrangement dynamics. For example, how do alliance dynamics relate to business ecosystem dynamics, and vice versa? How do ecosystem members' network positions influence business ecosystem growth?

Learning and discussion questions

1 How would you describe the differences and similarities between alliances, alliance portfolios, alliance networks, and business ecosystems?
2 All four views on collaboration share the cooperation-competition tension. Explain how and why this tension becomes manifest, albeit differently across the four views.
3 How would you describe the differences and similarities among the four change logics: life-cycle, teleological, dialectical, and co-evolutionary?
4 Consider you are a business leader, how and why would you approach the adaptation of a collaborative arrangement?

Exercise: The Walt Disney Company

In 2019, the Walt Disney Company (Disney) announced that it would end its content partnership with Netflix and roll out its own streaming service: Disney+. CEO Bob Iger characterized this move as 'an extremely important, very, very significant strategic shift'.

Disney is an American-based diversified multinational mass media and entertainment conglomerate headquartered at the Walt Disney Studios complex in Burbank, California. It is currently comprised of four main business segments: (i) studio entertainment; (ii) media networks; (iii) parks, experiences and products; and (iv) direct-to-consumer and international. Through these business segments, Disney owns and operates a wide range of brands, products, and services, including Walt Disney Pictures, Walt Disney Animation Studios, Pixar, Marvel Studios, Lucasfilm, 20th Century Studios, ABC broadcast network; Disney Channel, ESPN, Freeform, FX, National Geographic, and 14 theme parks around the world.

In 2005, Bob Iger replaced Eisner as Disney's CEO. Iger spent his first decade at Disney getting the creative engine spinning again so that it could generate fresh intellectual property at a constant rate. Preceding the launch of Disney+, he enacted several strategic moves to support Disney's growth ambitions. For example, Disney's US$7.4 billion acquisition of Pixar in 2006 was vital in terms of helping Disney revitalize its creative process. Disney's US$4 billion acquisition of Marvel in 2009 and US$4.1 billion acquisition of LucasFilm (*Star Wars*) in 2012 showed how Disney understood the synergies that drive Disney's growth. Disney announced an intention to leverage the *Star Wars* franchise across its divisions In April 2011, Disney broke ground on the US$4.4 billion Shanghai Disney Resort that opened on 16 June 2016. In 2017, Disney agreed to acquire most assets from 21st Century Fox, including 20th Century Fox, for US$52.4 billion. The merger included many of Fox's entertainment assets, such as filmed entertainment, cable entertainment, and direct broadcast satellite divisions in the UK, Europe, and Asia. Together, these corporate decisions reinforced Disney's growth engine by investing in content development and delivery, and also enabled Disney to better monetize (new) content.

In 2017, Disney announced that it had exercised an option to increase its stake in BAMTech to 75 percent, and would launch a subscription video-on-demand (VOD) service called Disney+ in 2019 that would feature its entertainment content. Disney+ replaced Netflix as the subscription VOD rights holder of all Disney film releases. As Netflix treated Disney's content exactly the same as every other piece of content, there was no opportunity to leverage any synergies to connect that distribution to grow the rest of Disney, whether via cross-sells to toys and merchandise or upsells to a physical experience or event. By moving content onto a platform it controls, Disney created the ability to innovate on new ways of presenting its content that drives deeper integration with the rest of Disney. Product changes that would encourage viewers to buy more toys or visit theme parks would allow for deeper monetization, putting Disney in an even more superior position to acquire or develop new IP.

In sum, it appears that Disney has, over time, been able to strike a balance between cooperation and competition, in support of building and sustaining its competitive advantage.

Case questions

1. Explain why (or why not) Walt Disney's constellations of enterprises, divisions, and partners represents a business ecosystem.
2. Explain how Walt Disney is able to create synergies well beyond the scope of what Netflix can create.
3. Explain why Disney launched its own streaming service (Disney+) and seeks to compete against Netflix instead of continuing and extending the existing partner agreement with Netflix.

Note

1. This section detailing on the four types of collaborative arrangements draws on the book *Strategic Alliance Management* written by Tjemkes, Vos, and Burgers (2017).

References

Aarikka-Stenroos, L. and Ritala, P. (2017) 'Network management in the era of ecosystems: Systematic review and management framework'. *Industrial Marketing Management*, 67: 23–36.

Adner, R. (2006) 'Match your innovation strategy to your innovation ecosystem'. *Harvard Business Review*, 84(4): 98–109.

Adner, R. (2012) 'Amazon vs. Apple: Competing Ecosystem Strategies'. Available online at https://hbr.org/2012/03/amazon-vs-apple-competing-ecos (accessed 25 June 2020).

Adner, R. (2017) 'Ecosystem as structure: An actionable construct for strategy'. *Journal of Management*, 43(1): 39–58.

Adner, R. and Kapoor, R. (2010) 'Value creation in innovation ecosystems: How the structure of technological interdependence affects firm performance in new technology generations'. *Strategic Management Journal*, 31(3): 306–333.

Ahuja, G. (2000) 'Collaboration networks, structural holes, and innovation: A longitudinal study'. *Administrative Science Quarterly*, 45: 425–455.

Albers, S., Wohlgezogen, F., and Zajac, E. J. (2016) 'Strategic alliance structures: An organization design perspective'. *Journal of Management*, 42: 582–1614.

Ariño, A. and de la Torre, J. (1998) 'Learning from failure: Towards an evolutionary model of collaborative ventures'. *Organization Science*, 9: 306–325.

Ariño, A., de la Torre, J., and Ring, P. S. (2001) 'Relational quality: Managing trust in corporate alliances'. *California Management Review*, 44: 109-131

Baum J. A. C., Calabrese T., and Silverman B. S. (2000) 'Don't go it alone: alliance network composition and startups' performance in Canadian biotechnology'. *Strategic Management Journal*, 21: 267-294.

Beltagui, A. Rosli, A., and Candi, M. (2020) 'Exaptation in a digital innovation ecosystem: The disruptive impacts of 3D printing'. *Research Policy*, 49(1): [103833].

Brandenburger, A. M. and Nalebuff, B. J. (1995) 'The right game: Use game theory to shape strategy'. *Harvard Business Review*, 73(4): 57-71.

Büchel, B. (2002) 'Joint venture development: Driving forces towards equilibrium'. *Journal of World Business*, 37: 199-207.

Burt, R. S. (1982) *Toward a Structural Theory of Action: Network Models of Social Structure, Perception, and Action*. New York: Academic Press.

Coleman, J. S. (1990) *Foundations of Social Theory*. Cambridge: Harvard University Press.

Das, T. K. and Rahman, N. (2001) 'Partner misbehaviour in strategic alliances: Guidelines for effective deterrence'. *Journal of General Management*, 27: 43-70.

Das, T. K. and Teng, B.-S. (2000a) 'Instabilities of strategic alliances: An internal tensions perspective'. *Organization Science*, 11: 77-101.

Das, T. K. and Teng, B.-S. (2000b) 'A resource-based theory of strategic alliances'. *Journal of Management*, 26: 31-61.

Das, T. K. and Teng, B.-S. (2001) 'Trust, control, and risk in strategic alliances: An integrated framework'. *Organization Studies*, 22: 251-283.

Das, T. K. and Teng, B.-S. (2002) 'The dynamics of alliance conditions in the alliance development process'. *Journal of Management Studies*, 39: 725-746.

De Rond, M. and Bouchikhi, H. (2004) 'On the Dialectics of Strategic Alliances'. *Organization Science*, 15(1): 56-69.

Dekker, H. C. (2004) 'Control of inter-organizational relationships: Evidence on appropriation concerns and coordination requirements'. *Accounting Organizations and Society*, 29: 27-49.

Dittrich, K., Duysters, G., and de Man, A. P. (2007) 'Strategic repositioning by means of alliance networks: The case of IBM'. *Research Policy*, 36: 1496-1511.

Dyer, J. H. and Nobeoka, K. (2000) 'Creating and managing a high-performance knowledge-sharing network: The Toyota case'. *Strategic Management Journal*, 21: 345-367.

Dyer, J., Singh, H., and Kale, P. (2008) 'Splitting the pie: Rent distribution in alliances and networks'. *Managerial and Decision Economics*, 29: 137-148.

Gilsing, V., Cloodt, M., and Rooijakkers, N. (2016) 'From birth through transition to maturation: The evolution of technology-based alliance networks'. *Journal of Product Innovation Management*, 33: 181-200.

Gulati, R. (1995) 'Social structure and alliance formation patterns: A longitudinal analysis'. *Administrative Science Quarterly*, 40(4): 619-652.

Gulati, R., and Gargiulo, M. (1999) 'Where do interorganizational networks come from?' *American Journal of Sociology*, 104(5): 1439-1493.

Hennart, J. F. (1988) 'A transaction costs theory of equity joint ventures'. *Strategic Management Journal*, 9: 361-374.

Hoffmann, W. H. (2007) 'Strategies for managing a portfolio of alliances'. *Strategic Management Journal*, 28: 827-856.

Ireland, R. D., Hitt, M. A., and Vaidyanath, D. (2002). 'Alliance management as a source of competitive advantage'. *Journal of Management*, 28: 413-446.

Jacob, J. and Duysters, G. (2017) 'Alliance network configurations and the co-evolution of firms' technology profiles: An analysis of the biopharmaceutical industry'. *Technological Forecasting and Social Change*, 120: 90-102.

Jarvensivu, T. and Moller, K. (2009) 'Metatheory of network management: A contingency perspective'. *Industrial Marketing Management*, 38: 654-661.

Jiang, R. J., Tao, Q. T., and Santoro, M. D. (2010) 'Alliance portfolio diversity and firm performance'. *Strategic Management Journal*, 31: 1136-1144.

Kavusan, K. and Frankfort, H. T. W. (2019) 'A behavioral theory of alliance portfolio reconfiguration: Evidence from Pharmaceutical biotechnology'. *Strategic Management Journal*. 40: 1668-1702.

Knight, L. and Harland, C. (2005) 'Managing supply networks: Organizational roles in network management'. *European Management Journal*, 23: 281-292.

Lavie, D., and Singh, H. (2011) 'The evolution of alliance portfolios: The case of Unisys'. *Industrial and Corporate Change*, 21(3): 763–809.

Majchrzak, A., Jarvenpaa, S., and Bagherzadeh, M. (2015) 'A review of interorganizational collaboration dynamics'. *Journal of Management*, 41: 1338–1360.

Mayer, K. J. and Argyres, N. S. (2004) 'Learning to contract: Evidence from the personal computer industry'. *Organization Science*, 15: 394–410.

McFadden, C. (2020) 'The Fascinating History of Netflix'. Available online at https://interestingengineering.com/the-fascinating-history-of-netflix (accessed 25 June 2020).

Moore J. F. (1993) 'Predators and prey: a new ecology of competition'. *Harvard Business Review*, 71(3): 75–86.

Moore, J. F. (1996) *The death of competition: leadership and strategy in the age of business ecosystems*. New York: HarperBusiness.

Moore, J. F. (1998) 'The rise of a new corporate form'. *The Washington Quarterly*, 21(1): 167–181.

Niesten, E. and Stefan, I. (2019) 'Embracing the paradox of interorganizational value Co-creation and Value Capture: A literature review towards Paradox Resolution'. *International Journal of Management Reviews*, 21: 231–255.

Pahwa, A. (2019) 'Netflix Business Model: How does Netflix make money?' Available online at https://www.feedough.com/how-does-netflix-make-money/ (accessed 25 June 2020).

Parise, S. and Casher, A. (2003) 'Alliance portfolios: Designing and managing your network of business-partner relationships'. *Academy of Management Executive*, 17: 25–39.

Sherman, A. (2019) 'Netflix has now lost two of its most popular shows as old media companies flex their muscle'. Available online at https://www.cnbc.com/2019/07/09/netflix-faces-new-competition-as-old-media-companies-flex-their-muscle.html (accessed 25 June 2020).

Simonin, B. L. (1999) 'Ambiguity and the process of knowledge transfer in strategic alliances'. *Strategic Management Journal*, 20: 595–623.

Than, T. (2020) 'Amazon Ecosystem Vs Apple Ecosystem'. Available online at https://thegeniusreview.com/amazon-vs-apple-ecosystem/ (accessed 25 June 2020).

Tjemkes, B. V., Vos, P., and Burgers, K. (2017) *Strategic alliance management*. Abingdon: Routledge.

Van de Ven, A. H. and Poole, M. S. (1995) 'Explaining development and change in organizations'. *Academy of Management Review*, 20: 510–540.

Volberda, H. W. and Lewin, A. Y. (2003) 'Guest editors' introduction – Co-evolutionary dynamics within and between firms: From evolution to co-evolution'. *Journal of Management Studies*, 40: 2111–2136.

Wassmer, U. (2008) 'Alliance portfolios: A review and research agenda'. *Journal of Management*, 36: 141–171.

White, G. O., Joplin, J. R. W., and Salama, M. F. (2007) 'Contracts and conflict resolution strategies in foreign ventures: A transaction cost perspective'. *International Journal of Conflict Management*, 18: 376–390.

Wieringa, R. (2019) 'A business model of the Netflix Ecosystem'. Available online at https://www.thevalueengineers.nl/what-is-an-ecosystem-business-model/ (accessed 25 June 2020).

Williamson, O. E. (1985) *The economic institutions of capitalism*. New York: Free Press.

Williamson, P. J. and De Meyer, A. (2012) 'Ecosystem advantage: How to successfully harness the power of partners'. *California Management Review*, 55(1): 24–46.

Wilson, J. and Hynes, N. (2009) 'Co-evolution of firms and strategic alliances: Theory and empirical evidence'. *Technological Forecasting and Social Change*, 76: 620–628.

7 Strategizing corporate social responsibility

Christopher Wickert

Summary

This chapter begins with a discussion of the changing expectations about companies' responsibilities towards society. As companies increasingly need to respond to societal challenges and ethical issues, they resort to corporate social responsibility (CSR) to improve transparency, accountability, and legitimacy. The chapter presents various CSR approaches and discusses how these are influenced by a differentiation-compliance tension. Furthermore, the chapter presents several relational tactics that help organizational leaders to garner support for and acceptance of their CSR actions.

Case: climate change and the airline industry

Imagine you are part of the top-management team of a global airline that offers both short-haul and long-haul flights, for instance, the classical flagship carrier of a country. You already have sustainability on the agenda and have some measures in place, such as managing the waste of your operations, investing in fuel-efficiency, and making sure that your fleet is on top of things by using the most modern aircraft available on the market. Despite of these efforts, a new buzzword has reached the boards of most players in the industry, whose consequences are alarming, to say the least: *Flygskam*. The Swedish word for 'being ashamed of flying' because of its enormous environmental impact and negative contribution to climate change. The term has been popularized by Swedish climate change activist Greta Thunberg and is being carried around the world by millions of protestors going on the streets every Friday as part of the Fridays-for-Future social movement. Will it eventually become a lasting trend and 'hip' among the younger generation not to fly? Has the entire airline industry been blind to its environmental footprint and massive impact on the climate? Have major players missed out on engaging in meaningful activities to mitigate its harm on the planet by blowing massive amounts of greenhouse gases into the atmosphere?

Progressive thinking and imagination are urgently needed. Indeed, for some airlines, this seems to be a very serious issue. The CEO of Dutch national carrier KLM asked people in a campaign in summer 2019: 'Could you take the train instead?', suggesting that at least short-haul flights should be substituted by more environmentally friendly means of transportation. Similarly, the CEO of Emirates, one of the largest global carriers, admitted to the audience during the Dubai Air Show in the fall of 2019 that he has only now begun to fully realize the climate crisis: 'I quite like Extinction Rebellion and Greta Thunberg for having brought a real focus to the issue; a focus on the fact that we are not doing enough at the speed we should be'. Clark went on to state that 'I'm not condoning some of their methods. But Extinction Rebellion and Greta have a role to play... We really need this kind of thing to force us to make decisions'.

Are these airline CEOs going crazy, jeopardizing jobs and economic growth? Or are they, rather, a good example of airliners with progressive thinking, who recognize the magnitude of the climate crisis? Do they, perhaps, simply want their firms to survive in the long-run and act out of pure business interest? No matter what their true motivation might be, airlines are reacting in ways which might in the long run substantially shake up their traditional business model. In fact, European low-cost carrier easyJet announced that with immediate effect it would go 'net carbon neutral' with its entire fleet by offsetting all of its CO^2 emissions. As easyJet's CEO Johan Lundgren stated, offsetting is only an interim measure, but in light of the climate crisis the airline needs to take immediate action to cut carbon emissions now, rather than hiding behind the usual excuse that 'more time is needed' in order to delay substantive action. Nevertheless, easyJet's 'priority is to continue to work on reducing our carbon footprint in the short term, coupled with long-term work to support the development of new technology, including electric planes, to reinvent aviation'. easyJet is the world's first major airline to take this step, but it is probably only a matter of time until others follow.

Like other industries that have a substantive environmental or social footprint, the airline industry is under ever-tighter stakeholder scrutiny. Companies are more than ever urged to demonstrate that their actions are truly making a positive impact on people and the planet and are not just another case of greenwashing covering business as usual. Progressive CEOs and business leaders need to anticipate those challenges and kick-off corporate transformation sooner rather than later. But the journey is not an easy one, specifically as business and societal interests don't always fully align.

Questions:

1 What is the main controversy regarding sustainability in the airline industry?
2 What are the airlines' responses to calls for more sustainability?

Source: Wilson (2019)

Learning objectives

1 To understand the importance of approaching issues of social, ethical and environmental responsibility strategically, and how contemporary CSR has moved from 'how the money is spent' to 'how the money is made'.

2 To understand the motives that drive companies' CSR engagement, and which are mainly driven by instrumental consideration as well as a response to stakeholder pressure for greater responsibility.
3 To recognize that a key tension in CSR lies in balancing the need for compliance in order to act according to standardized templates of CSR and meet societal expectations, and the need for differentiation in order to be perceived as 'more sustainable' than the competition.
4 To anticipate future challenges in CSR such as digitalization and the sustainable development goals (SDGs) that will dominate the debate about the limits of CSR in the future.

Introduction to corporate social responsibility

The contemporary understanding of CSR and the roles and responsibilities of business firms towards society have fundamentally changed over the last few decades. Up to the 1990s, CSR was by many firms considered a philanthropic exercise that was about donating some money to charity, in other words social responsibility was fundamentally about 'how the money is spent'. According to this logic, companies would maximize their profits without costly adjustments in core business operations. Then, they would simply compensate for issues such as pollution of the environment of exploitation of workers by making a few donations to a local charity.

Today, such behavior still exists and may follow very sincere and noble intentions. Philanthropy in itself is not to blame. However, it becomes problematic if 'giving back' becomes a firm's rationale for understanding its responsibilities. Today, CSR is elevated to a strategic level and has become fundamentally about 'how the money is made'. As such, CSR has turned away from 'giving back to society' towards a strategic idea about how value is created by a firm. This includes asking what the social, environmental and ethical implications of the firm's value creating processes are within its immediate boundaries and also beyond, throughout its supply chain. Integrating CSR principles into business strategy would thus include paying fair wages to workers in distant supplier factories and making sure that production processes are socially and environmentally responsible. At the same time, this includes recognizing opportunities for social value creation along the supply chain, and becoming a CSR leader doesn't have to be based on being responsible in the home market only. In essence, the scope of CSR is no longer constrained to the headquarters of a company, but instead stretched along its entire, and often global, supply chain and production network (Wickert and Risi 2019).

This stretched understanding of CSR notwithstanding brings new complications, which will be discussed in this chapter. While globally integrated firms with complex supply chains typically benefit from efficiency gains and cost reductions, it becomes a more challenging task to monitor and control what is going on in distant supplier factories, such as whether labor practices follow basic human rights. Stakeholders also attribute responsibility for business processes not only *upstream* to problematic issues along the supply chain. Expectations also increasingly go *downstream* to consumers and include the product life cycle. Thus, to approach CSR strategically, business leaders need an understanding of its scope and implications. Figure 7.1 illustrates those changes and how the scope of CSR has expanded.

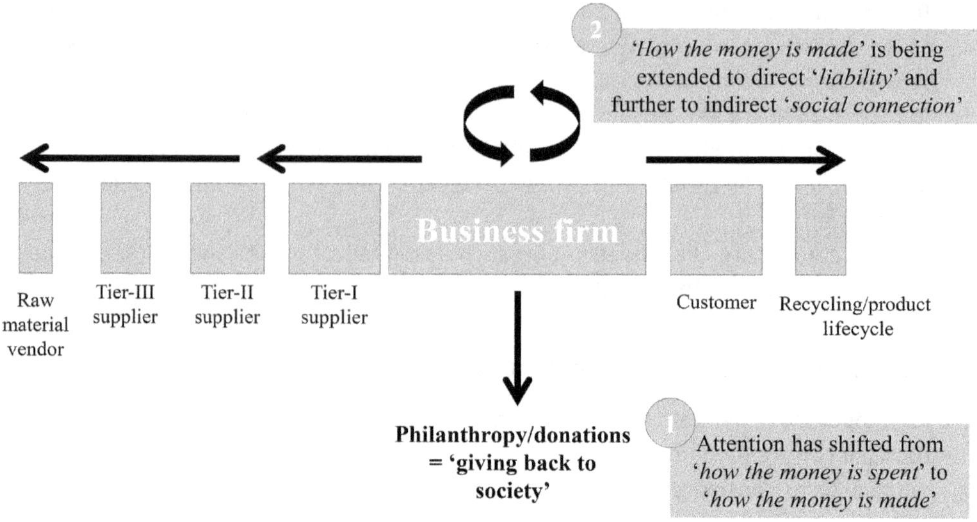

Figure 7.1 CSR: from philanthropy to liability to a social connection responsibility

Source: Wickert and Risi (2019: 6)

Because of the complexity of the social, environmental and ethical challenges that confront business firms, as well as the multiplicity of stakeholders that raise their voice, it is difficult to find a simple definition of CSR. This is because of three main reasons. First, even though there is some consensus among experts what CSR entails exactly and how far its scope may stretch, this can nevertheless be defined differently by different stakeholders – think about how a critical NGOs vs. a business firm may each think about how far responsibility should go. To businesses, this might even bring some advantages. For instance, by considering only those CSR topics which they can easily address, and simply disregarding those which are more difficult and costly to manage.

Second, it should be acknowledged that there are multiple concepts that each address the role of business in society and its social, ethical, and environmental responsibilities. While different terminology may be able to capture different nuances of this discussion, such as business ethics, corporate sustainability, or corporate citizenship, here we suggest to use CSR as an umbrella term for this debate. Moreover, among those terms, CSR is the most widely used and accepted and thus it makes it easier to reach a common understanding when the same language is spoken by firms and their stakeholders (see Bansal and Song 2017 for an overview).

Third, CSR must be understood as a dynamic phenomenon whose scope may change over time, just as the discussion above and its transformation from 'how the money is spent' to 'how the money is made' shows. In a decade from now, different responsibilities may appear on the radar and others may no longer be considered relevant. For example, what we witness now is that both the topic of digitalization as well as the challenge of sustainable development, as encapsulated in the SDGs of the United Nations, have garnered substantial attention in the CSR debate and are increasingly recognized as key topics to address by many businesses.

Despite these challenges it is important to have an, albeit broad, working definition for CSR. Here, we define CSR as follows: 'Corporate Social Responsibility (CSR) is an umbrella term to describe how business firms, small and large, integrate social, environmental and ethical responsibilities to which they are connected into their core business strategies, structures and procedures within and across divisions, functions as well as value chains in collaboration with relevant stakeholders' (Wickert and Risi 2019: 22).

This definition captures some key features of CSR. First, it denotes that CSR is not a completely voluntary concept with actions that go 'beyond the law'. What we see in how CSR is currently treated is that it become a de facto requirement for business firms and is thus rather semi-voluntary or quasi-mandatory to ensure legitimacy and a firm's social license to operate. Also, governments that once withdrew from the regulation of social and environmental issues in favor of business-led initiatives under the umbrella of CSR are becoming increasingly active and putting forward new regulations, for example regarding non-financial reporting practices. The fact that CSR has become a mainstream management concept also includes that CSR now goes much beyond purely voluntary actions.

Second, CSR implies considering the interests of multiple actors and it is fundamentally a stakeholder-driven concept. Companies are embedded in webs of stakeholder relationships and need to navigate through the oftentimes competing interests of those stakeholders, not simply their shareholders. The argument that a firm has a responsibility to its shareholders is typically not questioned, but because the same firm relies on the contribution of many other stakeholders such as consumers, employees, suppliers, and local communities in order to survive and prosper, their needs and expectations also require attention.

Third, while the term CSR includes the word 'corporation', in broader discussions using the term other forms of business are also included; specifically, CSR applies, albeit in different ways, to both large and small firms, which don't necessarily have to be incorporated or multinational but can, for instance, also be owner-managed and very local in scope. Even some government authorities refer to the term CSR when describing how they make their own operations more sustainable. In fact, the same basic principles about human rights, labor norms, environmental protection or anti-corruption equally apply to all business firms regardless of their size or the geographic location of their activities.

Fourth, while the term CSR includes the word 'social', it should be understood as a multi-dimensional construct that grants equal importance to environmental and ethical issues that appear in business conduct. This mirrors the globally recognized scope of responsibilities of business firms that comprise four key issue areas: (i) human rights (as determined in the Universal Declaration of Human Rights); (ii) labor rights (as stated in the International Labour Organization's Declaration on Fundamental Principles and Rights at Work); (iii) environmental principles (as agreed upon in the Rio Declaration on Environment and Development); and (iv) anti-corruption (as stated in the UN Convention Against Corruption). The United Nations Global Compact, the world's largest CSR initiative (www.unglobalcompact.org) has incorporated these issue areas in its 'Ten Principles'. While they should not be seen as exhaustive or definitive, they nevertheless provide a valuable moral compass for business leaders that outline the most important expectations of stakeholders.

Importantly, what CSR entails and which issues are prioritized by important stakeholders is inherently dynamic. Two megatrends have moved on the agenda of many companies only very recently, namely *digitalization* and *big data*, alongside the SDGs. Both trends are gradually being taken up by businesses around the globe, and CEOs need to understand their

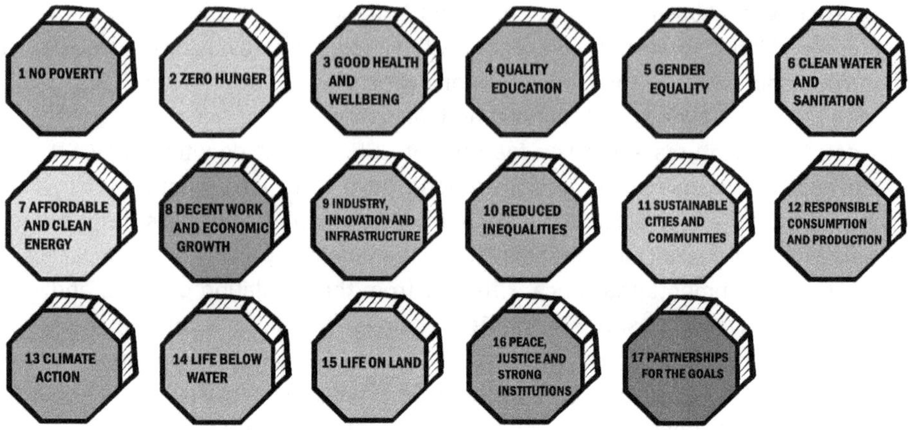

Figure 7.2 The 17 Sustainable Development Goals (SDGs)

Source: Based on United Nations (2020)

implications, not only in terms of creating business opportunities, but also how they create a new set of CSR-related challenges. What, for instance, does 'corporate digital responsibility' really mean? How can firms responsibly deal with artificial intelligence and big data, as such technologies have not only been praised, but also condemned as a threat to democracy, fostering racism and inequality and bringing more harm than good to society? Also, the 17 SDGs (see Figure 7.2) have entered the boardroom of sustainability leaders, and there is currently discussion regarding how the private sector can make a meaningful contribution to those goals, which include: the achievement of gender equality and empowering women and girls; eradicating hunger; contributing to biodiversity and maritime life; and other social and environmental issues that significantly stretch the boundaries of what is commonly considered the scope of responsibility for a business firm.

In fact, some MNCs have taken the lead in addressing some of the SDGs and incorporated them into their broader CSR strategy. Dutch multinational Unilever, for instance, has launched its 'Sustainable Living Plan' (Unilever 2020) and takes a firm stance in showing how its business operations have an impact on the SDGs, and at the same time how the issue areas outlined by the goals can impact their business success. Many SDGs are indeed directly relevant for businesses and are consistent with the 10 principles of the UN Global Compact, including 'decent work and economic growth' (SDG 8), 'responsible consumption and production' (SDG 12), 'good health and well-being' (SDG 3), and 'gender equality' (SDG 5). It can be expected that the SDGs will become something of a new gold standard for CSR policies and strategies around the globe, making it a necessity for leaders to engage with them and to show how their business can contribute to sustainable development.

Tensions in strategic CSR: balancing compliance and differentiation

An important tension pervades how business firms approaches CSR, namely between compliance with societal expectations in order to not fall behind and reduce risk and differentiation in order to stand out from the competition (see Figure 7.3). Here, we refer to this tension as

Figure 7.3 Compliance-differentiation tension

the 'managerial fallacy of CSR' (see Wickert and Risi 2019 for a more detailed discussion). This fallacy exists, because CSR has moved from the margins of top-managers' attention into a mainstream issue that can no longer be neglected by CEOs. What we observe in the business world is that almost every larger firm and also a significant number of smaller firms takes a firm stance towards CSR (Wickert, Scherer, and Spence 2016). Often, companies follow broadly accepted and highly standardized frameworks to organize their CSR activities, such as the guiding principles of the UN Global Compact, or the ISO 26000 CSR implementation scheme. Obviously, from a social and environmental point of view it seems to be a good thing that everyone is doing CSR. However, this creates a number of complications for those in charge of rolling a CSR strategy inside an organization.

Exactly because more and more firms follows comparable approaches to how they implement CSR into strategies, practices, and procedures, it is more difficult for each individual firm to stand out and be perceived as 'more sustainable' than the competition – an important feature when it comes to attracting talent, consumers, or being a supplier of choice because of an above-average CSR profile.

As CSR matures, opportunities to create a business case for some social or environmental initiative become more scarce and managers face a dilemma: the higher the societal and competitive pressure to engage in CSR, the more challenging it is to create a unique CSR profile that generates and sustains a competitive advantage from CSR. The more firms that engage in CSR because they see opportunities to create value for themselves and for society, but in doing so follow the same standardized templates, the more complicated it becomes to maintain exactly those opportunities.

A look at the theory helps to better understand this tension. In fact, a core principle of the resource-based view of the firm proposes that competitive advantage can only be obtained if resources are, amongst others, rare, inimitable, and unique (Barney 1991). This suggests that, to create such an advantage, only few companies could engage in CSR, each having a distinct approach that is highly idiosyncratic to each company. As such, it would allow firms to differentiate themselves from the competition, for instance by offering more sustainable products, or being a more responsible employer, etc. All of this, however, becomes increasingly difficult for firms the more 'everyone' is following the same standardized templates when trying to differentiate themselves from the competition. What can be observed more and more, however, is that CSR reports of major multinationals and how they portray their CSR strategies, policies, and activities looks very much alike (imagine the green tree on a lush mountain meadow, bright blue skies and smiling families – a picture can be easily found in quite a few CSR reports).

If all competitors pledge to follow the same or at least fairly similar CSR principles, it becomes more challenging to be perceived as 'the most responsible employer' to job seekers, or to have the 'most responsible product portfolio' in the eyes of consumers. From a theoretical point of view, this tension is reflected in a faulty base assumption about how CSR can become a source of sustainable competitive advantage. If, but only if, a CSR profile is unique, rare, and hard to imitate, as the resource-based view suggests it needs to be, then CSR can add substantial value to a firm by informing its product-differentiation strategy. The challenge for managers here is to develop a strategy that, on the hand, picks up those expectations that are commonly raised by societal stakeholders and which reflect what it means to 'be responsible' and, on the other, are innovative and difficult for competitors to imitate. This is tricky, because differentiation by definition includes an element of comparison, where a company is seen as more responsible than another company. In consequence, comparability also needs to be ensured, because CSR is evaluated by stakeholders relative to what competitors do for social and environmental sustainability, and hardly in isolation. Thus, the very nature of CSR asks for a high degree of transparency and proactive communication of a firm's strategy, as well as internal practices and procedures, to external stakeholders. The very visible nature of CSR therefore makes it easier for competitors to develop similar strategies or follow what might be considered a best-practice in a particular industry.

The mainstreaming of CSR into a 'must have' for business firms is an important factor that exacerbates the tension of compliance vs. differentiation (i.e., uniqueness) of a CSR profile (for example see box 7.1). The fact that CSR has become a mainstream business practice has turned into the number one motive that explains why so many firms feel urged to engage in CSR: it is now seen as a necessity, rather than an voluntary act. Business firms engage in CSR, not because they necessarily see a quantifiable business case for it, but because all or at least most of the competition does so. The evidence that underscores this argument is vast. A survey by KPMG published in 2017 concludes that CSR reporting is now a standard practice for large and mid-cap companies around the world (Blasco and King 2017). The question that companies need to find answers for is 'how' to report, and not 'whether' to report (p. 4). Similarly, self-regulatory initiatives that exist in different industries, such as the UTZ for tea and cocoa products, the FSC for sustainable forestry, or the MSC for fishery, should be better characterized as 'semi-voluntary', because participation in these initiatives is more of a corporate priority than a choice. It is important to note that there is factually no legal obligation to join such CSR initiatives, but they are 'quasi-mandated' by public and consumer expectations about what is considered a socially acceptable business practice.

Research provides support for this view. For example, the study by Bitaraf (2015) shows that in 2005, justifications for CSR, as portrayed in the opening statements of an annual report, have mainly emphasized the business case ('we engage in CSR because it enhances our profits'). In 2015, in contrast, justifications that stated a company's commitment to meet stakeholder expectations for responsible business conduct came to dominate ('we engage in CSR because our stakeholders expect it'). The research of Flammer (2013), who studied

Box 7.1 Balancing compliance and differentiation at Unilever

Dutch FMCG multinational Unilever is one of those companies which take the need to balance compliance and differentiation very seriously. On the one hand, Unilever subscribes to many of the popular CSR frameworks and thus signals to its stakeholders compliance to generally accepted norms of what it means to have 'good' socially and environmentally responsible business practices at the heart of their strategy and operations. For example, Unilever is a participant of the United Nations Global Compact, it uses the reporting framework of the Global Reporting Initiative, it is a member of the Carbon Disclosure Project to monitor and disclose its carbon emissions, and it has also commissioned the assurance providers PricewaterhouseCoopers (PwC), DNV, and KPMG to audit its activities and reporting. Compliance to external expectations of societal stakeholders more generally, along with externally provided CSR management frameworks, is thus a central building block of Unilever's approach to CSR.

On the other hand, an because compliance alone would do little to allow Unilever to stand out of the crowd of multinational committed to sustainability, the company has created a unique CSR profile, called its Sustainable Living Plan. While many of the actions and activities subsumed in this plan do reflect, for example, the issue areas outlined by the United Nations Global Compact, Unilever is one of the forerunners when it comes to translating the SDGs into more concrete corporate practice. The company's Sustainable Living Plan has elevated itself to a best-practice that many other firms jealously look at - while at the same time Unilever signals the impression of being aware that they must continue to stay ahead of the crowd in order to maintain their unique competitive advantage in how to live up to sustainability. In fact, as suggested by many media reports, Unilever's Sustainable Living Plan has been at the heart of its business model for more than a decade. With this plan, Unilever does not have a sustainability strategy that coexists with a financial and corporate strategy, but it takes an integrated approach: 'the sustainable business strategy is our strategy', says the company's CFO Graeme Pitkethly, emphasizing that they 'do not have another separate strategy'. In practice, this means that in discussions at board and executive level, and in discussions around Unilever brands, the focus is always on the sustainable business strategy. Crucially, having such management systems and practices in plans that are also reflected in the culture of the organization and in the mindsets of all of their employees is not something a competitor can easily copy.

Sources: ICAEW (2020); Unilever (2020)

reactions of shareholders to CSR initiatives, shows that positive stock-market reactions to 'good' CSR have become less notable over time, while negative reactions to 'bad' CSR have proliferated. In other words, as social and environmental responsibility have become the new normal, CSR has come to be seen in the same terms as hygiene, where demonstrating a baseline engagement is no longer rewarded, while being irresponsible and having no CSR (or hygiene) is increasingly punished.

Understanding the motives for CSR

We have discussed above that CSR has become mainstream and that business firms nowadays can hardly afford not to engage in CSR and incorporate it in their strategies and internal practices and procedures. In discussing the tension between compliance and the strive for differentiation we have already scratched the surface of some of the underlying motives as to why firms would be triggered to seriously consider CSR as part of their strategy. The literature generally distinguishes two distinct motives for CSR: a business case-driven motive and a stakeholder-driven motive. We will explain those in detail below. We may call it unfortunate, but ethical motives for CSR - while being discussed extensively in the literature from a normative point of view - that prescribe how businesses ought to behave and what is 'the right thing to do' are relatively marginal in terms of making their way up to the boardroom and managerial decision-making more generally. It all comes down to either finding a business case for CSR, or being exposes to such pressure from stakeholders that not engaging in CSR isn't an option.

The business-case motive for CSR

The essence of the business-case motive for CSR is encapsulated in the slogan 'doing well by doing good'. The idea of this is that being environmentally or socially responsible will ultimately result in higher financial returns or share prices. The literature provide for factors that explain why CSR might enhance long-term value and create a competitive advantage for firms (for an overview see, for instance, Vishwanathan et al. 2020).

First, internally, CSR initiatives can attract talent, increase employee engagement, motivation and satisfaction, and reduce employee retention, factors that are beneficial for job performance and productivity. Millennials, for example, are said to prefer working for companies that put high emphasis on their social responsibility, and might even accept a salary discount when earnings are spent for CSR initiatives.

Second, externally, consumers and investors value CSR and it can be beneficial for the creation of trust in brands and products, all of which are useful in creating a good reputation, which may lead to increased sales, allow for charging a price-premium on products, or being an investment of choice for socially oriented investors that screen for companies that meet certain CSR criteria.

Third, CSR can also help to reduce operational costs, for instance when implementing eco-efficiency, waste reduction, or recycling programs. Fourth, good CSR allows to better manage social and environmental risks. This includes being prepared for scandals or accidents when appropriate precautionary measures have been installed that give the sincere image that a firm did 'the best it could' to prevent such instances. Also, CSR programs maybe also work to forestall regulation, for instance when industry-specific self-regulatory standards are created to reduce pollution, rather than governmental intervention.

The idea of a business case for CSR has inspired a vast number of studies that have tried to establish a link between CSR and financial performance, both theoretically, asking 'why and how are CSR and financial performance related?' (e.g., McWilliams and Siegel 2001; Jensen 2002), and empirically, asking what the actual contribution of CSR to financial performance, or vice versa, is (e.g., Orlitzky, Schmidt, and Rynes 2003; Wang, Dou and Jia 2016; Vishwanathan et al. 2020).

In a seminal study, McWilliams and Siegel (2001) propose a supply-and-demand model for CSR. They argue that managers should determine an optimal degree of CSR based on a traditional cost-benefit analysis, as they would do for any other investment decision. This model, they suggest, allows to maximize financial returns and simultaneously meet stakeholder expectations. The demand for CSR depends on factors such as consumer awareness, preferences, and willingness to pay a price premium for products with CSR attributes (such as a fair-trade label or eco-certification). The supply for CSR depends on the higher costs of labor, machinery and production processes, if they follow certain higher social or environmental standards (e.g., more environmentally friendly equipment). An important point that McWilliams and Siegel make, however, is that CSR can create a sustainable competitive advantage if those CSR attributes of products or services are valuable, rare, inimitable, and difficult to substitute – some of which have been shown above to be problematic.

Jensen's (2002) idea of enlightened self-interest has also been influential in shaping the debate about the business case for CSR. Jensen suggests that businesses should accept certain social and environmental responsibilities insofar as doing so promotes their own self-interest. The assumption here, grounded in neoclassical economics, is that if all firms would maximize their long-term value it would automatically lead to higher overall social welfare. CSR is then viable as a business strategy, if it is able to contribute to the primary objective function of business firms to maximize profitability. This, in essence, reflects the underlying ideology of the business-case view of CSR that many advocates of CSR seem to accept. There is, however, a fairly opportunistic element in this perspective, something that we shall discuss further on in this chapter.

Based on this theoretical perspective, management guru Michael Porter and his co-author Michael Kramer (2006; 2011) have translated the business case for CSR into a now popular management framework called 'creating shared value' (CSV). Many businesses around the world have picked up the idea of CSV and took it as a framework to put CSR into strategy and practice. According to Porter and Kramer, CSV aims to elevate social and environmental issues to a strategic level, at it focuses attention on those relevant issues that affect a company's operations or its long-term competitiveness. Companies hence focus on the positive social impacts they can create along their value chain, based on a social opportunity analysis. Also, considering the competitive context of a firm is critical, as there are, according to Porter and Kramer, many social issues in the firm's external environment that substantially impact the drivers of competitiveness where it operates. The CSV concept, then, suggests to prioritize those social issues along the value chain that have the highest impact and to turn them into business opportunities, to create shared value for the business and society. For instance, firms would install CSR attributes in those products that have the highest visibility on the market or where they can expect the highest reputational gain, or they would aim to become more sustainable where stakeholder attention is most salient.

On the research side of things, many scholars have tried to examine empirically the link between CSR and financial performance (meta-analyses include Orlitzky et al. 2003; Vishwanathan et al. 2020; Wang et al. 2016). Finding support for this relationship has even been called the 'holy grail' of CSR research (Devinney 2009). Hundreds of studies hence illustrate the relationship between CSR and corporate financial performance (CFP) – the direction however remains inconclusive. Many studies indeed report a positive relationship, where CSR is

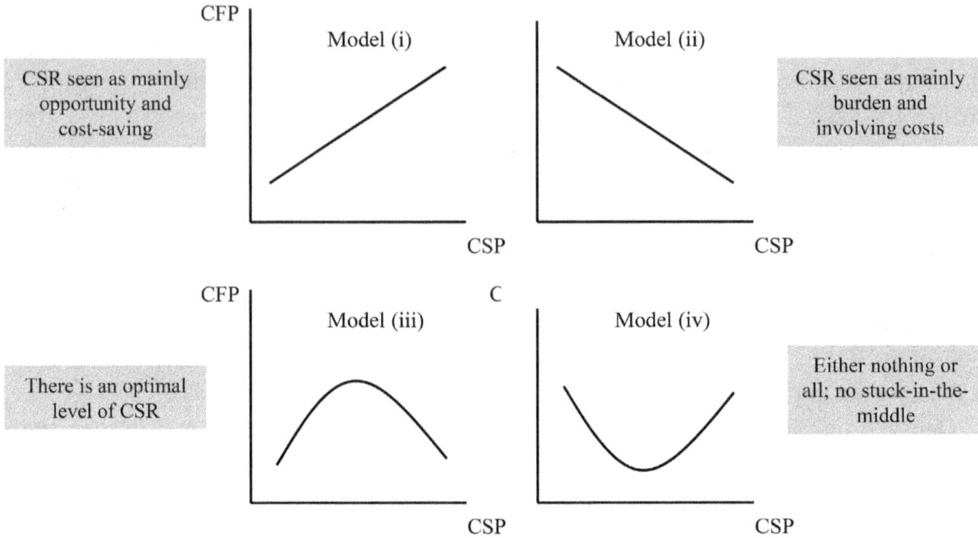

Figure 7.4 Multiple directions of the CSR-CFP link. CFP = corporate financial performance; CSP = corporate social performance.

Source: Brammer and Millington (2008)

either a means to enhance profits by selling more products or a way to save costs by installing more efficient practices. Some studies, however, find a negative relationship. This means that CSR is mainly something that implies higher costs that do not necessarily lead to higher profits - at least in the short-term. In line with the arguments by McWilliams and Siegel we reviewed above, other studies show a U-shaped relationship. This means in fact that there is an optimal level of CSR from a business case point of view. A company should thus not over- or underinvest in CSR, as too little CSR is below stakeholder expectations, and too much is simply beyond what stakeholders are able to reward. A few studies even find an 'inverted' U-shaped relationship. The highest return from CSR would accrue if a firm either does nothing, assuming that there is a large enough segment of the market that simply 'doesn't care', or to really implement CSR substantively in order to stand out and be perceived as a leader in sustainability (see Brammer and Millington 2008). Figure 7.4 summarizes the multiple directions the CSR (also commonly described as CSP - corporate social performance) and CFP can take.

Empirically, and due to the inconsistent findings in the literature, the relationship between CSR and CFP remains a puzzle. The conclusion of Barnett (2007: 794) from more than a decade ago probably still applies: 'after more than thirty years of research, we cannot clearly conclude whether a one-dollar investment in social initiatives returns more or less than one dollar in benefit to the shareholder'. This difficulty in establishing a clear causal link might be due to methodological problems. On the one hand, we have seen above that finding a clear-cut definition of CSR is challenging, and thus many studies compare apples and oranges. Some studies examine philanthropy (how the money is spent), and others look at supply-chain CSR (how the money is spent), which obviously would lead to different results. Others base their findings on more symbolic accounts of CSR, such as the existence of a commitment or a CSR report, while other examine more substantive measures, such as supply-chain monitoring systems that are certainly more costly and also more difficult to precisely measure (Wickert et al. 2016). Beyond methodological problems, however, lies another problem that challenges the prevalence of the business-case view of CSR. Is it really that CSR is driven by instrumental calculations of business firms where they engage in CSR whenever they see a business case? Or might most firms be inclined to commit to CSR for other reasons?

CSR as a response to stakeholder expectations

What CSR means and entails, and where its limits are, is increasingly shaped by the expectations of different societal stakeholders, such as consumers, investors, employees, civil society organization, suppliers and buyers, governments, and the media. Thus, CSR initiatives are less likely to be simply a result of some businesses' internal cost-benefit calculation, but instead a strategic response to stakeholder expectations - independent of whether they see an immediate business case or not. Evidence for such behavior is the prevalence of large-scale boycotts or media campaigns in which critical NGOs target typically well-known multinationals and call upon the broader public to avoid buying a product because of its poor social or environmental performance. Greenpeace is a well-known NGO whose 'most favorite' enemies are companies such as Nestlé (linked to environmentally damaging production of palm oil in the rainforest) or Shell (linked to oil exploration in the Arctic). Whether a boycott is justified or not, what we can increasingly observe is that companies put great effort in reacting to accusations, typically not by denying any responsibility, but rather by acknowledging some sort of previous wrongdoing and by committing to do better in the future. Nestlé for instance became a member of the Roundtable on Sustainable Palm Oil, and LEGO stopped the sales of a construction kit for children where they could build an oil platform because it didn't want to be associated with Shell's dirty business and feared negative publicity. Such boycotts and reactions not only by consumers but also by affected companies show the increasing influence of CSR-related decisions, and how social and environmental issues make it onto the top-management agenda. It is increasingly stakeholders and their judgement about what it means to be responsible that determines how companies react.

Stakeholder theory (e.g., Freeman 1984; Freeman, Harrison, and Zyglidopoulos 2018) provides the theoretical basis for what those stakeholders are, what they commonly expect and how they can influence business firms in their CSR agendas. Stakeholders are defined as actors who are affected by or can affect a businesses' actions, objectives, and operations, independent of whether they have a legal relationship or not. They can have different degrees of power and legitimacy in terms of how widely accepted and supported their claims are by the broader public, and some issues that are raised may have varying degrees of urgency (Mitchell, Agle, and Wood 1997). Consumers are a key stakeholder group. For example, fair-trade products, such as coffee, tea, or cocoa, that are demanded by so-called 'ethical consumers' are a market segment with above-average growth rates that in 2017 comprised more than 8 billion Euros globally (Statista 2020). Specifically, firms with valuable reputations cannot afford not to consider this market segment, for instance by attaching certifications or labels on their products to signal that their raw materials are sourced in a sustainable manner.

As the example from above demonstrates, NGOs, activists, and civil society groups are another stakeholder group that has become very influential in influencing the CSR agendas of business firms. Typically, NGOs are formed to fight for certain social or environmental causes, such as the elimination of child labor and human rights (e.g., Amnesty International), protection of the rain forest (e.g., Greenpeace), or mitigating climate change (e.g., Carbon Disclosure Project). Notable differences exist in how NGOs choose to approach the corporate world. Some, such as the WWF (Worldwide Fund for Nature) have a more collaborative stance and launch joint projects with companies, such as Coca-Cola to save water resources, for example. Other NGOs are more confrontational in their stance and engage in 'naming and shaming' companies whom they deem particularly evil, as the example of Greenpeace targeting Nestlé demonstrates. Both approaches are influential in shaping corporate responses to those pressures.

Governments and other regulatory agencies continue to be important stakeholders that shape businesses' CSR agendas (Kourula et al. 2019). This is because an important trigger for putting CSR on the agenda is to prevent future regulation about some social or environmental concern. Typically, the private sector prefers so-called 'soft-law' that reflects voluntary commitments and self-regulation over 'hard-law' imposed and enforced by governments. While many NGOs see exactly this as problematic, business firms prefer soft-law because those standards are typically lower and less strict, for instance when it comes to pollution control. What we have also witnessed in recent years is that governments have re-entered the CSR arena, from which many have retreated in the past, in favor of industry self-regulation. The European Commission, for example, has been active in putting forward new CSR regulation that requires companies to annually report on their social and environmental achievements.

Socially responsible investors are another group of stakeholders that has gained substantial influence in recent years. Those investors make their investment decisions based on social, environmental, and ethical criteria that companies have to fulfil and, for instance, exclude certain industries (such as weapons or gambling) from their portfolios, or only invest in those companies that have made sincere CSR commitments. Net assets under management by so-called socially responsible investing (SRI) funds have risen to more than 4 trillion Euros (Eurosif 2018). According to other research, specifically the millennial generation supports this trend of 'impact investing', where more than half of the population would consider social factors when making investment decisions. Even important wealth management companies such as BlackRock take a stance on CSR, and call on companies to strategically address it if they want to remain an investment of choice (Sorkin 2018).

Employees are important stakeholders as well. Today, many firms seek to meet their expectations by positioning themselves as responsible employers that sell sustainable products - who wants to work for a company that would systematically disregard human rights or damage the environment? Next to those key stakeholder groups, CSR decisions are also driven to a great extent by large buyers. For instance, textile brands expect that their supplier meet certain labor norms, or retailers sell only products which fulfil some sustainability standards. Thus, specifically for firms in the 'middle' of a supply chain, the expectations for CSR of their buyers are important triggers, as consumers often attribute both positive and negative CSR to those brands from which they bought the final product.

To conclude, we can observe that the business case for CSR has become a less important driver than the pressure of various societal stakeholders to engage in relevant CSR issues. Companies are expected to follow the 'rules of the game' and engage in social and environmental responsibility to maintain their social license to operate.

Approaching sustainability transformation strategically

Many of the CSR managers we interviewed reported that a major difficulty in their work is to convince other employees and decision-makers in their company about the importance of CSR. While many leaders and CEOs have recognized that CSR is a 'must have', many middle managers in particular seem not to have embraced it yet. Oftentimes they lack motivation or sheer interest in sustainability topics, or perhaps feel overburdened by their daily agendas and thus refrain from kicking off new CSR projects. Take, for instance, a procurement manager who is asked to include complicated new CSR standards in her decision-making and which may not necessarily be in line with previous financially oriented objectives. Others might indeed be 'into' sustainability, but simply do not know how to incorporate abstract issues such as climate change or human rights into their daily jobs. Collectively, evidence shows that while a CEO commitment is essential, it is not at all an automatism for successful CSR implementation. Rather, it is the CSR manager's task to pick up people for the CSR journey.

Although CSR is high on most large companies' agendas, it still takes considerable effort for it to be accepted and implemented at every level of the company. Business firms nowadays must position themselves with regard to CSR and communicate their activities to stakeholders. While formal structures, such as codes of conduct, policy documents, and certification schemes, are important for the successful implementation of CSR, their formal endorsement by CEOs alone often has little effect. In the worst case, public commitments to CSR without proper implementation easily backfire and lead to accusations of greenwashing or the symbolic construction of a CSR façade that lacks any substance. Leadership by CSR managers plays a crucial role to avoid such problems, because their responsibility is to implement CSR practices internally and spread a CSR mindset within the company. Most companies these days have employed a CSR or sustainability manager, or have even installed an entire department responsible for pushing the company towards greater responsibility.

> To create momentum for CSR, sustainability leaders need to make use of multiple relational strategies to sell social change.

The challenge for those responsible for the integration of sustainability issues internally then becomes: how to convincingly argue for such change within a company? Our previous research reveals a range of strategies for getting people onboard - and getting the company to 'walk the talk' (see also Wickert and de Bakker 2018; Wickert and de Bakker 2019; Wickert and Risi 2019). By interviewing a cross section of CSR managers, we found that the people who most effectively sell social change often perceive themselves as powerful change agents. They're dissatisfied with the status quo, and take personal responsibility for their organizations' movement towards social change. But, despite powerful self-perceptions, these change agents are also excellent at tempering their expectations, resisting the temptation to pursue more change than the organization can sustain.

To create momentum for CSR, sustainability leaders need to make use of several relational strategies to sell social change. CSR managers see themselves as issue sellers focused on building networks of like-minded people, enabling them to leverage their sometimes weak organizational positions. They also became adept at accepting small wins and adapting to the worldviews of their buyers, enabling them to chip away at change over time, all the while processing how others view social change. We found five relational tactics that successful CSR managers commonly employ. Although they are not necessarily equally present in each and every company, these five tactics represent recurring patterns that were highlighted by the majority of the CSR managers we interviewed. What they emphasized is that systematic application of these tactics is an important component of successful CSR implementation, and helps to better circumvent internal barriers and resistance to change.

Tactic 1: building a network of internal allies and achieving small wins. The creation of an internal network and the identification of likeminded others - those acting as allies in the quest for greater sustainability - is a key component of successful CSR implementation. Support from influential decision-makers who are embedded in the operational sphere helps CSR managers to launch pilot projects. For example, if the CSR manager can win the support of the head of procurement and the head of marketing, they can join forces to initiate a new CSR project. This makes it easier to give CSR a strategic edge and can be scaled up to other parts of the company.

Tactic 2: creating emotional and functional proximity. CSR managers able to connect abstract ideas of CSR and sustainability to the daily business routines of employees can create an important lever to foster commitment and support. It means explaining what sustainability means, not only for the company but also for specific people doing specific jobs. This can happen on the emotional level, where employees develop a sense of personal responsibility for different CSR aspects (such as accident reduction in their factory, or considering their own carbon footprint). Equally important, functional proximity means to make the sustainability impact of specific jobs in the company understandable. For instance, showing how tasks of the procurement or marketing function bring about social problems and which steps are necessary to address them (such as measuring the carbon footprint of the company's car fleet and adjusting procurement decisions for more efficient cars).

Tactic 3: identifying adequate incentives. In order to 'catch people where they can be caught'', CSR managers need to identify different and oftentimes heterogeneous incentives for and motivations of employees within the company, and adjust the underlying arguments in favor of particular CSR projects. This is important when convincing employees of different backgrounds of the importance of CSR for the company. In fact, many people have a different view of the role of business in society, and CSR managers need to identify what motivates people for social change. For example, employees in different divisions of a company, such as accounting, production, sales, or PR, oftentimes differ considerably in how they can be motivated for CSR. Our research shows that employees with managerial functions, in particular with a strong finance background or business education, are more likely to be convinced if CSR can be quantified and a strong business case presented. In contrast, arguments with regard to reputation and long-term effects on stakeholders, such as future employees or consumers, resonate stronger when the CSR manager is dealing with marketing, investor relations, and HR staff. We also found that, according to the CSR managers we studied, shop-floor employees and blue-collar workers can often be more easily motivated by presenting CSR as the 'right thing to do', independent of the effect this might have on profits.

Tactic 4: external and internal benchmarking. Creating benchmarks against which progress of CSR projects can be measured is another important tactic. Who wants to be the laggard when it comes to the implementation of CSR projects? CSR managers can leverage this in a twofold manner: (i) internal benchmarking; and (ii) external benchmarking. Internal benchmarking aims to compare different divisions within a company on related grounds, such as the carbon emissions or recycling quotas per unit for multiple production lines. It works well to create internal competition for the best CSR performance. For instance, decision-makers may be more motivated to engage in CSR projects if there is an incentive to be the best (or at least not the worst) among all divisions or locations. External benchmarking is broader and aims to compare the CSR performance of an entire company against that of its competitors. For instance, this can be measured by looking at the placement in reputed CSR rankings such as the Dow Jones Sustainability Index.

Tactic 5: creating holistic awareness. Finally, the effectiveness of these tactics can be leveraged if CSR managers are able to integrate CSR topics holistically into the awareness of employees. This is an important precondition to foster proactivity among employees, enabling them to detect CSR-relevant issues without the constant presence of the CSR manager. Creating holistic awareness starts by addressing ethics and sustainability in training and education programs, as well as by introducing internal communications tools or corporate volunteering programs.

Reflection

We have argued above that CSR is motivated either by business-case driven cost-benefit calculations or by pressure from stakeholders that urge companies to engage with their social and environmental responsibilities. An important ethical dilemma surrounds these motives for CSR that is worthy of some reflection. This dilemma is reflected in the essential question: if social responsibility is assumed under the condition that it pays off financially, what if it does not pay? Alternatively, if social responsibility is assumed under the condition that stakeholders are powerful enough to exert such pressure on a firm that it might be financially harmful to not pay attention to their claims, what if that is not the case and a stakeholder group has a legitimate claim but no power of influence?

The notion of CSV presented above lends itself as a case in point to reflect on the ethical tension inherent in the business-case view of CSR specifically, but applies similarly to the stakeholder view. CSV intends to address societal problems by enhancing profitability while solving those problems, in other words, so-called 'win-win' scenarios are created where everybody benefits: both the company and society. According to Porter and Kramer (2006: 6; our emphasis), for CSV '…the essential test that should guide CSR is *not whether a cause is worthy* [or ethical] but *whether it presents an opportunity to create shared value* – that is, a meaningful benefit for society that is also valuable to the business'. In consequence, '…strategic CSR (i.e., CSV) is far more selective. Companies are called on to address hundreds of social issues, but *only a few present opportunities* to make a real difference to society or to confer a competitive advantage' (Porter and Kramer 2006: 13; our emphasis).

From a corporate perspective, this may sound like a good deal, and who doesn't want to address social opportunities and identify win-win solutions? However, the idea behind CSV specifically, and the business-case or 'powerful stakeholder' approach more generally raises a fundamental ethical question: what should a company do if a cause is ethically desirable but does not create a business case, or there are only weak stakeholders that cannot substantially threaten that company? (Imagine, for instance, a tribe in the rainforest in fear of a planned oil exploration project, and which have no powerful lobby group behind them to give them a voice.) What the idea of CSV cannot answer is what will happen if paying attention to the interests of stakeholders yields consequences that do not contribute to the profit-maximizing aspirations of the company's shareholders? CSV clearly shows that profits come first, and ethical issues only enter the game if they are consistent with concerns for profitability. In essence, the ethical tension here is thus that ethical behavior and accepting some form of social responsibility is limited to its value-creation potential, and not to either solving or avoiding important ethical concerns in the production process. 'Real' ethical tensions and some more systemic forms of injustice (such as the exploitation of workers in emerging markets, environmental destruction in areas without strong state intervention, or systematic tax avoidance) tend to be ignored.

Scholars have indeed criticized CSV as well as the broader instrumental approach to CSR. Crane and colleagues (2014), for example, accuse CSR of ignoring the tensions between social and economic objectives, and they suggest that assuming the easy creation of win-win situations is simply naïve within our current economic system. To the contrary, they draw on the research about the link between CSR and financial performance and its yet ambiguous and inconsistent findings to argue that we have '…no evidence that behaving more virtuously makes firms more profitable' (p. 136; citing Vogel 2005). While in fact *some* firms may find a business case or be subject to strong stakeholder pressure for *some* or even many of their CSR actions, 'the market for virtue is not sufficiently important to make it in the interest of *all* firms to behave more responsibly' (ibid; emphasis added). What this means is that while some market participants, including firms and consumers, might care about some CSR issue and *might* be willing and able to pay a price premium for it, the major share of the market simply does not. A simple walk to the local supermarket and the share of the growing but still fairly small fair-trade vs. conventional products underscores this argument. Reality shows indeed that ethical tensions are much more common than win-win situations, which often remain wishful thinking.

The normative deficiency of the instrumental approach to CSR is thus that, predominantly, the interests of those stakeholders are attuned to who have the most power, and these are typically shareholders that often overrule the interests of other stakeholders.

From an ethical point of view, the problem is that taking up some social or environmental responsibility is simply another 'success factor' of a business, without much intrinsic value to 'do good' because it might be the right thing to do, and with less attention to not-so-powerful stakeholders. This would also encourage the opportunistic behavior of businesses, because they can switch on or off their CSR engagement depending on the existence of a business case, not depending on the existence of an urgent ethical problem. CSV as a management concept, critics argue (e.g., Crane et al. 2014; Scherer and Palazzo 2007), falls short in providing guidance to companies about what they *should* do in situations where accepting some responsibility would *not* contribute to profitability to the satisfaction of a powerful stakeholder group.

To sum up, our research suggests that formal structures, such as a code of conduct, a CSR strategy, or policy documents for environmental or social aspects, alone affect little, even if paired with strong CEO endorsement. They are important building blocks to start the 'CSR journey', but need to be activated by a range of relational tactics. Employees and decision-makers in the company need to be carefully picked up and subtly nudged in order to bring CSR to life. As we better understand CSR through the lens of relational endeavor, managers may better relate to the complexity of enacting social change within large organizations. Obviously, CSR managers and all those interested in pushing sustainability in business firms need profound background knowledge of the contemporary understanding of the social and environmental responsibilities of the private sectors. In this chapter, we delve into these issues and provide a snapshot of key debates in CSR.

Learning and discussion questions

1. How far should corporate responsibility go? Is it better leave it at 'how the money is spent' or to expect a commitment to 'how the money is made'? Discuss the limits and prospects of the expanded understanding of CSR.
2. How should responsibility for sustainability be shared among societal actors (i.e., firms, governments, civil society, consumers, and other stakeholders)? Who is responsible for what?
3. How should the managerial tension in CSR be reconciled and how can firms balance the need for differentiation with the need for compliance?
4. What are the ethical implications of the business case for CSR? Should a company only be responsible if it pays? What if it does not pay?
   a) Discuss how to make more firms follow CSR because it is the 'right thing to do'.
   b) How can the ethical tension in CSR be reconciled?
5. Future challenges and how to address them:
   a) What should the role of private business firms be in tackling the SDGs?
   b) Digitalization and the 'ethics of AI': what are the new responsibilities that emerge in the era of digitalization?
   c) Societal attention to climate change is rising again, and corporations need to respond strategically - and sincerely - to the expectations of the young generation such as *Fridays for Future*, if they want to keep attracting the best talent: what is the best response?

Exercise: working with global sustainability standards

Research shows that most of the well-known and publicly traded multinationals nowadays employ a CSR or sustainability manager, and some of them have even created a standalone CSR department in charge of developing the CSR strategy (Risi and Wickert 2017). Oftentimes, however, these departments reside at the fringes of the organizations to which they belong, and CSR managers are confronted with some of the challenges highlighted above in this chapter in their endeavor to push CSR forward internally. Some CSR managers have developed a range of relational tactics that they apply to mobilize support for CSR topics and to get other managers on board; a CEO commitment is often only the first step, and more concrete actions need to follow in order to live up to the promise of transitioning a company towards greater sustainability (Wickert and de Bakker 2018). At the same time, CSR management frameworks, such as those offered by the UN Global Compact or ISO 26000, or reporting templates, such as the indicators of the Global Reporting Initiative (GRI), need to be diffuse through the company and be filled with life. CSR managers have a challenging task to not only create relationships with influential and likeminded others, but also to create adequate management systems, incentive schemes, and internal processes and procedures to make CSR happen in the unique context of the organization in which they work. It is then up to the skills and creativity of those CSR managers to come up with solutions - backed by external support systems - not only to develop but also to realize the CSR strategy, such that each and every employee buys-in and acts accordingly.

Case questions

1 Discuss what CSR managers should do to implement CSR substantively in their organizations such that it is reflected in management practices, processes, and procedures to enable other employees to live up to the promise of becoming a sustainable company?
2 What are the key challenges and obstacles that CSR managers might face internally and how can they overcome them?
3 Discuss the potential and pros and cons of more informal (e.g., convincing and creating the right mindset) vs. more formal (creating rules and compliance expectations) means of pushing CSR forward in an organization.

Recommended background reading

- Wickert, C. and Risi, D. (2019) *Corporate Social Responsibility* (Elements in Business Strategy). Cambridge: Cambridge University Press.
    - o https://www.cambridge.org/core/elements/corporate-social-responsibility/E2694D5DE28DE75AD8D3D48A92D06EE5#fndtn-information
- Wickert, C. and de Bakker, F. G. A. (2019) 'How CSR managers can inspire other leaders to act on sustainability'. *Harvard Business Review*, 10 January 2019.
    - o https://hbr.org/2019/01/how-csr-managers-can-inspire-other-leaders-to-act-on-sustainability

References

Bansal, P. and Song, H.-C. (2017) 'Similar but not the same: Differentiating corporate responsibility from sustainability'. *Academy of Management Annals*, 11: 105–149.

Barnett, M. L. (2007) 'Stakeholder influence capacity and the variability of financial returns to corporate social responsibility'. *Academy of Management Review*, 32: 794–816.

Barney, J. B. (1991) 'Firm resources and sustained competitive advantage'. *Journal of Management*, 17: 99–120.

Bitaraf, K. (2015) 'The evolution of CSR drivers'. Unpublished working paper. Amsterdam: Vrije Universiteit.

Blasko, J. L. and King, A. (2017) 'The road ahead: The KPMG Survey of Corporate Responsibility Reporting 2017'. Available online at https://assets.kpmg/content/dam/kpmg/xx/pdf/2017/10/kpmg-survey-of-corporate-responsibility-reporting-2017.pdf. (accessed 25 June 2020).

Brammer, S. and Millington, A. (2008) 'Does it pay to be different? An analysis of the relationship between corporate social and financial performance'. *Strategic Management Journal*, 29: 1325–1343.

Crane, A., Palazzo, G., Spence, L., and Matten, D. (2014) 'Contesting the value of "Creating Shared Value"'. *California Management Review*, 56: 130–153.

Devinney, T. M. (2009) 'Is the socially responsible corporation a myth? The good, the bad, and the ugly of corporate social responsibility'. *Academy of Management Perspectives*, 23: 44–56.

Eurosif (2018) 'European SRI study 2018'. Available online at http://www.eurosif.org/wp-content/uploads/2018/11/European-SRI-2018-Study-LR.pdf (accessed 25 June 2020).

Flammer, C. (2013) 'Corporate social responsibility and shareholder reaction: The environmental awareness of investors'. *Academy of Management Journal*, 56: 758–781.

Freeman, R. E. (1984) *Strategic Management: A Stakeholder Approach*. Boston: Pitman.

Freeman, R. E., Harrison, J. S., and Zyglidopoulos, S. (2018) *Stakeholder Theory: Concepts and Strategies*. Cambridge: Cambridge University Press.

ICAEW (2020) 'Sustainability: business as usual out of the question'. Available online at https://www.icaew.com/insights/features/2020/mar-2020/sustainability-business-as-usual-out-of-the-question (accessed 25 June 2020).

Jensen, M. C. (2002) 'Value maximization, stakeholder theory, and the corporate objective function'. *Business Ethics Quarterly*, 12: 235–256.

Kourula, A., Moon, J., Salles-Djelic, M. L., and Wickert, C. (2019) 'New roles of government in the governance of business conduct: Implications for management and organizational research'. *Organization Studies*, 40: 1101–1123.

McWilliams, A. and Siegel, D. (2001) 'Corporate social responsibility: A theory of the firm perspective'. *Academy of Management Review*, 26: 117–127.

Mitchell, R. K., Agle, B. R., and Wood, D. J. (1997) 'Toward a theory of stakeholder identification and salience: Defining the principle of who and what really counts'. *Academy of Management Review*, 22: 853–886.

Orlitzky, M., Schmidt, F. L., and Rynes, S. L. (2003) 'Corporate social and financial performance: A meta-analysis'. *Organization Studies*, 24: 403–441.

Porter, M. E. and Kramer, M. R. (2006) 'Strategy and society: The link between competitive advantage and corporate social responsibility'. *Harvard Business Review*, 84: 78–92.

Porter, M. E., and Kramer, M. R. (2011) 'The big idea: Creating shared value'. *Harvard Business Review*, 89: 62–67.

Risi, D. an Wickert, C. (2017) 'Reconsidering the 'symmetry' between institutionalization and professionalization: The case of corporate social responsibility managers'. *Journal of Management Studies*, 54(5): 613–646.

Sorkin, A. R. (2018) 'BlackRock's Message: Contribute to Society, or Risk Losing Our Support'. Available online at https://www.nytimes.com/2018/01/15/business/dealbook/blackrock-laurence-fink-letter.html (accessed 25 June 2020).

Statista (2020) 'Revenue of fair trade products worldwide since 2004'. Available online at https://www.statista.com/statistics/271354/revenue-of-fair-trade-products-worldwide-since-2004/ (accessed 25 June 2020).

Scherer, A. G., and Palazzo, G. (2007) 'Toward a political conception of corporate responsibility: Business and society seen from a Habermasian perspective'. *Academy of Management Review*, 32: 1096–1120.

Unilever (2020) 'UN Sustainable Development Goals'. Available online at https://www.unilever.com/sustainable-living/our-strategy/un-sustainable-development-goals/ (accessed 25 June 2020).

United Nations (2020) 'The 17 goals. United Nations'. Available online at https://sdgs.un.org/#goal_section (accessed 25 June 2020).

Vishwanathan, P., van Oosterhout, H. J., Heugens, P. P. M. A. R., Duran, P., and van Essen, M. (2020) 'Strategic CSR: a concept building meta-analysis'. *Journal of Management Studies*, 57: 314-350.

Vogel, D. J. (2005) 'Is there a market for virtue? The business case for corporate social responsibility'. *California Management Review*, 47: 19–45.

Wang, Q., Dou, J., and Jia, S. (2016) 'A meta-analytic review of corporate social responsibility and corporate financial performance: The moderating effect of contextual factors'. *Business & Society*, 55: 1083–1121.

Wickert, C. and Risi, D. (2019) *Corporate Social Responsibility* (Elements in Business Strategy). Cambridge: Cambridge University Press.

Wickert, C., Scherer, A. G., and Spence, L. J. (2016) 'Walking and talking corporate social responsibility: Implications of firm size and organizational cost'. *Journal of Management Studies*, 53: 1169–1196.

Wickert, C. and de Bakker, F. G. A. (2018) 'Pitching for social change: Towards a relational approach to selling and buying social issues'. *Academy of Management Discoveries*, 4: 1-24.

Wickert, C. and de Bakker, F. G. A. (2019) 'How CSR managers can inspire other leaders to act on sustainability'. *Harvard Business Review*, 10 January 2019.

Wilson, A. (2019) 'Dutch airline KLM calls for people to fly less'. Available online at https://www.theguardian.com/travel/2019/jul/11/dutch-airline-klm-calls-for-people-to-fly-less-carbon-offsetting-scheme (accessed 25 June 2020).

PART 4

Responsibility and globalization

8 Navigating leadership teams

Martijn van der Kamp

Summary

This chapter explores issues related to what makes leadership teams (for example, boards and top-management teams (TMTs)) effective, by considering how team composition and team processes affect performance in a global context. The tension under investigation pertains to similarity and diversity, which has implications for the dynamics and performance of boards and TMTs. As upper echelons increasingly need to strategize for the global stage rather than solely for their domestic arena, new factors arise that affect the strategic decision-making process (such as multiple headquarters, multi-cultural TMTs, and conflicting strategic demands). This chapter combines concerns of leadership teams with new forms of organizing in global organizations. To advance understanding about how to reconcile the diversity-similarity tension in leadership teams, the chapter delves into group faultlines, managing team boundaries, and transactive memory systems.

Case: TankTerminal international joint venture leadership team

TankTerminal Limited is a storage and handling facility for petroleum products and crude oil located in the United Arab Emirates. With a capacity of over 1.5 million cubic meters, the facility is the largest in the area. UAE Terminals, TankNet, the regional government, and the Petrol Group established TankTerminal as joint venture partners in 1998. The joint venture meant an enlargement of the production capacity of the United Arab Emirates partners and an international expansion opportunity for the European partner, TankNet.

The TankTerminal joint venture is managed by a board at the highest strategic level, an executive coordination committee consisting of senior managers, and management teams at the operational level. Here we focus on the executive coordination committee, which is responsible for the day-to-day management of the terminal. This leadership team consists of delegates from UAE Terminals and TankNet, the two largest shareholders. On a daily basis, the major tasks of the team are the decision-making about the management and strategic development of the facility, and preparing decision documentation for the board.

The coordination committee came together for the first time in early 2009. Two members had been with their parent company for years, and the other three were relatively new (< 1 year) to their parent company and the joint venture. The team is quite homogenous in terms of gender, age, and race – all team members are males, in their forties, who have an economic or finance background. From the beginning, this team worked together quite effectively because of their strong shared understanding of the overall team goals and focused work manner. As one TankNet representative stated: 'They are very tough in their stands and in their negotiating position. But they would consider [...] what is the best for the joint venture?, and place the needs of the joint venture above the single shareholders' needs. To me, it doesn't really matter *how* we reach our goals, as long as we reach our goals!'

During the first year, this team spent a lot of effort and time on getting to know each other, on intensive communication, and on building transparency and trust. In contrast to Western cultures, Middle Eastern culture strongly prefers relationship-building over getting straight into business. Managers regularly switched offices between Dubai and Europe to become acquainted with each other's organizations. The team also got together over several activities organized to mark the 10th anniversary of the joint venture. As a result, members indicated that they experienced a positive team climate in which all managers got along very well and in which they easily adapted to one another.

After approximately a year, all team members were facing the same direction and had built a robust relational base on which to work together. The speed and quality of decision-making improved because of the intense focus on the objective of coordinating the parent company's mutual interest and the shared joint venture's goals. There was an exceptionally strong willingness among the team members to make things work in the joint venture. Their strong sense of purpose resulted in precise goal-setting and ongoing effective collaboration between the delegates. Transparency about every aspect of the business appeared to be crucial to the cooperation at this stage, and any disagreements were solved quickly. All team members agreed about the lack of conflicts between the partners in this team. As one TankNet representative stated: 'So we may come from different poles, but [...] the success factor of this team is the willingness of the partners to make something work. This brings us closer to each other and conflicts between us would only restrain the performance of our team.'

The team members were selected for their leadership skills and ability to work as an autonomous workgroup. They realized they could only succeed in their common goal if they were one team. After setting themselves a clear task in the first year, they focused on the social aspect of teamwork to become one team. The social events and office switches were meant to keep stimulating communication and transparency in order to build trust in the team and for team members to become acquainted with each other's organizations. Possible interpersonal biases and prejudices based on demographic differences were dealt with through intensive communication and openness towards one another, which prevented subgroup formation and conflict. As the team leader stated:

'I think that the first thing you have to do, is to create a good working environment, so that people understand each other, that they get along, know their differences and adapt to that, and manage those differences. Once you have a clear mind, and all prejudices are gone, you can take a more professional stand on things'.

This case portrays a senior leadership team that is responsible for the management of an international joint venture. What is exceptional about this case is that this leadership team worked together collaboratively and successfully, despite the fact that researchers estimate that roughly half of all joint ventures are destined to fail. Senior leadership teams are responsible for leading entire organizations - with budgets of millions of dollars and hundreds of staff - while managing dozens of stakeholders in a world characterized by environmental, economic, and social challenges, as well as increasing public scrutiny. All this amounts to high stakes and a lot of pressure on leadership teams. The odds of success for this particular team further decline because it works across organizational boundaries with national cultural differences, often in different locations, but especially because all these challenges lie between the representatives from UAE Terminals and those representing TankNet.

Questions:

1 How would you describe the relationships between the members of the coordination committee?
2 What mechanisms did the coordination committee employ to work effectively?

** Company names in this case are anonymized*

Learning objectives

The learning objectives of this chapter are to:

1 Provide insights into how leadership teams differ from other management teams
2 Identify the main challenges that diversity introduces to leadership teams
3 Discuss the diversity-similarity in leadership teams and how it affects their effectiveness
4 Offer insights into how leaders can navigate diversity in leadership teams.

Introduction to leadership teams

Leadership teams are often seen as the people listed in an organization's annual reports as being on the board of directors and TMT (also known as the executive team, or the C-suite). Unsurprisingly, in the popular press extant attention has been devoted to leadership teams. We read about 'rock-star' CEOs and their teams in the news, and many students have serious ambitions of being part of one of these teams someday, often sooner rather than later. In addition to financial and other organizational outcomes, leadership teams are responsible for providing leadership and holding up ethics, values, and culture. Yet the news is also full of stories of abuse of power, faulty executive team decisions, and multi-million-dollar ventures failing. Sometimes it seems that not enough is done to understand and learn about leadership teams before giving them the 'highest office' in business. The leadership teams mentioned under these headlines seem to have forgotten about leadership, ethics, values, and the 'high-office' they occupy, or are unable to live up to its demands.

The exact roles and governance structures of boards and TMTs can differ by country and by organization. The TMT is a small group of influential directors and executives that is not always clearly defined in terms of a team or committee but can simply represent the collective at the top of an organization (Finkelstein et al. 2009). Team members often represent different fields of expertise as reflected in C-level functions, such as chief financial officer, chief operational officer, chief human resources officer, etc. This group of people manages the day-to-day running of an organization at the strategic level, which involves tasks such as strategy setting and implementation, stakeholder management, and strategic decision-making.

Boards of directors differ from TMTs in that they are not directly responsible for the day-to-day operations of an organization, but rather review major strategic decisions. The sphere of influence of these teams pertains to executive hiring and compensation, review decisions on mergers and acquisitions, investments, R&D spending, and overseeing business conduct in general (Finkelstein et al. 2009). Boards of directors consist of executive and non-executive directors who bring in a variety of expertise and combine internal and external views on the organization. As such, boards form an essential link between organizations and their external environment. The influence and role of boards vary from highly engaged, active, and influential to operating more at a distance and being more inactive. Overall, there appears to be a trend of boards becoming the highest-level governance mechanism with increasing responsibility for the economic, cultural, and ethical conduct of an organization.

Through their decision-making, leadership teams strongly influence the systems, structures, and processes that together determine an organization's outcomes and its development (Hambrick 2007; Hambrick and Mason 1984). Given that no single person has the knowledge, expertise, time, or capacity to make all these decisions alone, executive teams combine the cognitive ability of multiple people to address a multitude of challenges and decisions. Each of these senior leaders, in turn, relies on their expertise, values, beliefs, skill-set, and interpretations. Therefore, each senior leadership team is unique in terms of the abilities it brings together. With decision-making being the bread and butter of senior leadership teams, their primary challenge is to achieve the cognitive and behavioral integration required to turn the team's unique abilities into decisions.

Tension: the double-edged sword of diversity

Diversity poses a particular tension for leadership teams. Diversity can be defined as 'any difference between individuals that may lead to the perception that another person is different from yourself' (Van Knippenberg and Schippers 2007). Initially, this often comes down to (readily visible) individual characteristics such as gender, age, ethnicity, nationality, physical ability, and organizational representation (for example, in joint venture teams). Later, as the team works together, it refers to less visible characteristics, such as expertise, functional roles, marital status, political beliefs, and religion. These characteristics are proxies for the underlying values, beliefs, and attitudes that senior leaders bring to the team, and on which they rely for interpreting situations and making decisions (Hambrick 2007; Hambrick and Mason 1984). These characteristics also trigger a variety of social processes and biases that affect teams, for better or worse. The key question is: how does diversity (or its opposite, similarity) affect team processes and outcomes, and particularly decision-making?

Social categorization theory helps to explain the diversity–similarity tension in teams. This theory describes how groups of people build relationships, create a sense of belonging, and behave towards each other in the workplace. Social categories are the groups that we are part of; they can vary from a team or a department to an organization or even a country. Social categorization processes help us to make sense of the web of social relationships around us. Relationships with others matter to us because they provide us with meaning, reduce uncertainty, and affect our sense of self-esteem, safety, and belonging (Tajfel and Turner 1986). Which social categories matter most to us depend on the context and varies over time (Leavitt and Sluss 2015). Social categorization processes shed light on the tension that exists between low and high levels of diversity through the similarity–attraction paradigm and information–decision-making perspective.

On one hand, birds of a feather flock together; in other words, we generally like to work with others who are similar to us (van Knippenberg, De Dreu, and Homan 2004). Diversity characteristics such as age, gender, and cultural background mostly immediately stand out and form part of our first impressions. Other diversity characteristics, such as expertise, values, beliefs, and attitudes, are not as prominent and only become apparent over time, as we engage more with others. For example, working with others who have a similar background in terms of culture, education, or expertise is often more comfortable than working with others who are different. We can more easily understand what similar others need and what they are talking about (especially when using jargon). Because it is easier to understand what they mean, it is also easier to agree with them and to collaborate. This similarity comes in handy in situations where speed and efficiency are of the essence. For example, consider how firefighters with similar training and backgrounds can work together more readily under the pressure of emergencies.

However, teams with high levels of similarity are also more prone to suffer from groupthink and intergroup biases. To fit in better with the group, people tend to agree with others rather than disagree, and to voice ideas that closely align with those of others. Low team diversity facilitates this tendency because it is usually easy to agree with someone who has similar views on the world and approaches to the task at hand. As a result, these homogenous teams develop less distinct viewpoints and solutions and short-cut decision-making processes. In time-poor situations or with relatively straightforward tasks, it is not necessarily much of an issue and could even work as an advantage. However, when facing a complex task, such as developing a driverless car, which has many possible solutions that benefit from diverse viewpoints and robust debate, similarity can be a disadvantage. Because it is easier to work with others who are similar, homogenous groups more easily develop a strong group identity, but also stereotypes about those who are dissimilar to them, which stand in the way of collaborating with other groups.

On the other hand, diversity brings a variety of perspectives to the team that can flow into decision-making, but can also generate conflict and misunderstanding. Diverse teams bring together individuals who are different in terms of, for example, age, gender, cultures, and expertise. Specifically, because of their varied knowledge, experience, and expertise, they have more viewpoints and ideas related to any particular problem. Therefore, they have the potential to solve more complex issues and to be more creative and innovative than more homogenous teams (Homan et al. 2008; Van Knippenberg and Schippers 2007). However, these outcomes depend heavily on the team's ability to share knowledge, to understand and combine different viewpoints, to argue constructively, and to make decisions that might not reflect any one individual's view. It also means that team members have to be comfortable with being (slightly) uncomfortable when it comes to understanding and dealing with others. It generally takes time to build these skills and to understand the diversity present in the team, and to benefit from it. A substantial investment in time, resources, and effort is required to make diverse teams work effectively. As such, diverse teams can be highly effective but are often less efficient than their more homogenous counterparts.

When we apply these social mechanisms to leadership teams, we see that they are often relatively homogenous. They are more likely to consist of men who have similar backgrounds and long experience within a particular organization or industry, which leads them to approach tasks and situations similarly. For high-pressure, time-bound, or relatively straightforward situations, similarity has its advantages. Leadership teams often face long-term, complex situations, and could therefore benefit from similarity between members. Similarity stimulates the selection and hiring of similar others, allowing for expedient and coherent decision-making. It restricts however the access of diverse others to leadership teams, potentially invoking blind-spots and one-sided decisions (see Box 8.1). Restated, diversity in leadership teams could positively influence decision-making, as members of diverse teams put forward different views, tend to arrive at out-of-the-box solutions, and are likely to receive support as their composition represent the organizations' population. As such, there is tension within leadership teams between similarity and diversity. Next, we will discuss how this tension plays out in a variety of ways.

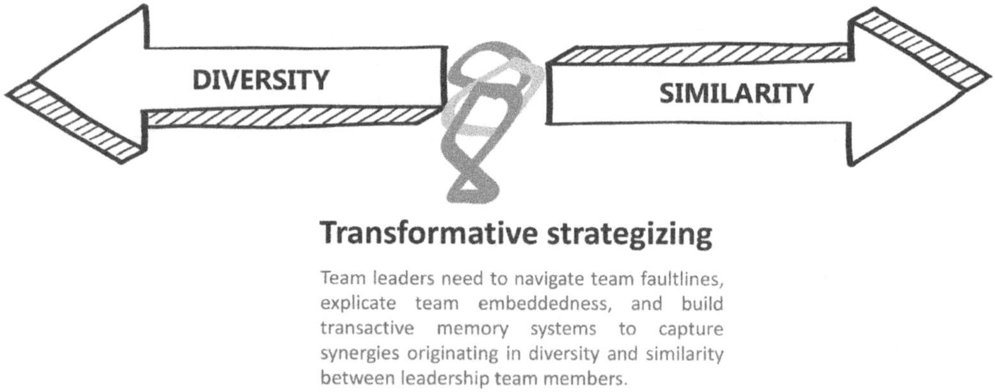

Figure 8.1 Diversity-similarity tension

Box 8.1 On board with gender diversity

In Australia, only 3.5 percent of ASX200 companies had female CEOs in 2013. This figure, which had barely moved in a decade, was one of the lowest rates in the Western world. By 2019, however, this number had increased to about 30 percent, although it remains lower for smaller organizations and for the management levels under the board. While this is an improvement for Australia, women are still underrepresented globally in boards and executive teams. In many countries there are more women enrolled in universities than men; in Australia, 58 percent of domestic students were female in 2016 (Larkins 2018). So why is it so hard to change the gender makeup of (senior) leadership teams?

Structural (unconscious) biases against women continue to restrict the progress of women into the ranks of senior leadership. Biases affect how we evaluate women's CVs differently than men's (even if they are exactly the same), the opportunity we give to women, and how we evaluate women differently compared to men in terms of their performance. When asked to draw a leader, most of us (both men and women) will instinctively draw a man. On top of that, many of us are biased in that we prefer to work with people that are similar to us. This means that senior leadership teams that are mostly comprised of men are likely to hire more men. As a result, the culture and processes of senior leadership teams are often male-oriented, making it hard for women to establish themselves in these teams, especially when they are the only female on the team. Research shows that women are talked over more often than men in organizations; as a result, female voices are less heard and therefore less influential then male voices.

Besides the fact that women deserve to be in leadership roles as much as men, that there is no shortage of women available to fill these roles, and that providing equal opportunity is a virtue, there is also a business case for increasing the number of women on senior leadership teams. The basic premise here is that women bring more and different viewpoints to senior leadership teams and, with that, increase the ability of the team to anticipate and deal with a broader variety of challenges and to generate a broader range of solutions. The link between female participation in senior leadership teams and organizational profit has been investigated many times and found to be practically non-existent. However, researchers seems to agree that this is because team processes link board composition to profits, so it is more worthwhile investigating the contributions women make to team processes (Choudhury 2015).

Research by Dezsö and Ross (2012) indicates that female participation on boards increases entrepreneurial outcomes for their organizations. While the board itself becomes more entrepreneurial, the female leadership style, which is arguably higher in inclusion, collaboration, and sharing knowledge than the male style (see Book 2000; Dufwenberg and Muren 2006) stimulates the entrepreneurial activity further down the organizational hierarchy. Other studies show organizational benefits from female participation in senior leadership teams in terms of stimulating the amount of effort each team member is expected to put in, generating and dealing with cognitive conflict about board tasks, and improved decision-making through the increase in viewpoints and opinions (Choudhury 2015).

Tackling the challenges of diversity in leadership teams

Diversity in leadership teams affects all aspects of team functioning and outcomes. Teams are social systems with a function to turn resources, information, and knowledge into team products and outcomes via a series of processes, all which is influenced by the context in which the team operates (Ilgen et al. 2005; Jehn and Bezrukova 2004). Team inputs, such as team size, functional diversity, level of interdependence between members, and geographical dispersion will all affect how team processes and outcomes will unfold. Important team processes for senior leadership teams evolve around decision-making, conflict management, and behavioral integration. The context in which leadership teams operate is often characterized by strong time-pressures, scrutiny by stakeholders, and rapid changes in the economic, social, and environmental climate. Below we will unpack some of these challenges, explore how they relate to team diversity, and make recommendations on how to manage accordingly (see Table 8.1 for an overview).

Managing leadership team faultlines

The diversity and composition of senior leadership teams affects how prominent team processes, such as team conflict and behavioral integration, will evolve. We have seen that team composition can, to some degree, be planned for before a team comes together. Team processes only come around after the team has been established and the team starts working together. How a leadership team addresses problems, communicates, builds trust, and collaborates will affect which outcomes it is able to realize. Team processes are the crucial link between team diversity and team outcomes. Research on leadership teams noted that team

Table 8.1 Leadership teams: faultlines, embeddedness, and transactive memory system

	Description	*Actions*	*Reconciliation diversity-similarity*
Leadership team faultlines	Strong team faultlines divide teams into factions; weak team faultlines depict homogenous or heterogeneous teams	Identify faultlines, assess their consequences, and use activators and deactivators to mitigate/reinforce team processes	The leadership team should become a reflexive dialogue-driven entity that embraces diversity while exploiting similarities
Leadership team embeddedness	Relative stable decision-making unit intertwined with a dynamic group of stakeholders and direct reports	Explicate multi-team system, define goal hierarchy, establish inter-team linkages, and promote shared understanding across system	The leadership team (often non-diverse) should interact with wide-range of diverse teams, challenging the team to embrace diverse views
Transactive memory system (TMS)	A TMS enables leadership teams to enhance their readiness to deal with contextual opportunities and threats	Ensure that team members share knowledge and information, guided by members' interdependencies and needs	The leadership team should build a shared memory and understanding, enabling it to capture similarity and diversity benefits

faultlines affect key team processes, such as team conflict and behavioral integration, which in turn affect team decision-making. The following section discusses group faultlines and their management.

A group faultline is a hypothetical division between team members, based on the alignment of diversity attributes such as age, gender, expertise, etc. (Lau and Murnighan 1998). Faultline strength is the extent to which two or more diversity attributes align between potential subgroups. For example, a team consists of two male German engineers, and two female Arabic finance managers. It has a strong faultline on gender, nationality, and functional background. Weak faultlines exist when the team is homogenous, meaning it has little diversity. Faultlines are also weak when a team is highly heterogeneous, meaning that all team members are different from each other. In both cases there is little alignment of diversity attributes between potential subgroups.

Considerable evidence suggests that team faultlines strongly influence leadership team processes and outcomes. People prefer to bond with others who are similar to them and are likely to form biases against different others; therefore, not surprisingly, leadership teams with strong faultlines are more likely to break into conflicting subgroups (Barkema and Shvyrkov 2007; Li and Hambrick 2005) than those with weak faultlines. Other research suggests that group faultlines affect product diversification (Hutzschenreuter and Horstkotte 2013), firm financial performance (Cooper, Patel, and Thatcher 2014; Kaczmarek, Kimino, and Pye 2012; Ndofor, Sirmon, and He 2015), productivity and profitability (Van Knippenberg et al. 2011), and can even lead to higher abnormal CEO compensation (Van Peteghem, Bruynseels, and Gaeremynck 2018).

Team faultlines will affect team outcomes even more when they are activated (Jehn and Bezrukova 2010). Faultlines are activated when they are made salient due to external triggers. In an international collaboration, for example, different cultural practices would emphasize the difference between potential subgroups. Particularly relevant for senior leadership teams are factional faultlines; these are faultlines between representatives of different groups or organizations such as in joint venture boards, Mergers and acquisitions (M&A) teams, or even representatives of internal groups (Crucke, Moray, and Vallet 2015). These groups are considered as 'pre-activated' because team members rely on the organizations they represent for their livelihoods and are tasked with 'defending' the stakes of their organization, which adds an element of competition (Li and Hambrick 2005).

In some cases, however, faultlines can have positive outcomes. In particular, information-based faultlines - those based on diversity in experience, education, and expertise - can contribute to product expansion (Hutzschenreuter and Horstkotte 2013), but these effects depend on the organizational context (Cooper et al. 2014), goal setting (Van Knippenberg et al. 2011), and CEO characteristics (Georgakakis, Greve, and Ruigrok 2017). For example, information-based faultlines only contributed to firm performance in industries with low environmental dynamism, high complexity, and high munificence (Cooper et al. 2014). Because group faultlines have mostly detrimental effects on leadership, teams must manage group faultlines and their effects carefully to make them work to their advantage.

When managing team faultlines, we must consider how we can minimize the salience of activated faultlines; or, in other words, how we can deactivate faultlines (Van der Kamp, Tjemkes, and Jehn 2013; 2015). By shifting the attention away from activated faultlines,

faultlines become less salient as a basis for subgroup formation. Research suggests that shifting the attention away from faultlines can be done by making other social categories salient. For example, shifting the attention from subgroups (such as executive vs. non-executive directors) towards an overarching team identity (such as we are all board members) by focusing on overarching team and organizational objectives (Crucke and Knockaert 2016; Van Knippenberg et al. 2011) can help to mitigate the negative effects of faultlines in senior leadership teams. Executive pay contingencies (Kaczmarek et al. 2012), CEO characteristics (Georgakakis et al. 2017), and meeting informality (Tuggle, Schnatterly, and Johnson 2010) have all been shown to stimulate cohesiveness and collaboration in senior leadership teams with strong faultlines.

Taken together, team faultline research tells us that the selection of leadership team members on boards or TMTs has an impact on which faultlines may form in the team and, therefore, which challenges are more likely to arise then others. Teams can then prepare accordingly. In some teams, faultlines are unavoidable. Team members might then consider which 'activators' are most likely to trigger the activation of faultlines based on the diversity characteristics of the faultline and the context in which the team operates. Having an overview of potential challenges, and the triggers activating these challenges, helps teams to devise approaches than can reduce or take away the triggers or can help to deal with the challenges. Going through such an exercise could itself be a deactivating experience for a team that has just formed and is becoming aware of its faultlines. Building on team composition and faultlines, the next challenge for leadership teams is to manage the effects of external pressures and circumstances on the team.

Managing leadership team embeddedness

The traditional composition of senior leadership teams as consisting of the most senior people, with educational backgrounds relevant to the organization and long-term experience within an industry, is now shifting. The boundaries of leadership teams are blurring, with people working across multiple teams and participating in the team only around a specific topic, time, or project. In addition, with the increasing number of mergers and acquisition, joint ventures, and other types of strategic alliances, leadership teams are often composed of people who represent their 'partner organization' and look after the interests of the alliance as well as the partner. These changes in the composition of leadership teams introduces challenges regarding the management of boundaries between senior leadership teams and other teams.

Leadership teams are remarkably hard to define, both for academics and the senior leaders in those teams. Especially in larger organizations, the directors of business units, country branches, or advising managers close to these teams could be considered part of the senior leadership team. Following on from this, it may not come as a surprise that only seven percent of senior leadership teams are in full agreeance about who is on the team, when asked individually (Wageman et al. 2008).

While teams are often perceived as people who work interdependently towards one or more shared goals (Kozlowski and Bell 2003), it might be more productive to think about leadership teams as having a stable core and dynamic periphery (Roberto 2003). The core is a relatively stable decision-making unit that is advised by a dynamic group of people who introduce external knowledge (such as stakeholder views or industry dynamics), or expertise (such as knowledge from different departments or subject matter expertise such as legal advice). This does raise a number of questions: who is in or out of this circle? How do executives manage and maintain relationships with this dynamic periphery such that they are involved close enough without being on the exact same team?

Research around multi-team systems offers useful insights to address these questions. A multi-team system (MTS) is a network of interdependent teams that work together collaboratively towards common goals (Mathieu, Marks, and Zaccaro 2001). For example, leadership team members are also part of teams within their particular business, business unit, or task responsibility, and interface with middle management (Raes et al. 2007). Teams in this network not only pursue organizational objectives, but also pursue team objectives that are often at odds with each other. For example, setting up a new business unit will take away resources from other business units. While this might make sense on the organizational level, it can create tensions between business units.

Luciano, Nahrgang, and Shropshire (in press) reconceptualized the interface between the top management team and the board as a leadership multi-team system. The independence of these teams is traditionally considered a main strength of this system. Both teams have different functions for the organization - one is more internally focused, the other more externally focus - and their tasks can be at odds in terms of matters such as executive remuneration. However, in 'unprecedented' times, boards and top management teams may benefit from more interdependence. Monitoring the environment is a crucial task that is better executed with both the board and TMT on top of it. The integration of multiple perspectives across both teams increases the benefit of diversity in terms of coordinating understanding, search for information, and responding to change (see also 'transactive memory systems' below).

To realize the benefits of this leadership system, clear boundaries need to be established and managed. Whether it is the dependence-interdependence tension between board and TMT, or working with other teams inside or outside the organization, clear team boundaries stimulate both within and between group performance (De Vries et al. 2016). The CEO is traditionally seen as a key boundary spanner between board and TMT, but having multiple TMT members in boundary-spanning roles can help manage interdependencies with the board on different matters, with committees and other teams within the organization. Because senior leadership team composition changes through natural turnover and hiring, managing team boundaries and coordination across teams helps to prevent confusion with newcomers (Desai 2016).

Taken together, in order to benefit from diversity within leadership teams and the teams that they work with, it is essential to first clearly define who is on these teams, and to create a shared understanding of team membership across the team(s). This understanding can then be applied to develop within- and between-team collaboration and coordination and to making optimal use of diversity across teams. Role clarity, particularly relating to boundary spanning, helps team members to identify with their team and work effectively with others in and outside of their team. The overall diversity and coordination of the leadership system have significant input in considering new hires on the team, and with helping people that work in more than one team.

Managing leadership team context

Natural disasters, global pandemics, terrorist attacks, cyber threats, increasing media scrutiny, and broad ethical responsibility are just some of the external pressures facing senior leadership teams. As we have seen, diversity in teams can be both a threat and an opportunity, but under high time-pressure and in strong situations as the ones mentioned, it becomes difficult to bring out the best in people, let alone invest the time and energy necessary to make diversity work in a team. It is particularly important during these times and under these circumstances to be on the same page and to move quickly. This section explains how having a sense of what knowledge is available in the team and how that knowledge is deployed helps people to perform under pressure, as well as what teams can do to manage the influence of strong contexts and utilize their inherent diversity.

Group context can be defined as the situational opportunities and constraints that affect the occurrence and meaning of team member behavior (Johns 2006). Therefore, strong contexts are those that provide far-ranging opportunities and constraints, but also that sincerely affect the perception of team members and their behaviors. For example, consider how a strong context such as the Abu Ghraib prison in Iraq allowed a culture of torture and abuse to arise. A more relatable example might be how working on an advertising campaign for men's razorblades (a gender-specific task) could lead to conflict between subgroups of men and women as they differ in their experience of what razorblades mean to them and how they are used (Pearsall, Ellis, and Evans 2008). Because the team context affects team members' perception and behavior, it can activate group faultlines (Chrobot-Mason et al. 2009), make it harder to stay on the same page (Cannon-Bowers, Salas, and Converse 1993; Mathieu et al. 2000), and result in an inability to bring the right information to the table at the right time (Nadkarni and Barr 2008). Rather than trying to prepare for everything, research suggests that a team should not organize itself in one particular way, but rather develop an awareness of the system it is in (Williams 2011). This includes an awareness of the resources it has available and the skills it has to draw upon these resources when required. This is where a team's transactive memory system (TMS) comes in.

A TMS is the shared division of cognitive labor with respect to the encoding, storage, retrieval, and communication of information from different domains that often develops in close relationships (Hollingshead 2001; Lewis and Herndon 2011). A TMS builds on the notion that not everyone on the team needs to have the same knowledge in order to solve a problem. Instead, a TMS helps to use the diversity in a team and increases interdependence between team members. Any particular situation or problem is easier to solve with systems and structures in place that facilitate strong relationships and teamwork in storing, retrieving, and communicating relevant knowledge. The TMS includes having a shared understanding about what knowledge is present or lacking in the team (who knows what), and builds on both shared and unique knowledge to solve complex issues (Lewis and Herndon 2011). Having knowledge is not the same as having the ability to apply that knowledge effectively, hence, a TMS also includes processes relating to learning and knowledge retrieval.

TMSs sustain leadership teams in a variety of ways. Particularly volatile environments both demand and facilitate the development of a TMS in senior leadership teams (Bachrach et al. 2019). These environments call for knowledge coordination and integration, and for tasks to be divided among knowledgeable team members. Volatile environments also require teams to gather knowledge and develop expertise. Particularly in context where senior leadership teams are globally distributed, or work virtually, TMSs have been shown to increase information-sharing and decision quality (McLeod 2013). Crisis management also greatly benefits from having a strong TMS that develops before the crisis emerges (Waller, Zhike, and Pratten 2014). TMSs can further support leadership teams in integrating outsider perspectives, especially in highly dynamic contexts (Heavey and Simsek 2015) and in dealing with organizational ambidexterity (Heavey and Simsek 2017).

To develop an effective TMS, leadership teams should primarily consider whether they have the right people on the team. Is the variety of expertise and access to networks and resources on the team sufficient to deal with tasks ranging from ethical issues, to dealing with shareholders, all the way to crisis response? Leaders who have worked across domains will be more likely to build a wider TMS as opposed to functional specialists (Heavey and Simsek 2017). To increase the accuracy and sharedness of the TMS, it is necessary to eliminate differences between perceptions of others' expertise and their actual expertise (Bachrach et al. 2019). This can be done through learning about the information-exchange patterns in the team and the related technological platforms used for information exchange (Adibhatla et al. 2009). Mapping a team's knowledge base and identifying gaps in it can direct team learning and further team-member specialization (Hollingshead 1998). Working across locations, or virtually, slows the development of TMS; therefore, teams should be well-socialized through face-to-face meetings and spending time together (Heavey and Simsek 2017). Given that leadership teams regularly face team-member turnover, it is worth considering how that affects the TMS and how new leaders can be included in the established TMS (Lewis et al. 2007).

Taken together, team context creates boundaries, constraints, and opportunities that facilitate or block the functioning and processes of the group and its members (Crawford and LePine 2013; Joshi and Roh 2009). Because contexts are volatile and often unpredictable, a stream of group studies posits that there is no 'one best way' to organize a group (Hollenbeck et al. 2002; Johns 2006). TMSs can help leadership teams to develop a state of readiness that allows them to engage with many different situations, as they have an awareness of who knows what, not only in the team but also in the team's extended networks. With systems that allow the retrieval, distribution, and recombination of that knowledge in place, senior leadership teams become bigger and more resilient than the sum of their individuals.

Reflection

We are slowly witnessing a shift in terms of senior leadership teams being 'old boys networks' of gray-haired men approaching the end of their careers. Senior leadership teams are becoming as diverse as any other team. With new people flowing into the contemporary boardroom, a need arises to flush out some of the old ways of working and collaborating. New voices bring different questions, different answers, and often have different needs from those already established. Managing a senior leadership team is already hard enough as it is; who has time to pay attention to these new requirements and changing dynamics? – 'Let's get on with the work already!' Changes in team composition and team process often detract from tasks that require immediate responses. To facilitate this change and to help grow the attention for teamwork in leadership teams and improve their functioning, this chapter has detailed how leadership teams can manage faultlines and embeddedness and use a transactive memory system to reconcile the diversity-similarity tension.

Leadership teams need to navigate team composition, team embeddeness in the organization, and team context to reconcile the diversity-similarity tension.

Leadership teams are facing challenges at a more rapid pace than ever before, and are more visible than their predecessors. They also have more diverse talent available to draw on in addressing these challenges. We are witnessing a shift in leadership teams as they become more diverse. However, this shift also results in tensions relating to this diversity. It is easier and often more efficient to work with others who are relatively similar to us. Diversity brings broader perspectives on many fronts, from expertise and work experience, to culture and connections. This give these teams advantages in dealing with more complex issues, although ongoing effort is required to capture the value in diversity. Therefore, managing this double-edged sword matters to the processes and outcomes of senior leadership teams and, through their influence, also to broader organizational outcomes.

Diversity is like a complex algorithm that requires an active and broad approach. Diversity characteristics such as gender, age, expertise, and nationality are proxies for underlying values, beliefs, attitudes, and knowledge. These values, beliefs, and attitudes are so deeply rooted that we are often not consciously aware how they translate into our day-to-day behaviors and social interactions, as well as those of others. Our social interactions are strongly influenced by the implicit biases we hold about different others, as reflected in team selection, subgroup formation, how we communicate to different others, and the extent to which we trust them. These implicit assumptions are so strong that the mere intention of being inclusive is not enough, which necessitates a more structural approach to the topic.

Building on the notion that teams are social systems in which different aspects of their functioning are highly intertwined (Ilgen et al. 2005; Jehn and Bezrukova 2004), this chapter has outlined a range of strategies to manage diversity and intergroup-biases in leadership teams. Combined, the strategies act as a more comprehensive toolkit to address different aspects of team functioning and make the whole more inclusive. Part of the tension is that the management of diversity takes time and effort, and therefore comes at a premium. Leadership teams need to weigh which and how many of these strategies to implement. Close consideration of the team composition, current processes, and team context can help to determine which strategy to prioritize over others.

The general logic of managing team diversity evolves around bringing diverse minds together and keeping them on the same page. Because of the time and effort required to make diversity work, the first question senior leaders often ask themselves is, 'do we need a diverse team to get the task done?' In the case of senior leadership teams, the answer is almost always a resounding 'yes' (Wageman et al. 2008). If the team does not already exist, their next question is would be, 'who should be on the team?' Again, the team task will be a main driver, although prior experience with diversity and with other team members might drive the selection. Once the team is formed, there is an opportunity to set the team boundaries and to form a TMS. Next, its team members need to realize that people and circumstances continually change, so their team boundaries and transactive memory system need to change continually in order to stay on the same page. Therefore, diversity is an ongoing conversation. Regular board reviews can help to ensure the quality of these conversations and their timeliness.

The central tenet of 'upper echelon theory' is that senior leadership teams strongly influence the rest of the organization they work in, as they set the systems and processes (Hambrick and Mason 1984; Hambrick 2007). When it comes to the management of diversity, senior leadership teams have two crucial roles in creating organizations and organizational cultures that are truly inclusive. Primarily, their teams are a role model to the rest of the organization. If senior leadership teams expect their organizations to be inclusive and equitable, they must show their organizations how that is done, recognizing that the effort it takes to set up and manage diverse teams, and also to maintain them, is considerable and an ongoing effort. Through leading by example, leadership teams can make managing diversity more simple, practical, and accessible to the rest of the organization. In addition, leadership teams can help to reduce the structural biases present in every organization. Systems, structures, and processes, which guide team selection, formation, and teamwork, as well as other aspects of organizations, can help to open up pathways for others who are often left out.

While there have been decades of research on diversity, research on how to effectively manage the tensions of diversity in leadership teams is in its early days. This chapter has presented a series of interventions that are specific to senior leadership teams and relate to different aspects of teamwork. Furthermore, we have attempted to do this in a pragmatic manner. With that, it supports a more holistic approach to managing diversity that will hopefully inspire senior leaders, students of leadership, and researchers to tackle the challenges that diversity brings to teamwork. Perhaps even more so, we hope the approaches outlined here can contribute to more productive and effective senior leadership teams, characterized by a general sense of inclusion and belonging, and that serve as an example to teams within their organizations and beyond.

Learning and discussion questions

1. How does diversity provide a tension for leadership teams? And how does it affect team processes and outcome? Should leadership teams always aim to be diverse?
2. How can the perspective of multi-team systems help leadership teams to manage diversity?
3. What are group faultlines and why do they matter to leadership teams? Which steps would you take to manage the challenges related to faultlines?
4. What is a transactive memory system and how can it help to manage the tension of diversity? How would you go about setting up a transactive memory system?
5. How do unconscious biases prevent the participation of women (or other groups) on boards?

Exercise: ING management banking board

The ING Group is a Dutch multinational banking and financial services corporation headquartered in Amsterdam. Its primary businesses are retail banking, direct banking, commercial banking, investment banking, wholesale banking, private banking, asset management, and insurance services. It is regularly ranked among the 30 largest banks globally. ING has a two-tier board structure consisting of the executive board and the supervisory board. In ING's view, a two-tiered board is the best way to create the proper checks and balances in the company. The supervisory board is responsible for controlling management performance and advising the executive board. The supervisory board is made up exclusively of outside directors. The management banking board, comprised of the executive board (two members) and board members (five) is responsible for day-to-day management of the business and long-term strategy. See Table 8.2 for an overview of the Management Banking Board and board member attributes.

ING embraces diversity and inclusivity. As stated on the ING website (ING 2020b):

> We promote diversity at ING not just because it is the right thing to do. We promote diversity because it's essential for delivering on our strategy. In order to stay a step ahead, we need teams with a healthy mix of contrasting perspectives and backgrounds. These kinds of teams are more creative, faster to adapt and more inventive with their solutions.

In other words, ING has taken initiatives to deal with systemic organizational biases and, for example, increase female participation in leadership teams. Such an approach starts with

Table 8.2 ING management banking board

Surname (first name)	*Function*	*Gender*	*Birth date*	*Nationality*	*Education* **(***highest***)**	*ING tenure*
Van Rijswijk (Steven)	Chairman/CEO Member of executive board	Male	1970	Dutch	Business Economics Master	1995
Phutrakul (Tanate)	CFO Member of executive board	Male	1965	Thai	Engineering Master	2008
Abay (Pinar)	Head of leaders	Female	1977	Turkish	MBA degree	2011
Bogdaneris (Aris)	Head of challengers & growth markets	Male	1963	Canadian	International Economics Master	2015
Fernandez Niemann (Isabel)	Head of wholesale banking	Female	1968	Spanish	Law Master	2016
Louwhoff (Roel)	COO/CTO	Male	1965	Dutch	Business Administration Master	2014
Temporary position	CRO					

CEO = chief executive officer; CFO = chief financial officer; COO = chief operations officer; CTO = chief transformation officer
Source: ING (2020a)

inclusive leadership attitudes and approaches in senior leadership teams. Taking a stance and actively pursuing female participation and equality requires changing organization-wide beliefs, values, and attitudes towards women, as well as reconfiguring systems and processes that guide decision-making in hiring, promoting, mentoring, and training employees. Developing systems and guidelines, such as blind CV evaluation and visualizing leadership pipelines, can help to support more objective decision-making processes that are essential to reinforce career pathways for women all the way to the top team.

Case questions

1 To what extent do you consider the management banking board a diverse team? What member attributes do you consider relevant in your assessment? What are team process and performance implications?
2 What faultlines exist in the management banking board, do you think they are 'activated,' and how would you manage them?
3 What relationships does the management banking board have with other teams within ING, and what recommendations would you offer to manage these relations?
4 To what extent do you believe that diversity practices applies to the management banking board? How would you organize the appointing of the chief risk officer (CRO)?

References

Adibhatla, V., Shapiro, A., McNeese, M. D., and Balakrishnan, B. (2009) *'Design and development of a Transactive memory system prototype for geocollaborative crisis management'*. Paper presented at the Proceedings of the Human Factors and Ergonomics Society Annual Meeting.

Bachrach, D. G., Lewis, K., Kim, Y., Patel, P. C., Campion, M. C., and Thatcher, S. (2019) 'Transactive memory systems in context: A meta-analytic examination of contextual factors in transactive memory systems development and team performance'. *Journal of Applied Psychology*, 104(3): 464.

Barkema, H. G. and Shvyrkov, O. (2007) 'Does top management team diversity promote or hamper foreign expansion?' *Strategic Management Journal*, 28(7): 663–680.

Book, E. W. (2000) *Why the best man for the job is a woman: The unique female qualities of leadership*. New York, NY: HarperBusiness.

Cannon-Bowers, J. A., Salas, E., and Converse, S. (1993) 'Shared mental models in expert team decision making'. In Castellan Jr., N. J. (ed.), *Individual and group decision making: Current issues*. Lawrence Erlbaum Associates, Inc.

Choudhury, B. (2015) 'Gender diversity on boards: Beyond quotas special issue: Key corporate governance themes and issues in a globalised and internationalised world'. *European Business Law Review*, (1): 229–248.

Chrobot-Mason, D., Ruderman, M. N., Weber, T. J., and Ernst, C. (2009) 'The challenge of leading on unstable ground: Triggers that activate social identity faultlines'. *Human Relations*, 62(11): 1763–1794.

Cooper, D., Patel, P. C., and Thatcher, S. M. (2014) 'It depends: Environmental context and the effects of faultlines on top management team performance'. *Organization Science*, 25(2): 633–652.

Crawford, E. R., and LePine, J. A. (2013) 'A configurational theory of team processes: Accounting for the structure of taskwork and teamwork' *Academy of Management Review*, 38(1): 32–48.

Crucke, S., and Knockaert, M. (2016) 'When stakeholder representation leads to faultlines. A study of board service performance in social enterprises'. *Journal of Management Studies*, 53(5): 768–793.

Crucke, S., Moray, N., and Vallet, N. (2015) 'Internal representation and factional faultlines as antecedents for board performance in social enterprises'. *Annals of Public and Cooperative Economics*, 86(2): 385–400.

De Vries, T. A., Hollenbeck, J. R., Davison, R. B., Walter, F., and Van der Vegt, G. S. (2016) 'Managing coordination in multiteam systems: Integrating micro and macro perspectives'. *Academy of Management Journal*, 59: 1823–1844.

Desai, V. M. (2016) 'The behavioral theory of the (governed) firm: Corporate board influences on organizations' responses to performance shortfalls'. *Academy of Management Journal*, 59(3): 860–879.

Dezsö, C. L. and Ross, D. G. (2012) 'Does female representation in top management improve firm performance? A panel data investigation'. *Strategic Management Journal*, 33(9): 1072–1089.

Dufwenberg, M. and Muren, A. (2006) 'Gender composition in teams'. *Journal of Economic Behavior and Organization*, 61(1): 50–54.

Finkelstein, S., Cannella, S. F. B., Hambrick, D. C., and Cannella, A. A. (2009) *Strategic leadership: Theory and research on executives, top management teams, and boards*. Oxford: Oxford University Press.

Georgakakis, D., Greve, P., and Ruigrok, W. (2017) 'Top management team faultlines and firm performance: Examining the CEO-TMT interface'. *The Leadership Quarterly*, 28(6): 741–758.

Hambrick, D. C. (2007) 'Upper echelons theory: An update'. *Academy Management Review*, 32: 334–343.

Hambrick, D. C. and Mason, P. A. (1984) 'Upper echelons: The organization as a reflection of its top managers'. *Academy of Management Review*, 9(2): 193–206.

Heavey, C. and Simsek, Z. (2015) 'Transactive memory systems and firm performance: An upper echelons perspective'. *Organization Science*, 26(4): 941–959.

Heavey, C. and Simsek, Z. (2017) 'Distributed cognition in top management teams and organizational ambidexterity: The influence of transactive memory systems'. *Journal of Management*, 43(3): 919–945.

Hollenbeck, J. R., Moon, H., Ellis, A. P. J., West, B. J., Ilgen, D. R., Sheppard, L., Porter, C. and Wagner, J. A. (2002) 'Structural contingency theory and individual differences: Examination of external and internal person-team fit'. *Journal of Applied Psychology*, 87(3): 599–606.

Hollingshead, A. B. (1998) 'Communication, learning, and retrieval in transactive memory systems'. *Journal of Experimental Social Psychology*, 34(5): 423–442.

Hollingshead, A. B. (2001) 'Cognitive interdependence and convergent expectations in transactive memory'. *Journal of Personality and Social Psychology*, 81(6): 1080.

Homan, A. C., Hollenbeck, J. R., Humphrey, S. E., Van Knippenberg, D., Ilgen, D. R., and Van Kleef, G. A. (2008) 'Facing differences with an open mind: Openness to experience, salience of intragroup differences, and performance of diverse work groups'. *Academy of Management Journal*, 51(6): 1204–1222.

Hutzschenreuter, T. and Horstkotte, J. (2013) 'Performance effects of top management team demographic faultlines in the process of product diversification'. *Strategic Management Journal*, 34(6): 704–726.

Ilgen, D. R., Hollenbeck, J. R., Johnson, M., and Jundt, D. (2005) 'Teams in organizations: From input-process-output models to IMOI models'. *Annual Review of Psychology*, 56: 517–543.

ING (2020a) 'Management Board Banking'. Available online at https://www.ing.com/Newsroom/Media-kit/Board-members.htm (accessed 25 July 2020).

ING (2020b) 'Diversity & Inclusion'. Available online at https://www.ing.com/Sustainability/Our-own-operations/Diversity-inclusion.htm (accessed 25 July 2020).

Jehn, K. A. and Bezrukova, K. (2004) 'A field study of group diversity, workgroup context, and performance'. *Journal of Organizational Behavior*, 25(6): 703–729.

Jehn, K. A. and Bezrukova, K. (2010) 'The faultline activation process and the effects of activated faultlines on coalition formation, conflict, and group outcomes'. *Organizational Behavior and Human Decision Processes*, 112(1): 24–42.

Johns, G. (2006) 'The essential impact of context on organizational behavior'. *Academy of Management Review*, 31(2): 386–408.

Joshi, A. and Roh, H. (2009) 'The role of context in work team diversity research: a meta-analytic review'. *Academy of Management Journal*, 52(3): 599–627.

Kaczmarek, S., Kimino, S., and Pye, A. (2012) 'Board task-related faultlines and firm performance: A decade of evidence'. *Corporate Governance: An International Review*, 20(4): 337–351.

Kozlowski, S. W. J. and Bell, B. S. (2003) 'Work groups and teams in organizations'. In Borman, W. C, Ilgen, D. R., and Klimoski, R. J. (eds.), *Handbook of psychology (Vol. 12): Industrial and organizational psychology*. New York: Wiley-Blackwell.

Larkins, F. P. (2018) 'Male students remain underrepresented in Australian universities. Should we be concerned?' Available online at https://melbourne-cshe.unimelb.edu.au/lh-martin-institute/insights/gender-enrolment-trends-flarkins: https://melbourne-cshe.unimelb.edu.au/lh-martin-institute/insights/gender-enrolment-trends-flarkins (accessed 25 May 2020).

Lau, C. D. and Murnighan, J. K. (1998) 'Demographic diversity and faultlines: The compositional dynamics of organizational groups'. *Academy of Management Review*, 23(2): 325–340.

Leavitt, K., and Sluss, D. M. (2015) 'Lying for who we are: An Identity-based model of workplace dishonesty'. *Academy of Management Review*, 40(4): 587–610.

Lewis, K., Belliveau, M., Herndon, B., and Keller, J. (2007) 'Group cognition, membership change, and performance: Investigating the benefits and detriments of collective knowledge'. *Organizational Behavior and Human Decision Processes*, 103(2): 159–178.

Lewis, K., and Herndon, B. (2011) 'Transactive memory systems: Current issues and future research directions'. *Organization Science*, 22(5): 1254–1265.

Li, J. T., and Hambrick, D. C. (2005) 'Factional groups: A new vantage on demographic faultlines, conflict, and disintegration in work teams'. *Academy of Management Journal*, 48(5): 794–813.

Luciano, M., Nahrgang, J., and Shropshire, C. (in press) Strategic leadership systems: Viewing top management teams and boards of directors from a multiteam system perspective. *Academy of Management Review.*

Mathieu, J. E., Heffner, T. S., Goodwin, G. F., Salas, E., and Cannon-Bowers, J. A. (2000) 'The influence of shared mental models on team process and performance'. *Journal of Applied Psychology*, 85(2): 273–283.

Mathieu, J. E., Marks, M. A., and Zaccaro, S. J. (2001) 'Multi-team systems'. In Anderson, N. Ones, D., Sinangil, H. K. and Viswesvaran, C. (eds.), *International Handbook of Work and Organizational Psychology*. London: Sage.

McLeod, P. L. (2013) 'Distributed people and distributed information: Vigilant decision-making in virtual teams'. *Small Group Research*, 44(6): 627–657.

Nadkarni, S., and Barr, P. S. (2008) 'Environmental context, managerial cognition, and strategic action: An integrated view'. *Strategic Management Journal*, 29(13): 1395–1427.

Ndofor, H. A., Sirmon, D. G., and He, X. (2015) 'Utilizing the firm's resources: How TMT heterogeneity and resulting faultlines affect TMT tasks'. *Strategic Management Journal*, 36(11): 1656–1674.

Pearsall, M. J., Ellis, A. P. J., and Evans, J. M. (2008) 'Unlocking the effects of gender faultlines on team creativity: Is activation the key?' *Journal of Applied Psychology*, 93(1): 225–234.

Raes, A. M. L., Glunk, U., Heijltjes, M. G., and Roe, R. A. (2007) 'Top management team and middle managers – Making sense of leadership'. *Small Group Research*, 38(3): 360–386.

Roberto, M. A. (2003) 'The stable core and dynamic periphery in top management teams'. *Management Decision*, 41(2): 120–131.

Tajfel, H., and Turner, J. C. (1986) 'The social identity theory of intergroup behavior. In Worchel, S. and Austin, W. G. (eds.), *Psychology of Intergroup Relations*. Chicago: Nelson-Hall.

Tuggle, C. S., Schnatterly, K., and Johnson, R. A. (2010) 'Attention patterns in the boardroom: how board composition and processes affect discussion on entrepreneurial issues'. *Academy of Management Journal*, 53(3): 550–571.

Van der Kamp, M., Tjemkes, B., and Jehn, K. A. (2013) 'Putting Team Faultlines and Conflicts into Context: Faultline Activation and Deactivation'. Paper presented at the Academy of Management Proceedings.

Van der Kamp, M., Tjemkes, B. V., and Jehn, K. A. (2015) 'Faultline deactivation: Dealing with activated faultlines and conflicts in global teams'. In Wildman, J. L. and Griffith, R. L. (eds.), *Leading Global Teams: Translating Multidisciplinary Science to Practice*. New York: Springer.

Van Knippenberg, D., Dawson, J. F., West, M. A., and Homan, A. C. (2011) 'Diversity faultlines, shared objectives, and top management team performance'. *Human Relations*, 64(3): 307–336.

Van Knippenberg, D., De Dreu, C. K. W., and Homan, A. C. (2004) 'Work group diversity and group performance: An integrative model and research agenda'. *Journal of Applied Psychology*, 89(6): 1008–1022.

Van Knippenberg, D. and Schippers, M. C. (2007) 'Work group diversity'. *Annual Review of Psychology*, 58: 515–541.

Van Peteghem, M., Bruynseels, L., and Gaeremynck, A. (2018) 'Beyond diversity: A tale of faultlines and frictions in the board of directors'. *The Accounting Review*, 93(2): 339–367.

Wageman, R., Nunes, D. A., Burruss, J. A., and Hackman, J. R. (2008) *Senior leadership teams: What it takes to make them great*. Boston: Harvard Business Review Press.

Waller, M. J., Zhike, L. E. I., and Pratten, R. (2014) 'Focusing on teams in crisis management education: An integration and simulation-based approach'. *Academy of Management Learning & Education*, 13(2): 208–221.

Williams, E. A. (2011) *Towards an understanding of multiteam systems: Theorizing about identification, leadership, and communication in an emergency response system*. (Doctoral thesis). Purdue University.

9 A trans-cultural leadership paradigm

Fons Trompenaars[1]

Summary

In an increasingly dynamic and globalized business environment, sustained organizational performance depends on the development of leaders who are able to identify and take ownership of new opportunities. The growth of international business brings about new career paths and demands for a new group of strategic leaders. Leaders who possess capabilities to effectively navigate a multi-cultural landscape, who are able to inspire and empower followers, who are considerate and mindful, and who stand out from the crowd and are able to identify and resolve creatively tensions. This chapter juxtaposes traditional views on leadership with a new leadership paradigm - the trans-cultural leadership paradigm. The trans-cultural leadership paradigm stipulates that leaders need to develop and use a trans-cultural competency to guide their organizations and teams, effectuate change, and enact leadership as learning. Moreover, a trans-cultural competency enables leaders to effectively reconcile a multitude of leadership dilemmas.

Case: entering the 21st century as a manager or a leader?

What makes a good leader? The answer depends on who you ask or, rather, in which country you ask.

A quick scan through the literature on leadership reveals striking differences over time (Kotter 1996; 1999; Bennis 1994) as well as among French, American, and Japanese authors (Curtis 1999; Mannari 1986; Ockrent and Séréni 1998; Van Wolferen 1990). That is understandable. To be successful in France you need to be part of the right network, have the right education, and possess a certain amount of charisma. In Japan, being male, possessing seniority, and the right education (yes, even going to the right kindergarten) helps; wisdom certainly does not hurt. In the US, having a touch of vision, mission, and some business principles would suffice.

So, what makes a good leader in different countries? To investigate this, Trompenaars and Hampden-Turner (2001) asked a sample of 4,000 managers which of the following descriptions of a leader is most accurate:

A Good leaders are people who continuously help their subordinates to solve the variety of problems that they face. They are like parents, not teachers.
B Good leaders occupy a position between that of a private coach and a teacher. Their effectiveness depends on how they balance both roles.
C Good leaders get things done. They set goals, give information, measure results and let people do their work in that context.
D Good leaders give a lot of attention to work streams, so that goals, tasks, and achievements are aimed at improving those processes.
E Good leaders get things done. They set goals, give information and measure results so that everyone is embedded in continuous work streams.

The leaders described in answer 'A' look like those of the beginning of the last century: listen to father and everything will be okay. This style is still very popular in Latin America and Asia, where we have also conducted the research, and less so in Europe and the US. There is nothing wrong with that, but it is quite limited in its applicability outside these regions. Answer 'B' is a typical compromise and will not work very well anywhere. Answer 'C' is very popular amongst Anglo-Saxons and North-West European managers. The ever-popular 'management by objectives' is again applied recklessly. Add some vision and mission, and you're the modern leader; but the French would quickly argue: 'whose vision and mission is it?' Answers 'D' and 'E' are two alternative ways to integrate seemingly opposing values on a higher level. Answer 'D' suggests that good leaders guide people who make mistakes and learn from them, while 'E' integrates the dichotomy of task orientation with work streams in the opposite direction. The last two choices were made much more frequently by more successful leaders. Why all the fuss?

The diversity of perspectives on what good leadership looks like causes a great deal of confusion for the trans-cultural manager. If the French manage in France, the Japanese in Japan, and the Americans in the US, there is no problem. But increasingly we find that leaders have to deal with multi-cultural groups. Which paradigm should they follow? Which meaning should they create? Which principles should they follow if they need to act in a multi-cultural setting?

Questions:

1 Why is it challenging to lead a multi-cultural team or organization?
2 What makes a good leader in a global organization?

Learning objectives

The learning objectives of this chapter are to:

1 Provide insights traditional leadership paradigms and how these are different from an integrative leadership paradigm
2 Detail the various dilemmas that confront leaders navigating a globalized world

3 Showcase how and why dichotomous (i.e., productive vs. unproductive) leadership approaches are ineffective
4 Provide insights into how trans-cultural competence enables leaders to guide their organizations and teams, effectuate sustained change, and enact leadership as learning.

Introduction to leadership theories

The phenomenon of leadership has long been the focus of academic and managerial attention. In the last century, several leadership theories have been developed, which can be classified into three categories.

First, there is the ***trait theory,*** which examines whether there is a relationship between personal characteristics of leaders, varying from physical, to social, to psychological characteristics and the success with which they perform their tasks. In particular, Bennis and colleagues (e.g., Bennis and Nanus 1997) claimed to have found a relation between the effectiveness of leaders and properties as logical thinking (translating ideas into simple forms), persistence (learning from errors and swimming against the flow), empowerment (enabling and enthusing others), and self-control (working under high pressure and resisting intimidation). Criticism of the much-cited work of the trait theory focuses on the low correlation between effectiveness and personal properties. Moreover, it is frequently mentioned that such approaches do not consider contextual factors such as the type of industry and culture. Also, it does not seem likely that one can affect certain physical characteristics, such as height, gender, or skin color. All this has been very helpful for the supporters of the theory of those who say that leaders are born and not made. The effectiveness of a lot of properties also appears to be culturally dependent. It is improbable that the properties of a good American leader have the same impact in Japan or France.

The second stream of thought is known as the ***behavioral theory.*** This paradigm does not deal so much with the personal properties of the leader, but rather focuses on the behavior of the leader, particularly behavior that influences the performances and motivation of employees. Here, leadership style becomes the center of attention. It focuses on the behavior of leaders towards subordinates, the way tasks and functions of leadership are conducted. The famous Ohio State University study (see, e.g., Stogdill 1974) in the 1940s and 1950s concluded that an *initiating* style exists, for which performance-targeted behavior is initiated with clear supervision, a results orientation, and role clarification, and a more 'participative' *consideration* style exists, for which leaders aim their behavior at cooperation and satisfaction at work. This paradigm is very much developed around the research of scholars such as Tannenbaum and Schmidt (1973) and Blake and Mouton (1964), who respectively distinguished autocratic versus democratic or participative styles, and task-specific versus person-oriented styles of leadership. The weakness of this approach is that one hardly enters the complexity of the world of the relationship between both styles. Moreover, the behavior theory does not take the context (of culture, for example) into consideration.

It will not be surprising that the third stream of thought represents the ***situational theory.*** In case certain aspects of behavior and trait approaches are related to a certain context or situation, a new and promising predicting explanation of the effectiveness of leadership develops itself. The so-called contingency theories of Fiedler (1967), House (1971), and Vroom and Yetton (1973) show that environmental variables significantly influence the effectiveness of leadership. The 'one best way' is buried forever. For example, Fiedler (1967) hypothesized that leadership behavior interacts with the favorableness of a situation to determine effectiveness. He concluded that a focused task-oriented leadership does better in both extremely predictable and in very unpredictable situations, whereas people-oriented leadership does better in a situation of average complexity. Vroom and colleagues (1973) distinguished an autocratic, consultative, and group-based style of leadership, for which the choice would have to depend on the structure of the problem, the available information, and the required quality of the decision.

Although many situations are described by these three leadership paradigms, strikingly little attention is given to the cultural context within which leadership is practiced. In fact, the dilemmas that leaders are facing in the current world are hardly described. It is possibly the most important quality of a leader to reconcile the ends of a dilemma on a higher level. Both the trait and the behavior theory continue to be stuck with the dilemma of how certain culturally bound characteristics can be overcome, especially in a globalizing world. Situational leadership would stipulate different behaviors in different cultural surroundings. But how would leaders then deal effectively within multi-cultural surroundings? A new paradigm of leadership will have to tackle how leaders will deal with value dilemmas. We predict that a successful leader in the current time of very rapidly changing situations and multi-cultural surroundings needs to choose a people-oriented style to accomplish his or her task. The leader will have to be participative to be able to take autocratic decisions of a higher level. He or she will have to think logically, fed by an illogical intuition. Finally, a leader must be very sensitive to the situation to take consistent decisions regardless of the situation. Only then one can observe whether a person is born as a leader or becomes one.

A trans-cultural paradigm of leadership

A leader must inspire as well as listen. They must make decisions themselves, but also delegate, and must centralize their organization around local responsibilities. A professional needs to master his or her materials and, at the same time, be passionately at one with the mission of the whole organization. They need to apply their brilliant analytic skills to place these contributions in a larger context. They are supposed to have priorities and put them in a meticulous sequence, while parallel processing is in vogue. They must develop a brilliant strategy and at the same time have all the answers to questions in case their strategy misses its goals. No wonder there are so many definitions of effective leadership.

There is a need for a new leadership paradigm, for the development of a meta-theory of leadership that transcends culture - the trans-cultural paradigm of leadership. This new leadership paradigm is rooted in dilemma theory (Hampden-Turner 1990). Dilemma theory stipulates that differences between values function as a basis for learning. Business leaders who actively strive to embrace the behaviors and attitudes that feel most uncomfortable to them are those who can gently force engineers, marketers, managers, and other employees to embrace the unthinkable (Trompenaars and Hampden-Turner 2001). Although dilemma theory focuses primarily on cultural differences, at its core, the theory offers a foundation to explain and deal with the dynamics associated with any kind of business dilemma. Dilemma theory recognizes that differences can serve as the basis for intractable conflict and struggle. If values are diametrically opposed between two individuals, they have a tendency to fall into an 'us' versus 'them' and 'good' versus 'bad' dynamic. To curb polarization it is imperative that opposing values are identified and reconciled in a creative manner, such that the outcome accounts for the opposing forces. Research clearly shows that competence in reconciling dilemmas is the feature that most clearly differentiates successful and less successful leaders (Kaiser 2020; Trompenaars and Hampden-Turner 2001).

In short, the trans-cultural paradigm of leadership stipulates that in a globalized economic and social landscape, thriving leaders have an ability to reconcile dilemmas; in other words, these leaders possess a ***trans-cultural competence.*** Trans-cultural competence does not replace other leadership competencies (see e.g. Box 9.1), but must be viewed as a powerful and necessary skill in the leader's toolbox. It transcends the single culture in which it is developed and thus provides a robust approach for all cultures. Before providing detail on the organizational ramifications of leaders possessing a trans-cultural competency, we first detail trans-cultural dilemmas and explain how dilemma reconciliation works.

The trans-cultural competence is a leader's propensity to reconcile dilemmas. It transcends a single culture and it represents the real essence of leadership. This is the most discriminating feature that differentiates successful and less successful leaders.

Tensions: trans-cultural leadership dilemmas

Leaders who operate in an international world are continuously dealing with dilemmas - defined here as a choice between two options, both of which are attractive but appear to be mutually exclusive - that they need to reconcile on a higher level. Contemporary leadership

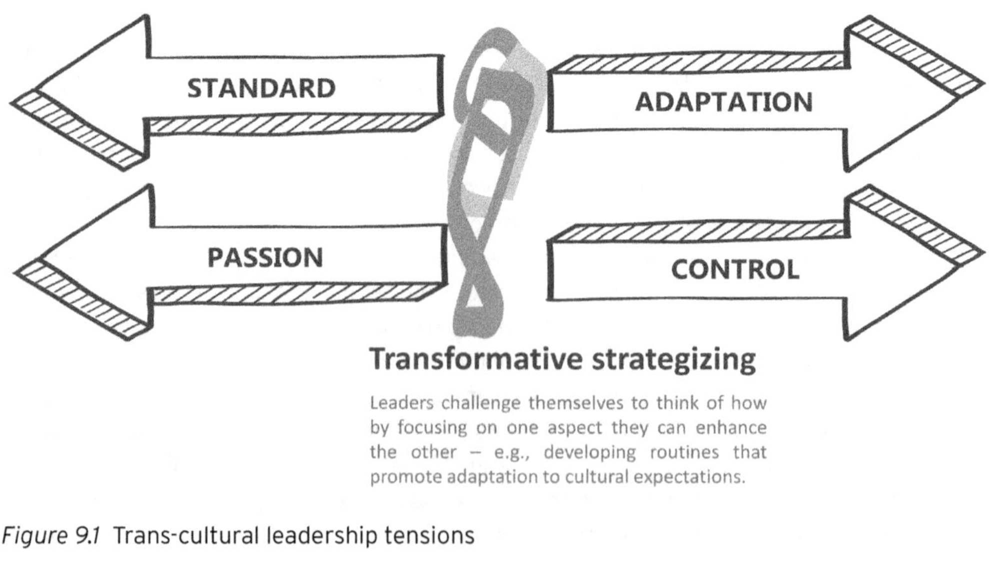

Figure 9.1 Trans-cultural leadership tensions

Box 9.1 Leadership in the 21st century

At least three big challenges characterize leadership today. First, there is the need to juggle a growing series of paradoxical demands. Second, the unprecedented pace of 'disruptive change' increases the pressure on organizations to adapt. Third, there is a call for diversity and inclusivity. These challenges have led to a reconsideration of what leaders are, and prompted new forms of leadership. Below are three illustrations:

Versatile leadership refers to a leader's capacity to read and respond to change with a wide repertoire of complementary skills and behaviors. It focuses on how to lead via 'forceful leadership' (asserting personal and positional power) and 'enabling leadership' (involving others and bringing out their best). This gives rise to pairs of behaviors: taking charge versus empowering, being decisive versus being participative, and being demanding versus being supportive. It also entails a focus on who to leads, by making a distinction between strategic and operational leadership. Both also include specific pairs of behaviors: setting direction versus driving execution, growing the business versus focusing resources, and introducing innovation versus providing order and stability.

Inclusive leadership ensures that all team members feel they are treated respectfully and fairly, are valued and sense that they belong, and are confident and inspired. It means having the courage to take conscious steps to break down barriers for people at risk of being excluded from society. It embodies an approach that appreciates diversity, invites and welcomes everyone's individual contribution, and encourages full engagement with the processes of decision-making and shaping reality. The aim of inclusive leadership is to create, change, and innovate whilst balancing everybody's needs.

Nimble leadership promotes self-management while balancing freedom and control in pursuit of innovation. A company functions efficiently and exploits new opportunities quickly as they minimize bureaucratic rules. It entails three types of leaders. Firstly, entrepreneurial leaders, concentrated at lower levels of an organization, create value for customers with new products and services. Secondly, enabling leaders, in the middle of the organization, make sure the entrepreneurs have the resources and information they need. Thirdly, architecting leaders, near the top, keep an eye on the whole game board, monitoring culture, high-level strategy, and structure.

Across these manifestations of leadership, a new leader is willing to: (i) learn from a variety of different and challenging work experiences; (ii) engage in ongoing feedback and development; (iii) continuously invest in becoming a more well-rounded person; (iv) live by a shared vision and purpose; (v) build meaningful relationships; and (vi) create change by valuing the world they live in.

Sources: Bortini et al. (2016); Ancona, Backman, and Isaacs (2019); Kaiser (2020)

research acknowledges such a tension approach and, for example, suggests that business leaders need to deal with taking charge versus empowering, being decisive versus being participative, being demanding versus being supportive, setting direction versus driving execution, growing the business versus focusing resources, and introducing innovation versus providing order and stability (Kaiser 2020). But what kind of dilemmas do leaders face? An interview study of more than 50,000 leaders found that the following two dilemmas are most common (Trompenaars and Hampden-Turner 1997); see Box 9.2 for other universal dilemmas.

Dilemma 1: standard and adaptation. The standard-adaptation tension affects leaders in various situations, such as deciding whether to globalize or localize a firm's approach or choosing between mass-production or focusing on specialized products. Effective leaders are those who can devise solutions that reconcile this tensions such the 'transnational organization' where best local practices are globalized continuously or 'mass customization' that combines standardized production with specialized adaptations.

Dilemma 2: passion and control. What makes a more effective leader - emotion and passion or controlling emotions? None of the extremes are useful, as leaders who are passionate

Box 9.2 Other trans-cultural dilemmas that leaders encounter frequently

- ***Individual creativity and team spirit.*** This dilemma is the integration of team spirit with individual creativity. An effective leader knows how to make an excellent team out of creative individuals. The team is stimulated to support brilliant individuals, while these individuals deploy themselves for the greater whole.
- ***Analysis and synthesis.*** Are the best leaders those who can divide the big picture into small modular pieces or those who put issues in the big picture and prioritize? Another important characteristic of the modern leader is the ability to know when and where to go in deep, as only analysis leads to paralysis, and overusing synthesis leads to a lack of action.
- ***Doing and being.*** This tension emphasizes that successful leaders are able to integrate doing and being. That is, their actions reflect who they actually are and they are one with the business they are undertaking. In other words, the excessive compulsion to perform, when doing so does not match an individual's true personality, leads to ineffective behavior.
- ***Sequential and parallel.*** Effective leaders can work both in a rigorous sequential way, but can also stimulate parallel processes. This reconciliation, manifests as 'synchronize processes to increase the sequential speed' - or 'just in time' management - and also seems to be very effective in integrating the long and short term.
- ***Push and pull.*** This core competence for today's leaders is the ability to connect the voice of the market with the technology the company has developed and vice versa. That is, leaders who can combine the technology push with market pull. For example, a computer that is capable of making complex calculations can also be user-friendly.

without reason are seen as neurotics and leaders lacking emotions are perceived as robots. The best leaders combine the two. For instance, while Richard Branson regularly checks his passion with reason, the more neutral Jack Welch (the former CEO of General Electric) gives his controlled reason meaning by occasionally showing passion.

How does dilemma reconciliation work?

While reconciling dilemmas may seem easy, if we repeatedly resolve dilemmas by choosing one option over the other, the option we choose becomes an unconscious preference. Over time, we stop being aware that we are making a choice; we simply assume it is the best course of action. These deeply internalized preferences become values that shape the decisions we make and the actions we take. Leaders tend to believe that their way of dealing with something is obviously superior, even when they encounter others who routinely make the opposite choice. In this situation, it is easy to characterize different choices as absurd or based on ignorance.

Two phenomena that often prevent leaders from engaging in dilemma reconciliation are skilled incompetence and schismogenesis (Ramsey 2020). Skilled incompetence means that leaders (like anyone else) can develop a tendency to prefer one alternative over the other; an unconscious preference, at the expense of the other. For example, for a long time, and even still today, corporate leaders pursued shareholder value while even consciously considering alternative interests, most notably climate change. Even if they acknowledge an opposite alternative, their preference guides their actions and behaviors. In other words, skilled incompetence describes the mismatch between what people say and what they do (Agyris 1986).

Schismogenesis refers to the splitting apart of complementary values (Bateson 1935). Schismogenesis occurs when an initially small difference becomes progressively bigger. Consider the example of a break-through innovation that may resolve a sustainable challenge and make the engineers involved excited. With great enthusiasm they communicate their work to their manager, who responds by calmly articulating concerns about marketability. In response, the engineers work harder, which leads the manager to strengthen his/her position, and so on. A minor difference in views has turned into a polarized debate.

So, how can leaders reconcile dilemmas? To mitigate the adverse impact of skilled incompetence and schismogenesis on dilemma reconciliation, leaders may engage in the following activities. A key part of achieving reconciliation is awareness of one's own thinking and behavior. From a cultural perspective, dominance on one value is often considered normal - people are rewarded for acting on the basis of an extreme of one value. However, organizational health requires the reconciliation of a range of values, so leaders should invest in developing awareness of other values, interests, and views. Leaders become polarized when they can see only the good in what they value and only the evil in the values of those who oppose them. It is important that they 'look for the whole' and practice seeing the whole picture by noticing the gains and losses to be made by pursuing each value represented in a dilemma. Values often lie hidden beneath the surface, which makes reconciliation difficult. Leaders should bring values to the surface; for example, by explicating and understanding the motives behind actions and behaviors.

Most importantly, reconciliation involves seeing the relationships between complementary values. To see how this relationship unfolds, it is important to practice sequencing. Leaders should replace the notion of 'either-or' with 'through'. How can innovation be attained through compliance to regulations or, alternatively, how can compliance be improved through innovation?

Leading with a trans-cultural competency

Thus far, we have described the need for a trans-cultural paradigm of leadership by transcending trait, behavioral, and situational theories. We have argued that trans-cultural dilemmas need to be reconciled to make leaders effective in particularly international environments. Simply rejecting opposite orientations will achieve nothing. Abandoning your own position and adopting the other extreme is like trying to impress on your first date by acting out an opposite unfamiliar role – you will soon be found out. The significance of our new leadership approach is that it enables us to determine the propensity for the individual to reconcile dilemmas and this trans-cultural competency is a direct measure of healthy and strong leadership. Next, we explain how adopting a trans-cultural competency approach (i) enables leaders to guide their organizations and teams, (ii) enables organizational change, and (iii) views leadership as learning.

The leader as leading a team

As another way to see how the trans-cultural paradigm of leadership might affect all aspects of organizational life, we now consider the leader as a team player. The anthropologist Margaret Mead once said, 'Small groups have changed the world. Indeed nothing else ever has'. The qualities of a leader, of the team, and the interaction between both are the most important factors in the success of an organization, and have been the subject of many books.

In my opinion, the most original thinker on management teams is the British author and consultant Meredith Belbin. In his first book, *Team Roles at Work* (1981), he defined an effective team as a group of people who aim for a shared goal and therefore go through several phases. After 40 years of research, he concluded that the effectiveness of a team is dependent on the fulfilment of eight complementary roles. They do not have to be proportional; nor does one individual need to play each of the roles, since one person can incorporate different ones.

In the first phase of the definition of the task, Belbin (1981) distinguished between the roles of the *shaper* and the *chairman*. Shapers are extroverted go-getters who integrate different aspects of relevant activities into a coherent whole. They will frequently test the ineffectiveness of a team in a very impatient way. Chairmen complement shapers in the first phase by their rest and patience, but simultaneously appreciate all potential contributions and meld them together in the context of a very strictly managed set of goals. In the second phase of generating ideas and gaining information, two new roles are dominant. The first is the unorthodox *plant*, which generates creative ideas. Plants are loaded with imagination and creativity and generate one proposal after the other. What the plants contribute in terms of content, the *resource investigators* add to the level of the process; they sell ideas enthusiastically and are able to negotiate extra budgets from management. In the third phase, there is a need for planning and collection of resources. Here, the specialized roles of the *team worker*

Box 9.3 A critique of Myers-Briggs Type Indicator (MBTI)

The MBTI is probably the most widely used personality inventory in history. HR professionals have seized on it to help their clients make important business, career, or personal decisions. The MBTI was 'designed to make Carl Jung's theory of psychological types understandable and useful in everyday life' (Myers 1991). Derived from Jung's insights (Jung 1971), the MBTI distinguishes four basic psychological processes that can each be plotted on a bipolar scale:

1. Extroversion-introversion (E versus I)
2. Sensing-intuition (S versus N)
3. Thinking-feeling (T versus F)
4. Judging-perceiving (J versus P)

The first scale describes where you tend to focus your attention and from where you get your energy. At one extreme is *extroversion*, where the source of energy comes from the outside world. *Introversion*, at the other extreme, is where one's power derives from within oneself. The second scale describes how one gathers information. This distinguishes *sensing* (when information is captured in a literal and concrete sense) and *intuition* (when we give meaning to our data by putting it in a larger context). The third scale captures the way we judge information and make decisions based upon how we perceive that information. Those who make decisions based on logic and ratio can be spoken of as having a preference for *thinking*. By contrast, when people prefer to make decisions based on values or things they stand for, we speak of a dominant *feeling* preference. The fourth scale describes a preference for how one orients oneself to the outside world and how one organizes information. At one extreme, there is a dominance of *perceiving* information, preferring flexibility and spontaneity. At the other extreme is *judging*, for those who have a preference for organizing things in an orderly and disciplined manner.

The fundamental concern with the classic MBTI is that each dimension is based on a single axis continuum. Does the MBTI logic ask if you are sensing *or* intuiting? The more you identify yourself as sensing, the less intuiting you must be. When seeking to apply the MBTI typology in an international context, we find that accretion to the extremities of each scale is constraining. We argue that global leaders are more effective when they are able to integrate seemingly opposing values on a higher level. Consider two very different leaders: Sir Isaac Newton observed and sensed his way into science. But he also generated deductive insights from intuiting his objective investigations. He scored high on sensing initially, which he then integrated with intuiting. By contrast, Albert Einstein started with his intuition and inspired guesses. Many of his breakthroughs initially came from 'thought experiments' that he and others later verified and demonstrated experimentally as well as theoretically. Einstein scored high on intuiting, which he then reconciled with sensing. The trans-cultural paradigm of leadership put forward in this chapter challenges leaders to move beyond binary thinking to find ways in which they can reconcile two opposing forces.

and the *company worker* are crucial. Team workers are emotionally intelligent people who have great social skills, reconciling the conflicts in the team and giving the necessary support, even if it means making the coffee. Company workers translate the ideas into concrete tasks and are also willing to execute them personally. They have analytical minds and love organizing. Finally, in the fourth phase, tasks need to be critically analyzed and completed. Here is where the *monitor evaluator* and the *completer/finisher* come in. The first role takes care of distant and mild criticisms, critically evaluating problem analyses. Completers/finishers are the conscientious and anxious perfectionists, who ensure, in a professional way, that the team completes all its tasks.

What we most appreciate in the Belbin model are the implicit values that are associated with diverse roles. In most theories about team roles, many characteristics of the differing roles are summed up as though they were stable and as if they could independently guarantee a certain continuity. In reality, however, the effectiveness of a team is fully dependent on how it takes advantage of the differences in roles, in which the dynamic of complementarity is essential. In particular, in the transitions between each of the four phases the differences between the roles become even clearer, and the reconciliation of the different orientations becomes essential.

Consider the example of the tension between the relaxed but task-oriented chairman and the opportunistic resource investigator who continuously looks for new possibilities. A team will be able to function effectively when the issues that the resource investigator introduces from the outside can be reconciled with the more inwardly directed goals of the chairman. A second dilemma that the leader needs to resolve is the tension between the deviating plant and the mediating team worker. A new idea from a plant will often initiate a conflict between deviation and consensus. However, if some members of the team support the idea, there is nothing that can stop them and the team will flourish. The third field of tension that a leader often finds is between the company worker and the completer/finisher. The former believes in the success of hard work, while the latter believes in a focus on details. This can result in many tensions that can be relieved if the worker can convince the completer that no details are being overlooked. Another dilemma is created between the skeptical view of the evaluator and the more optimistic approach of the action-oriented shaper, who is often irritated by the amount of time required for the process of evaluation and discussion. The must also transfer the apparent lack of inspiration and motivational image of the cool calculator into passionate enthusiasm.

One could suggest that Belbin (1981) depicted an outdated view on teams. This may be so, but the Belbin Model remains a vastly popular tool to design and navigate teams towards success. Furthermore, more contemporary approaches towards teams with a focus on team composition, leadership, and processes tend to negate underlying tensions. For example, extant research shows the importance of setting and articulating shared goals, but members' and leaders' goals are likely to embody a tension; a psychologically safe climate drives team performance, but what is considered safe most likely varies across cultures; self-management by teams and team members is deemed critical for steering teams towards success, but without procedures, rules, and regulations teams will become disconnected from the organization; and team performance assessments are recommended to enact change and improvements, but assessment content and procedures are inherently cultural sensitive. Identification of team dilemmas and engaging in dilemma reconciliation can lead to mold-breaking new solutions and tilt the team towards higher levels. Value is often created by the complementarity of roles within a team. The success of a team is dependent on whether all the roles are played by one or more of its members. This gives us a deeper meaning of the concept of diversity. The identification of these roles is only the beginning. The role of a leader needs to be particularly aimed at reconciling the crucial dilemmas created between the team roles, and in this way organizing the relationship between the roles. In such a way, the basic requirements for the team's success are well planted and ready to grow.

The leader as change agent

Another role of the leader is that of a change agent. How would the trans-cultural paradigm of leadership deal with the leader as a change agent? Here again we see a new approach to change emerging. It is striking how much the Anglo-Saxon model of change has dominated the world of leading change (Kotter 1996), based on a task-oriented culture and the idea that traditions need to be forgotten as soon as possible. This seems to be fine in an Anglo-Saxon environment: you formulate a bunch of new goals, preferably in the context of a clear vision, you hire some consultants for a marginal US$300,000 a year (excluding bonuses), and you dump the ones that do not believe in your set goals. In this 'guided missile' model, the organization is conceived as a task-oriented instrument at the disposal of shareholders, where managers have an MBA and employees are referred to as human resources (Trompenaars and Hampden-Turner 1997).

The challenge lies in what to do when the surrounding culture is not aligned with this type of change logic. Consider an American manager from Eastman Kodak who had launched a successful change program in Rochester, New York, and who, after launching the formula in Europe, explained:

> The French and Germans are unbelievably inflexible. I have done a whole round in Europe and in each of the countries, many people seemed to support our vision. Okay, the Germans had some problems with the process; they wanted to know all the procedural details and how these were connected to the change envisioned. The French were very worried about the unions. However, we, as internal consultants and management, left with the idea that we agreed on the approach. When I returned some three months later to check how the implementation was going, I noticed that in France and Germany nothing had been started. Nothing!

Anyone with a bit of sensitivity to cross-cultural affairs could have predicted this. Germans often believe in a vision, but without the proper structures, systems, and procedures that make this vision come alive, nothing will happen. Germans have a 'push' culture: you push them in a certain direction. Compared to North Americans, they are not easily 'pulled'. You give them a goal or task and they follow, particularly when you pay them well to do it. In Latin and Asian countries, management of change often means changing the management. In their power-oriented, family ideology, change will only happen when new points of departure are personalized. If 'Monsieur le Président Directeur Général' does not fully back these points of departure, no pull or push will be effective.

This is one of the areas that creates dilemmas for Western leaders who, in their efforts to globalize their activities, like to acquire and change foreign operations. Consider another example: an American organization thinks its Singaporean management takes too long to come to a decision. Consensus is nice, but doesn't work in these times of great speed. The Singaporeans, for their part, think that the Americans make decisions too quickly and without enough deliberation. They perceive that this will lead to major implementation problems, largely because too few people have been involved in the process. At one extreme, the desire of quick-on-their-feet managers often results in a 'follow me, follow me' attitude, causing a situation where, like lemmings, people all 'fall off a cliff' together. At the other extreme are the Asians, who spend their time involving all ranks to gain consensus: the 'lost democratic' model. Change is best directed towards the integration of both ways, guided by the trans-cultural leader. This would explain why father figures, so popular in both Latin and Asian cultures, derive their authority from the way they serve their teams through their colleagues' sharply formulated tasks.

The leader in a learning organization

How does the trans-cultural paradigm of leadership deal with learning in organizations? Leaders are increasingly confronted with questions from clients about how their knowledge can be embedded into the company's long-term learning processes, or how they can help the organization to build and sustain 'cultures of learning', 'cultures of continuous development', and 'cultures that embrace change and diversity'.

Many educational programs in our schools, universities, and within our organizations are based on presenting codified knowledge, which is dumped on the heads of the students. The teachers, who have developed or captured this knowledge, fulfill their roles as 'knowledge dumpers' with great gusto. Just look at the way that many classrooms and even professional conference centers are designed. The podium (preferably in an elevated position) contrasts with the uncomfortable chairs that are huddled behind folding tables in the rest of the room (Ackoff 1987). To break out from the imaginary square of the traditional principles of learning and to build a true learning organization, a leader must first distinguish a certain number of dilemmas that characterize an alternative learning process.

First, there is the dilemma of a universal team style versus a diversity of learning styles. In a recent research project within Heineken, we found that their employees' team styles differed more significantly than their cultural backgrounds. How can a business cope with this if it is necessary to develop and apply globally consistent learning programs? One suggestion is to globally apply the learning cycle, as developed and described by David Kolb (1993) in his book *Experiential Learning*. Kolb's cycle includes four stages: (i) experiencing; (ii) reflecting; (iii) conceptualizing; and (iv) planning and generalizing. He suggests that each culture needs to go through the full cycle. However, in the USA the case study or simulation seems to be the most effective starting point, whereas in France, a kick-off with theories and conceptualizations leads to better results because they tend to say, 'I see what happens in practice, but first prove to me that it will work in theory'. By choosing an approach, a learning organization can take better advantage of the diversity of its members. In this way, you can see that, within a learning organization, the learning cycle can be universalized while the points of departure within the cycle are culturally dependent. And what about universal, supply-driven training curricula versus particularistic, demand-driven, ad-hoc sessions?

A second dilemma that needs to be reconciled is that of the value of individual learning versus group learning. Many learning processes focus solely on the individual. The individual completes tests and receives feedback. The learning organization is dependent on the knowledge of individuals, but the organization will only increase its effectiveness when the individual is inspired by a surrounding group. One way of achieving this might be to have the individual salesperson or researcher compete for the best cooperation with the customer or fellow researchers. One could also have an approach aimed at stimulating the cooperation between colleagues to share best practices in such a way that everyone learns from each other. This reconciliation can be described as 'cooperative competitive learning', in which the best ideas are raised in a competitive context so that the entire organization cooperates around the best practices. Individual learning must be framed in a group context. A learning organization is also a changing one, in which you can only change individually if the organization around you changes in parallel, in a sustainable way. In other words, while individuals are trying to implement cultures of continuous development, which takes time and patience, their organizations can deal with a series of pressures that fly in the face of their original desire (cost pressures, the urgent need to deliver value to the customer today, etc.).

A third dilemma that arises when challenging traditional learning processes is that between action and reflection (see Figure 9.2). For a long time, it has been recognized that purely cognitive learning or 'reflection' results in limited learning. It creates the 'ivory tower' scientist. To counter this, many organizations opt for 'action learning', as can be witnessed by the increased popularity of the case-study approach in universities. However, action learning also has some constraints. Consider the example of a Harvard student in his first well-paid job, struggling with a particular problem. The only thing he could say to his boss, as an

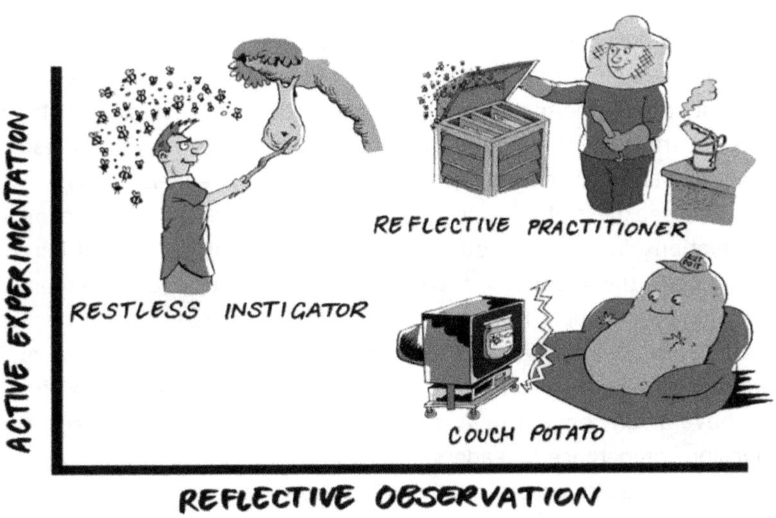

Figure 9.2 Reconciling reflective observation and active experimentation

excuse for his struggles, was that he had never worked on this kind of case before. The weakness and limitation of action-learning programs is that they are too often disconnected from any reflection on the overall context of the individual problems the organization is facing. A learning organization can benefit by having 'action learning' as a principle, where the action is undertaken on specific issues, and with workshops that are then used to share knowledge and reflection, but only to move into action once more - this time in a more informed and effective way. It was Donald Schön (1983) who beautifully described the effectiveness of a leader by combining action and reflection. This is another example of the importance of a leader to integrate seemingly opposing values on a higher level.

The tensions we have mentioned can all serve as challenges of a leader in creating learning organizations. But they can also definitely bring about real change if reconciled, which can result in companies becoming, for example, more diversity-minded or more global. In all these dilemmas, one discovers an organizational principle that is based on the idea of integration. One must leave the Cartesian and deductive model behind and bring a synthesis of the dilemmas that form the basis of learning.

Reflection

To conclude, the central premise put forward in this chapter is that the propensity to reconcile seemingly opposed values is the key competence behavior to be an effective leader in today's world. To support this premise, we have juxtaposed transitional leadership theories with an alternative one - the trans-cultural paradigm of leadership - and argued why the latter is more likely to be effective in a globalized world. The core tenet of the theory stipulates that successful leaders build and use a trans-cultural competence that enables them to identify and creatively reconcile (cultural) business dilemmas. The results are inspired people, collective sense-making, superior performance, and, most importantly, an effective resolution to the leaders' dilemmas permeating the VUCA world. Two final questions remain.

Does it work in theory? In this chapter we have sought to show that dominant theories of leadership - categorized in three main paradigms known as trait, behavioral, and situational theories - do not resolve the main dilemmas that leaders are facing. Trait theory claims a single best set of traits for the leader and ignores the culture in which these traits come to fruition. Behavioral theory claims that there are different leadership styles vis-à-vis task and followers. The weakness of this approach is that one hardly enters the complexity of the world of the relationship between both styles. Again, the cultural context is not taken into consideration. Finally, the situational theory of leadership introduces the (cultural) context as an important aspect of the effectiveness of leadership. However, one aspect that has not been resolved is how a leader can be effective in a multi-cultural environment. We believe the trans-cultural paradigm of leadership resolves most black spots in existing leadership theories. We have given conceptual and empirical evidence that it is necessary to focus on the reconciling competence of leaders.

Originally, the investigative work on dilemma theory was inductive. In an action learning exploratory phase over several years, Hampden-Turner (1990) undertook many interviews with senior international leaders. The interviews included the use of several challenges/decision options to leaders in situations with seemingly opposing views and values. We used similar methods, as well as questionnaire-based investigations in parallel on value dilemmas leading to the construction of a cross-cultural database of 55,000 managers/leaders (Trompenaars and Hampden-Turner 1997). This database and its principal questionnaire instruments have been widely used in training workshops and consultancy interventions across the world. Face and content validity have been constantly improved from qualitative and quantitative studies including internal formalized research and by university PhD students.

Does it work in practice? Following an interpretative and inferencing phase, the underlying schema of dilemma reconciliation and its relationship to leadership evolved. This was tested initially by the principal authors working both separately and in collaboration in preliminary research, consultancy, and training workshops with major global companies across the globe. Through consulting work we have found that the trans-cultural paradigm of leadership is effective in a variety of key business processes, ranging from selection, team building, and learning. Recruitment instruments need to be adapted to be able to 'scan' trans-cultural competence. We have also found that leaders can be more effective in practice by reconciling dilemmas raised within teams and learning environments. Resulting from these activities, several core propositions concerning the underlying behaviors that are characteristic of high performing leaders in the global workplace were assembled. The interest was in developing an underlying robust theory to explain the effective performance of the global leader (and global manager), thereby providing a model for improving professional practice through what we have described as intercultural competence.

Learning and discussion questions

1 What tensions should leaders of global organizations consider?
2 What makes a good leader for global organizations?
3 Explain what dilemma reconciliation is?
4 Why is it important to reconcile cultural dilemmas?
5 How can cultural dilemmas be reconciled?

Exercise: stimulating change in a South Korean subsidiary

In 1985, US-based Belly Electronics (BE) started to manufacture in South Korea. Early 1991 margins from the South Korean operations came under pressure because of Thai and Vietnamese competition. For the first time, BE flew in experienced US managers from the San Francisco Bay Area of California to determine why the South Korean managers were not getting the job done. Based on a continuous improvement program, South Korean managers were put under pressure to get 'their act together'. The American manager told the South Korean managers:

> You haven't been doing a good job of managing. I expect that you will correct your previous mistakes to achieve improvements in the numbers within six months. You must work harder to become a profit-generating company. I expect you to show me that Koreans can achieve measurable benchmarks for profitability and quality. This will be rewarded by significant monetary bonuses.

After six months of demands and very disappointing results, a second US manager was flown in, but his similar words made no difference. You are asked to come to the rescue of the Korean operation. What would you do?

1 I would reinforce the previous manager's positions. After all, the South Korean managers were not achieving the results BE was getting in other operations. I would find ways to pressure them more to achieve the improvements.
2 I would explain that I had been assigned to make improvements in the South Korean operation's results. Whatever has happened in the past was not important. I would ask each manager to work with me to create the necessary changes and take advantage of their actual attributed positions.
3 I would reinforce the previous manager's positions. However, I would not only reward the South Korean managers with measures of output, but also by promotion.
4 I would put them under slightly less pressure, but still maintain some minimal deadlines regarding certain prime objectives.
5 I would identify those South Korean managers who were most respected by the others. I would work with that group, create trust with those in charge, and thus support their efforts to improve the operations.

Case questions

1 What do you think of the US manager's approach to change? Is it about managing or leadership?
2 Why do you think the South Korean managers are resisting change?
3 Which of the above courses of action would you take? Why?
4 Discuss which of the different cultural dilemmas discussed in this chapter is relevant in this case.

Note

1. Parts of this chapter have appeared in: Trompenaars, F. (2002) 'The quest for a new paradigm of international leadership'. *Inauguration of the Van Rossum Professorship on European Multiculturality at the Solvay Business School.* Also a word of thanks for the great support of all colleagues at THT-consulting and in particular to the great minds of Charles Hampden-Turner and Peter Woolliams to whom I owe so much. Thank you colleagues at the Vrije Universiteit, Amsterdam, to allow me to communicate the insights in this important field of inquiry.

References

Ackoff, R. (1987) *The Art of Problem Solving Accompanied by Ackoff's Fables*. New York: Wiley & Sons.
Agyris, C. (1986) 'Skilled Incompetence.' *Harvard Business Review*, 64: 74–79.
Ancona, D., Backman, E., and Isaacs, K. (2019) 'Nimble Leadership.' *Harvard Business Review*, 97(4): 74–83.
Bateson, G. (1935) 'Culture Contact and Schismogenesis'. *Man*, 35: 178–183.
Belbin, M. R. (1981) *Team Roles at Work*. London: Butterworth-Heinemann.
Bennis, W. G. (1994) *On Becoming A Leader*. Reading, MA: Addison-Wesley Pub. Co.
Bennis, W. G. and Nanus, B. (1997) *Leaders: Strategies for Taking Charge*. New York: Harper & Row.
Blake, R. and Mouton, J. (1964) *The Managerial Grid The Key to Leadership Excellence*. Houston, TX: Gulf Publishing Company.

Bortini, P., Paci, A., Rise, A., and Rojnik, I. (2016) 'Inclusive leadership: Theoretical framework'. Available online at https://inclusiveleadership.eu/inclusive-leadership-manual-for-trainers/ (accessed 25 July 2020).
Curtis, G. L. (1999) *The Logic of Japanese Politics: Leaders, Institutions, and the Limits of Change*. New York: Columbia University Press.
Fiedler, F. (1967) *A Theory of Leadership Effectiveness*. New York: McGraw-Hill.
Hampden-Turner, C. (1990) *Charting the Corporate Mind: From Dilemma to Strategy*. Oxford: Blackwell.
House, R. J. (1971) 'A Path Goal Theory of Leader Effectiveness'. *Administrative Science Quarterly*, 16(3): 321–339.
Jung C. G. (1971) *Psychological Types*. London: Routledge and Kegan Paul.
Kaiser, R. (2020) 'The best leaders are versatile ones'. Available online at https://hbr.org/2020/03/the-best-leaders-are-versatile-ones (accessed 25 July 2020).
Kotter, J. P. (1996) *A Force for Change: How Leadership Differs from Management*. Cambridge, MA: Harvard Business School Press.
Kotter, J. P. (1999) *What Leaders Really Do*. Cambridge, MA: Harvard Business School Press.
Kolb, D. A. (1983) *Experiential Learning: Experience as the Source of Learning and Development*. Englewood Cliffs, NJ: Prentice Hall.
Mannari, H. (1986) *The Japanese Business Leaders*. Tokyo: University of Tokyo Press
Myers, I. B. (1991) *Gifts Differing*. Palo Alto, CA: CPP Inc.
Myers, I. B. and McCaulley, M. H. (1985) *Manual: A Guide to the Development and Use of the Myers-Briggs Type Indicator*. Marwal, CA: Consulting Psychologists Press.
Ockrent, C. and Séréni, J. P. (1998) *Les Grands Patrons. Comment ils voient notre avenir* Paris: Plon.
Ramsey, B. (2020) 'Learning Through Differences: Dilemma Theory in Action' Available online at https://thesystemsthinker.com/learning-through-differences-dilemma-theory-in-action/ (accessed 27 July 2020).
Schön, D. A. (1983) *The Reflective Practitioner: How Professionals Think in Action*. London: Taylor & Francis Ltd.
Stogdill, R. M. (1974) *Handbook of Leadership: A Survey of Theory and Research*. New York, NY: Free Press.
Tannenbaum, R. and Schmidt, W. H. (1973) 'How to Choose a Leadership Pattern'. *Harvard Business Review*, 51: 162–180.
Trompenaars, F. and Hampden-Turner, C. (1997) *Riding the Waves of Culture: Understanding Cultural Diversity in Global Business*. London: Nicholas Brealey Publishing.
Trompenaars, F. and Hampden-Turner, C. (2001) *21 Leaders for the 21st Century*. London: Capstone.
Van Wolferen, K. (1990) *The Enigma of Japanese Power*, New York, NY: Vintage Books.
Vroom, V. and Yetton, P. (1973) *Leadership and Decision-Making*. Pittsburgh, PA: University of Pittsburgh Press.

10 Working with transformative strategies

Transformative strategies in practice

The main idea we put forward in this book is that decision-makers need to shift their thinking from linear models to new flexible and complex models. This is due to the transformations in the business environment. The change in the business environment can be described by three characteristics: speed, magnitude, and the predictability of change. With today's increasing globalization and technological advancements, the environment is changing at increasingly fast rates, in higher magnitudes, and in ways that are difficult to predict due to destructive technologies. This makes traditional linear models of thinking about competitive strategies obsolete. Ideas of fit between the organization and environment are not easily implemented when the environment is changing quickly, drastically, and in ways that are difficult to predict. In this new normal, fixed and linear competitive strategies are bound to be disappointing. Instead, managers need to devise more flexible strategies that allow the organization to pivot quickly and in major ways when the environment changes.

However, developing such flexible strategies is difficult because it requires the incorporation of tensions in strategy-making and implementation. Organizations have been struggling to balance the exploitation of their current capabilities with the development of new ones for decades (e.g., Mihalache et al. 2014; Mihalache and Mihalache 2016). Even when organizations developed the next disruptive technology, they were often unable to bring it to market due to organizational inertia. Kodak, the US photography company, is a case in point. Steven Sasson developed a prototype of a digital camera as early as the 1970s. This new technology had the potential (as has become abundantly clear) to radically transform the photography industry. However, instead of using this new technology, Kodak decided to ignore it. Recounting that period, Sasson said that '. . . management's reaction was: that's cute, but don't tell anyone about it' (Deutsch, 2008). So, instead of leading the digital photography revolution, Kodak ended up almost disappearing because of it. So, how is it possible that Kodak chose not to use this new technology? The answer is simple: the tension between existing capabilities and new capabilities for the future. In the 1980s and 1990s, Kodak's main source of income came from the sale of film, not cameras.

In today's VUCA business environment, decision-makers need to shift their thinking from linear models to new flexible and complex models that allow them to accommodate tensions in multiple parts of the organization.

Also, most employees were involved in the development of film for cameras with a large contingent of chemists. The introduction of digital photography was perceived as threatening by many groups within Kodak, whose organizational standing depended on the development and sale of film. Bill Lloyd, Kodak's chief technology officer, said: 'I've been here five years, and I'm still learning about all the things they already have. It seems Kodak had developed antibodies against anything that might compete with film' (Deutsch, 2008). As Kodak's case shows, even when organizations develop the next disruptive technology, they might sometimes be unable to use it because of organizational forces entrenched in the old capabilities.

Other companies are much more able to engage in both exploitation and exploration. A stellar example of this is Apple, whose release of the iPhone essentially killed one of Apple's most successful products, the iPod. This is in line with the company's philosophy, as famously put by Steve Jobs: 'If we don't cannibalize ourselves, somebody else will' (Yarow, 2011). Apple is particularly proficient in venturing into new spaces, such as with the introduction of Apple TV and the Apple Watch, while at the same time exploiting current capabilities, as evidenced by the yearly iterations of iPhone or Apple Watch. Apple's success shows the importance of stimulating both the exploitation of current capabilities and the exploration of new ones for long-term survival. The cases of Kodak and Apple are two extreme opposites when it comes to dealing with the conflicts between existing and new capabilities.

We argue that, in today's VUCA world, these considerations need to be taken one step further to be explicitly incorporated in organizations' strategies. As organizations should account for the fact that it is often difficult to predict what will work in the future and that the future can come suddenly, they need to allow for higher levels of flexibility in their operations to pivot drastically and quickly when needed. To be able to do this, organizations must pursue multiple and often contradictory strategic avenues.

This book helps decision-makers to shift their mentality from linear to flexible models that incorporate multiple tensions. To this end, the various chapters present a new take on key areas of decision-making by highlighting the tensions that decision-makers need to consider (see Figure 10.1).

Incorporating inter-related tensions

The tensions presented in this book are experienced at multiple levels: individual, organization, and organization-environment. Further complicating matters are the interlinkages between the levels at which tensions are felt (see Table 10.1). That is, an organizational tension will reverberate at lower levels. For instance, the central tension of competing globally (Chapter 2), although it is an organizational tension, is also felt at the team and individual levels. A country manager who needs to deliver the highest possible sales would benefit

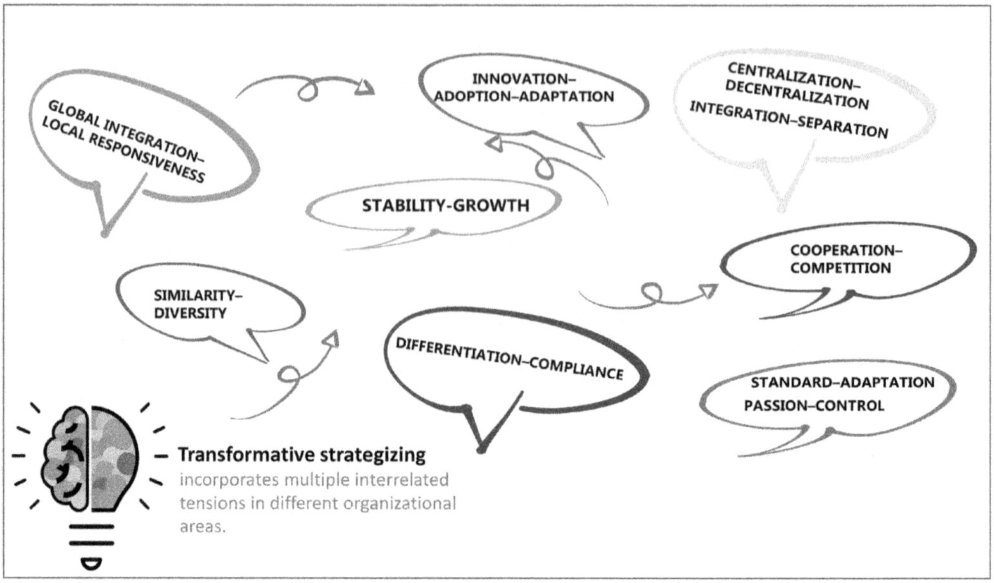

Figure 10.1 Incorporating inter-related tensions

from local responsiveness. However, the country manager also needs to interact with the headquarters and other subsidiaries to secure resources. As such, it needs to balance the local needs for responsiveness with the needs of global integration. The converse also holds - individual-level tensions carry over to the organizational level. An example is the tension felt by an international team leader who must consider that some of her team members prefer individual action, while others prefer collective action (Chapter 9). To successfully manage this tension between the individual and the collective, the manager needs the organization to support her with policies and routines, since, to allow the focus on the individual performance to stimulate rather than inhibit team spirit, changes need to be made in how employees are evaluated and rewarded. The leader might need the organization to introduce a new reward system that provides a bonus to the entire team when one individual performs well, such as coming up with a creative idea. Thus, even though the leader might be the first one to experience this tension, she needs organizational support to enable synergistic effects.

Furthermore, tensions are interlinked not only at different levels, but also between strategic (and organizational) areas. Although we presented the different areas as distinct chapters, it is important to acknowledge that, in practice, it is difficult, if not outright dangerous, to consider them in isolation. It would be naïve to consider changes in business models (Chapter 4) without considering consequences for one's CSR strategy (Chapter 6). Similarly, when developing or implementing a digital strategy (Chapter 5), decision-makers need to consider their leadership approach (Chapter 9). This is because changes in the centralization-adaptation tension are directly related to managing individual standardization-adaptation tensions. Alternatively, attempts to increase decentralization in some aspects of strategy-making, for instance, require leaders to leverage the individual creativity-team spirit tension in their individuals and teams.

Table 10.1 Transformative strategies, tensions, and inter-related tensions

Area	*Central tension*	*Key ideas and transformational strategies*	*Inter-related tensions (examples)*
Chapter 2 Competing globally	Local responsiveness-global integration	To compete on the global stage, organizations need to focus on both increasing revenues through local responsiveness and efficiency through global integrations. For this, they can decentralize customer-facing activities to increase local responsiveness and centralize back-office activities to increase global integration. Organizational design solutions can help organizations to develop locally relevant products and services at the same time as working efficiently.	• Organizations use global centralized platforms and decentralized and localized platforms (Chapter 5) • Organizations compete locally with rival firms while collaborating globally (Chapter 6) • Leadership tensions between standard and adaptation are created as leaders aim to localize practices for maximizing the effectiveness of employees with different backgrounds while, at the same time, they attempt to standardize practices to conform to global standards (Chapter 9)
Chapter 3 Transformative entrepreneurship	Stability-change	As they move through the different stages of the life-cycle, organizations need to manage the tension between stability, associated with the current capabilities, and change, associated with new capabilities and new ways of doing things. Growth requires continuous (re)alignment between changing strategic elements, firm size, and entrepreneurial roles.	• The changing leadership roles as organizations grow create a tension between similarity and diversity, as new leaders and other employees join the organization (Chapter 8). • Firms also need to engage with the innovation-adoption-adaptation tension of business model transformation as they advance though the life cycle stages (Chapter 4).
Chapter 4 Business model innovation	Innovation-adoption-adaptation	Business model innovation oftentimes requires organizations to modify multiple elements of the business model, as it is not always possible to fully leverage new products and services with the existing business model. This requires an understanding of what business model elements to innovate, how to assure adoption by internal and external stakeholders, and continuous adaptation of the new business model.	• Transforming business models requires considering the integration-separation tension (Chapter 5) • Business model transformation also requires a reconsideration of organizations' approach to CSR as their stakeholders are changing (Chapter 7)
Chapter 5 Leading digital strategy	Centralization-decentralization Integration-separation	Established firms encounter several tensions during their attempt to strategize in the context of digital technologies. Organizations may address these tensions by taking innovative approaches and management practices in strategy-making that is built on the principles of inclusivity and openness.	• Leaders need to work on reconciling the passion-control tension as strategizing in the digital era is increasingly expanded beyond the corporate suite (Chapter 9) • New ways of competing, such as platform competition, require firms to reconsider who their competitors and partners are (Chapter 6)

(*Continued*)

Table 10.1 (Continued)

Area	*Central tension*	*Key ideas and transformational strategies*	*Inter-related tensions (examples)*
Chapter 6 Collaborative transformation	Cooperation–competition	To manage this tension, decision-makers need to acknowledge the cooperative and competitive elements in the relationship and establish balanced governance to reconcile this tension, while incorporating different transformation logics to steer the relationship towards success.	• Collaborative arrangements invoke business model innovations creating new cooperative and competitive pressures (Chapter 4) • Business ecosystems enable members to attain corporate goals while serving stakeholders and societal interests (Chapter 7)
Chapter 7 Strategizing corporate social responsibility	Compliance–differentiation	Organizations face a tension in terms of how to design their sustainability practices to either conform or differentiate the organization. To deal with this tension, leaders can think in terms of both conformity and differentiation and identify ways in which these reinforce one another. Leaders play a key role in driving the organizations' CSR practices and they can garner support by employing relational tactics.	• Organizations at different stages in their life cycle can reconcile the CSR tension in different ways (Chapter 3) • CSR responses can depend on the extent to which organizations focus on integration versus local responsiveness in their global strategy (Chapter 2)
Chapter 8 Navigating leadership teams	Diversity–similarity	In order to benefit from both similarity and diversity in leadership teams, and steer away from negative consequences, it is important that leadership manages team faultlines, explicate how the leadership team is embedded in the organization, and invest in building a transactive memory system to capture and leverage prior learnings.	• Business model transformation requires a reconsideration of the extent to which the characteristics of the TMT are aligned with the new logics of creating and capturing values (Chapter 4) • Firms' choice regarding the similarity–diversity tensions affect their abilities to reconcile leadership tensions between standard and adaptation (Chapter 9)
Chapter 9 A trans-cultural leadership paradigm	Standard–adaptation Passion–control	(Global) leaders are confronted with trans-cultural dilemmas and need to change their frame of mind from 'either/or' thinking to 'both' and 'through' thinking. Leaders need to challenge themselves and their teams to think of how by focusing on one aspect they can enhance the other – such as developing routines that promote adaptation to cultural expectations.	• Leaders need to shift between leading a global company (universal dilemmas) and leading local subsidiaries (contextual dilemmas) (Chapter 2) • Digital transformation requires a consideration of the extent to which passion and control are incorporated in the organization (Chapter 5)

Therefore, the level of complexity in dealing with tensions comes from the interrelatedness of the tensions discussed in this book. These tensions are interrelated at different levels in the organization as well as between elements of strategy and organizing. So, does this mean that managing tensions for the entire organization is an insurmountable task? We have great belief in the ability of decision-makers to find ways to thrive amid tensions rather than be intimidated or defeated by them. While this might be easier said than done, the next section offers some thoughts on how decision-makers (i.e., leaders and followers) can make these shifts towards embracing tensions. As the concept of yin and yang suggests, both sides are needed to make a whole. This also applies to competition and, even more so, in today's VUCA business environment.

In pursuit of transformative strategizing

As the book shows so far, organizations need to incorporate multiple tensions in order to compete successfully in a VUCA world. Together, these tensions can be considered under the general concept of organizational hybridity, which refers to 'the combination of identities, forms, logics, or other core elements that would conventionally not go together' (Smith and Besharov 2019). As we have seen so far in this book, many organizations tend to work on reducing tensions rather than embracing them. And while some might be able to find ways to identify and implement synergies between conflicting strategic actions, they are rarely able to do so for long periods. Also, because organizations are likely to experience a different combination of tensions depending on, for instance, their life stage (Chapter 3) or degree of digitalization (Chapter 5), it is difficult to provide definite solutions on how to deal with tensions. What does help is to provide guiding principles for developing an organization where transformative strategizing thrives.

Incorporating tensions in organizations in the long term

An important way in which organizations can sustain transformative strategizing over time is through structured flexibility (Smith and Besharov 2019). Decision-makers start by identifying the tension's sides. Through discussion, they can explore these sides and their importance for the organization. The expertise decision-makers and other organizational members develop about these two sides can act as boundaries of action. As discussed so far in the book, the two sides are to be considered contradictory and desirable. That is, both are necessary for successful long-term competition, as is the case of global strategies where a focus on increasing revenues (through local responsiveness) needs to be balanced by consideration of costs (through global integration). Within these boundaries, organizations can establish enactment processes, including confronting strategic tensions, interpreting what they mean for the organizational members' identity, and experimenting with practices (Smith and Besharov 2019). In other words, after uncovering and clarifying the two sides of the tension, leaders should establish routines for experimenting with new practices that can potentially create synergies.

Importantly, this process of understanding the tension, its sides, and experimenting with new practices should be a continuous process since environmental changes mean that the tensions or their meaning can change over time.

Enabling the practice of management innovation

To be able to transform organizations in a way that allows the incorporation of tensions, it is necessary to introduce new ways to manage. Management innovation refers to the introduction of new management practices, processes, and structures that are new to the firm and intended to further organizational goals (Mol and Birkinshaw 2009: 1270). Famous examples of management innovation include the introduction of total quality management by Toyota or the virtual organization by Visa. These new ways to manage and organize introduced by Toyota and Visa are considered largely responsible for both companies' rise and their subsequent sustained performance.

There are three types of management innovation: new to the world, new to the firm and implemented with adaptation, or new to the firm and implemented without adaptation (Volberda, Van Den Bosch and Mihalache 2014). Management innovation does not come naturally for most organizations because it is more tacit than product innovation and its boundaries tend to be more difficult to identify (Birkinshaw, Hamel, and Mol 2008). Furthermore, unlike for product innovation, most organizations do not have routines for innovating in their management practices. This means that while many organizations actively try to develop new products and services that are relevant in a changing world, they do not engage in similar attempts to seek new ways to manage. Consequently, many organizations are stuck with traditional ways to manage that are not appropriate in today's VUCA environment.

Although difficult to achieve, new-to-the-world management innovation has the potential to provide long-term benefits as it tends to be valuable, rare, inimitable, and can be exploited by the organization (Hamel 2006; Mol and Birkinshaw 2009). Management innovation does not have to be new to the world, as organizations can adopt and adapt (if necessary) management practices of other companies. As the barriers to developing new management practices tend to be high (that is, a lack of internal routines and capabilities), many organizations adopt rather than develop management practices. In this process, both external and internal change agents play important roles and the successful implementation depends not only on their respective activities, but also on how they interact (cf. Volberda et al. 2014). External change agents such as management consultants can help an organization to implement new management practices, processes, or structures that they might not be able to identify by themselves.

> Management innovation is necessary because accommodating tensions within organizations requires new management principles, practices, and structures.

Developing new ways to manage is paramount for supporting tensions within the organizations, because existing management theories are developed with the opposite goal in mind; that is, that of creating alignment or removing tensions. Generally, the top management team (TMT) plays a key role in stimulating management innovation. Since management innovation tends to be systemic (Birkinshaw et al. 2008), organizational leadership needs to support such initiatives. Vaccaro et al. (2012) showed that leadership processes that introduce a system of challenging the status quo can stimulate management innovation. In line with this way of thinking, Mihalache et al. (2014) found that reflexivity and minority dissent in TMTs can help organizations to increase their levels of management innovation. Reflexivity is 'the extent to which team members collectively reflect on and adapt their team's objectives, strategies, and processes' (Tjosvold, Tang, and West 2004: 542) and minority dissent refers to 'instances in which a minority in a group publicly opposed the beliefs, attitudes, ideas, procedures, or policies assumed by the majority of the group' (De Dreu and West 2001).

Box 10.1 Crisis management

The COVID-19 pandemic created a health, social, and economic crisis. Taking a business perspective, one could argue that a crisis is nothing more than an extreme, yet temporary, VUCA environment, requiring decision-makers to reconcile tensions such as 'health versus economy', 'top-down decision-making versus bottom-up decision-making, and 'leveraging existing markets versus developing new markets'. To navigate a crisis, decision-makers may consider the following steps:

Resolve: Resolution entails an immediate and effective response to the crisis situation, preferably based on available crisis plans. For example, as the COVID-19 pandemic spread, businesses launched a large array of interventions, such as focusing on cost savings, securing supply, and employee safety.

Resilience: Leveraging organizational resilience is a necessity when faced with a crisis (e.g., secure liquidity). Companies need to effectuate resilience plans as the shock begins to upturn established industry structures and reset competitive positions. Leaders will need to make difficult decisions that balance economic viability and social sustainability.

Return: Returning businesses to operational viability after a crisis is extremely challenging. Leaders must reassess their entire business system and plan for contingent actions in order to return their business to effective production at pace and at scale.

Reimagination: A crisis will create a discontinuous shift in the preferences and expectations of customers. Reimagination results in a stronger sense of what makes business more resilient to shocks, more productive, and better able to deliver to customers. Leaders will need to reconsider the cost structure, assess how far to flex operations, and capture opportunities to push technology adoption.

Reform: Leaders need to anticipate changes to policies and regulations as stakeholders seeks to avoid, mitigate, and preempt a future crisis. The aftermath of a crisis will also provide an opportunity to learn from a plethora of social innovations and experiments.

Source: Sneader and Singhal (2020).

Both processes introduce a precipitating dynamic that stimulates change. Therefore, the introduction of new ways to manage is essential for developing transformative strategies that incorporate tensions.

Leadership for transformative strategizing and strategies

Leaders (across all echelons) play a key role in incorporating tensions because leaders' characteristics and actions affect both the strategy content and, subsequently, organizational outcomes (e.g., Cannella, Park, and Lee 2008; Hambrick and Mason 1984; Simons, Pelled, and Smith 1999). One of the key roles of organizational leaders in supporting tensions within the organization is to act as the glue that brings all perspectives together. To be able to achieve this, leaders' actions need to be based on the principles of *discovery* and *integration*. This will allow them not only to discover different points of view but also to integrate those diverse perspectives.

Shared leadership. One way in which the TMT can promote discovery and integration is by engaging in shared leadership. Shared leadership refers to the extent to which TMT members share the task of leadership (such as setting goals or motivating employees) rather than being concentrated in the CEO (Carson, Tesluk, and Marrone 2007). In an empirical study of over 200 Dutch organizations, Mihalache et al. (2014) found that organizations whose TMTs engage to a greater extent in shared leadership are more likely to exhibit higher levels of both exploiting current capabilities and developing new capabilities for the future. Such sharing of roles is particularly important in allowing the organization to incorporate and even leverage tensions because it holds the promise to overcome CEO biases.

Shared leadership promotes decision-making comprehensiveness as it gives voice to different people's perspectives. This is especially important as the TMT members tend to have different backgrounds and be responsible for different parts of the business, which means they are likely to see the world differently. Also, shared leadership stimulates the integration of different perspectives as it requires a more cooperative conflict management style. When sharing responsibilities, TMT members are more likely to perceive goals structure as collective rather than distinct (Tjosvold, Poon, and Yu 2005) and will, consequently, tend to look for win-win solutions (Rahim 1983).

Sharing leadership tasks within the top management team can also have the added effect of lowering the cognitive demands for the CEO. Leading organizations that incorporate tensions at multiple levels and that link multiple functional areas might be overwhelming for a single individual. Thus, shared leadership might provide the TMT with cognitive benefits to more easily understand and manage multiple tensions across the organization.

Leading by example. Leading organizations that incorporate tensions require leaders to juggle multiple leadership styles. The idea that leaders can use different leadership styles was put forward half a century ago in the situational leadership theory (Hersey and Blanchard 1969). The main point of the theory was that leaders need to adapt their leadership style to the level of their followers' sophistication. We believe that similar logic needs to be applied to leading organizations that incorporate tensions, with the difference that changes in leadership style depend not only on the maturity of followers but also on goals.

Since a tension implies contrasting elements, employing a single leadership style cannot achieve opposing goals. Consequently, we argue that leaders need to juggle between different leadership styles in order to be able to support competing strategic actions. This idea is supported in existing management research by studies showing that different styles of leadership lead to different innovation outcomes. Transformational leadership behaviors stimulate the development of new capabilities, as they encourage generative thinking, and transactional leadership behaviors stimulate the exploitation of current capabilities (Jansen, Vera, and Crossan 2009). When it comes to innovation, such changes in leadership style are important because leaders' actions affect the perceived support for experimentation (e.g., Damanpour 1991; West and Anderson 1992) or the learning culture through perceived tolerance of failed ideas (Shalley and Perry-Smith 2001).

Moral leadership. Moral leadership is about providing values or meaning for people to live by, inspiration to act, and motivation to hold oneself accountable (Blank 2019). Moral leaders guide themselves with values and ethics that they develop over time and with experience. They have a sense of self and are not threatened by others, as leading is about serving others. They do not impose their values on others, and instead consider other people's values. Moral leaders do not fear change; they have the courage and conviction to share a vision to try and bring about positive change. Moral leaders communicate and unite people around a (societal) purpose that inspires. Transformative strategizing associates with moral leadership. This is because reconciling tensions is inherently tied to being sensitive to minority interests, being appreciative of competing stakeholder interests, and being open to out-of-the box and unexpected contributions, all relevant to inspire, engage and give meaningful direction to organizational and societal members.

Taken together, we propose that leaders enacting transformative strategizing need to start by understanding the tensions within their organizations and then change their leadership behaviors to match contrasting needs. This is certainly not an easy task, as it might challenge leaders to go outside of their comfort zones. However, such leadership juggling can help the organization accept and pursue conflicting strategic actions.

Dualities in strategic communication

We propose that leaders can support tensions within the organization through dualities in strategic communications. The tendency of many corporate communications might be to provide a single clear message throughout the organization. However, just like employing a single leadership style, a single message might not be able to achieve conflicting organizational goals. An organization that incorporates inconsistencies is likely to require a complex communication strategy to ensure that stakeholders engage in the required actions. Since communication serves to legitimize different activities, attempts to support opposing strategic action require specific messaging that supports these conflicting actions. In other words, to enact transformative strategies, leaders might be better off disregarding the common wisdom of delivering a consistent message, as consistent communication can be biased towards a certain group of stakeholders.

An example of this type of inconsistent communication was exhibited by Ericsson's CEO in 2010. While in several communications he promoted 'full alignment of all regional and business unit strategies', in the company's annual report he emphasized the importance of a 'customer-first perspective' (Khanagha et al. 2018: 1104). The communications emphasizing a focus on global integration contrast with the annual report's focus on local responsiveness. While the CEO's messaging might initially appear to indicate a lack of clarity regarding the direction of the organization, upon further inspection, it might help the organization to pursue both global integration and local responsiveness, as discussed in Chapter 2. Thus, strategic ambiguity in corporate communication can support the pursuit of apparently conflicting strategic actions.

Transformative strategizing as reflexive practice

Decision-makers are confronted with accelerating rates of change, uncertainty, and ambiguity, and often work in politicized organizations where they have to deal with a variety of strategic, organizational, and ethical issues. To navigate these challenges, it is important that they continuously develop their ways of thinking and managing.

The starting point of a personal development process is understanding oneself. Reflexive practice provides opportunities to surface values, pressures, and interests by encouraging decision-makers to examine the assumptions that underpin choices (Cunliffe 2004). In examining assumptions, limitations and possibilities are uncovered, prompting decision-makers to steer away from institutionalized responses, as reflexive practices enable them to bridge theory (know-what) and practice (know-how). Reflexive practice is not just about looking back at past actions and events, but instead pertains to systematically investigating emotions, experiences, actions, and responses and use retrieved insights to enhance his/her knowledge foundation to reach a higher level of understanding (Schön 1983).

But how may one enact reflexive practice? Individuals construct social realities and a sense of self through interactions with others. Reflexive practice, therefore, demands from decision-makers that they think about how they construct realities and identities together with others. Departing from this understanding, decision-makers may then engage in reflective analysis, followed by reflexive questioning. Reflective analysis draws on the notion that an objective reality can be analyzed using logic and theory. In turn, reflexive questioning entails an effort to articulate subjective, multiple, and constructed realities. Critically reflexive questioning means exposing contradictions, doubts, dilemmas, and possibilities. To attain this, leaders may use a variety of techniques, including journaling, practicing observation, guided intervision, and group exercises (see Cunliffe 2004). When reflection and reflexivity guide action, a decision-maker will transition from single-loop learning - problem solving, and identifying and correcting errors - to double-loop learning -questioning assumptions, values and espoused theories and inventing and evaluating new theories in action (Argyris 1982).

Reflexive practice enables decision-makers to understand how they construct their realities and identities and how they can develop more collaborative and responsive ways of leading organizations. Enacting transformative strategizing successfully requires that strategists adopt systematic and deliberate approaches towards professional development. Though critical for personal development, experience, (external) consultation, and (formal) education are simply insufficient to fully embrace transformative strategizing. For example, engaging in reflexive practice enables leaders to become critical thinkers and moral practitioners; it assures that leaders will have a profound impact on followers, organizations, and society (Cunliffe 2004).

Concluding remark

In this book, we have put forward the idea that, to compete successfully in a VUCA environment, organizations need to develop and deploy transformative strategies. That is, they need to incorporate tensions in their strategy content and implementation so that they can pivot quickly and drastically when needed. The book identifies important tensions for several areas of strategy that decision-makers need to consider. Each chapter challenges the reader to translate these general tensions to their organization. The book concludes with a discussion on the interrelatedness of tensions and provides several guiding principles for engaging in transformative strategizing. We hope that these ideas will stimulate managers to shift their mindsets from reducing to leveraging tensions.

References

Argyris, C. (1982) *Reasoning, learning, and action: Individual and organizational*. San Francisco: Jossey-Bass.

Birkinshaw, J., Hamel, G., and Mol, M. J. (2008) 'Management innovation'. *Academy of Management Review*, 33(4): 825-845.

Blank, A. (2019) '5 ways to step up and become a moral leader'. Available online at https://www.weforum.org/agenda/2019/08/5-ways-moral-leader (accessed 27 July 2020).

Cannella Jr., A. A., Park, J. H., and Lee, H. U. (2008) 'Top management team functional background diversity and firm performance: Examining the roles of team member colocation and environmental uncertainty'. *Academy of Management Journal*, 51(4): 768-784.

Carson, J. B., Tesluk, P. E., Marrone, J. A. (2007) 'Shared leadership in teams: an investigation of antecedent conditions and performance'. *Academy of Management Journal*, 50(5): 1217-1234.

Cunliffe, A. L. (2004) 'On becoming a critically reflexive practitioner'. *Journal of Management Education*, 28(4): 407-426.

Damanpour, F. (1991) 'Organizational innovation: A meta-analysis of effects of determinants and moderators'. *Academy of Management Journal*, 34(3): 555-590.

De Dreu, C. K. and West, M. A. (2001) 'Minority dissent and team innovation: The importance of participation in decision making'. *Journal of Applied Psychology*, 86(6): 1191-1201.

Deutsch, C. H. (2008) 'At Kodak, Some Old Things Are New Again'. *The New York Times*. Available online at https://www.nytimes.com/2008/05/02/technology/02kodak.html (accessed 22 December 2020).

Hambrick, D. C., and Mason, P. A. (1984) 'Upper echelons: The organization as a reflection of its top managers'. *Academy of Management Review*, 9(2): 193-206.

Hamel, G. (2006) 'The why, what, and how of management innovation'. *Harvard Business Review*, 84(2): 72.

Hersey, P. and Blanchard, K. H. (1969) *Management of Organizational Behavior - Utilizing Human Resources*. New Jersey: Prentice Hall.

Jansen, J. J., Vera, D., and Crossan, M. (2009) 'Strategic leadership for exploration and exploitation: The moderating role of environmental dynamism'. *The Leadership Quarterly*, 20(1): 5-18.

Khanagha, S., Ramezan Zadeh, M. T., Mihalache, O. R., and Volberda, H. W. (2018) 'Embracing bewilderment: Responding to technological disruption in heterogeneous market environments'. *Journal of Management Studies*, 55(7): 1079-1121.

Mihalache, O. R., Jansen, J. J., Van den Bosch, F. A., and Volberda, H. W. (2014) 'Top management team shared leadership and organizational ambidexterity: A moderated mediation framework'. *Strategic Entrepreneurship Journal*, 8(2): 128-148.

Mihalache, M. and Mihalache, O. R. (2016). Organizational ambidexterity and sustained performance in the tourism industry. *Annals of Tourism Research*, 56: 142-144.

Mol, M. J., and Birkinshaw, J. (2009) 'The sources of management innovation: When firms introduce new management practices'. *Journal of Business Research*, 62(12): 1269-1280.

Rahim, M. A. (1983) 'A measure of styles of handling interpersonal conflict'. *Academy of Management Journal*, 26(2): 368–376.

Schön, D. A. (1983) *The Reflective Practitioner: How Professionals Think in Action*. London: Taylor & Francis Ltd.

Shalley, C. E. and Perry-Smith, J. E. (2001) 'Effects of social-psychological factors on creative performance: The role of informational and controlling expected evaluation and modeling experience'. *Organizational behavior and human decision processes*, 84(1): 1-22.

Simons, T., Pelled, L. H., and Smith, K. A. (1999) 'Making use of difference: Diversity, debate, and decision comprehensiveness in top management teams'. *Academy of Management Journal*, 42(6): 662–673.

Smith, W. K. and Besharov, M. L. (2019) 'Bowing before dual gods: How structured flexibility sustains organizational hybridity'. *Administrative Science Quarterly*, 64(1): 1–44.

Sneader, K. and Singhal, S. (2020) 'Beyond coronavirus: The path to the next normal'. *McKinsey & Company*. Available online at https://fedcapgroup.org/storage/2020/04/Beyond-coronavirus-The-path-to-the-next-normal.pdf (accessed 17 December 2020).

Tjosvold, D., Poon, M., and Yu, Z. (2005) 'Team effectiveness in China: cooperative conflict for relationship building'. *Human Relations*, 58(3): 341–367.

Tjosvold, D., Tang, M. M., and West, M. (2004) 'Reflexivity for team innovation in China: The contribution of goal interdependence'. *Group & Organization Management*, 29(5): 540–559.

Volberda, H. W., Van Den Bosch, F. A., and Mihalache, O. R. (2014) 'Advancing management innovation: Synthesizing processes, levels of analysis, and change agents'. *Organization Studies*, 35(9): 1245-1264.

Vaccaro, I. G., Jansen, J. J., Van Den Bosch, F. A., and Volberda, H. W. (2012) 'Management innovation and leadership: The moderating role of organizational size'. *Journal of Management Studies*, 49(1): 28–51.

West, M. A., and Anderson, N. (1992) 'Innovation, cultural values, and the management of change in British hospitals'. *Work & Stress*, 6(3): 293-310.

Yarow, J. (2011) 'The Best Steve Jobs Quotes From His Biography'. *Business Insider*. Available online at https://www.businessinsider.com/best-steve-jobs-quotes-from-biography-2011-10?international=true&r=US&IR=T (accessed 17 December 2020).

11 Appendix
Strategic management theories

Co-evolutionary perspective

Co-evolution is rooted in the tradition of population ecology and evolutionary theory and refers to the simultaneous development of organizations and their environment, both independently and interactively. Co-evolution assumes that change may occur in all interacting populations of organizations, which allows changes to be driven both by direct interaction and by feedback. The theory of co-evolution suggests that natural selection (that is, the argument that an organization that fits with its environment has a greater chance of survival) does take place, but that the change in organizations results in favorable inherited traits that bestow certain advantages. Co-evolution occurs in a population consisting of heterogeneous firms that have adaptive learning capability, and who are able to interact and mutually influence each other. In addition, some initiating event, which can be either internal or external, is present to trigger the co-evolutionary process. This dynamic interaction between organizations and environment implies that organizations represent adaptive entities that, based on learning and experience, engage in a continuous and interrelated self-renewal processes in an attempt to seek and maintain fit. A co-evolutionary view captures multi-directional causalities over a long period of time, in which the outcomes of co-evolution are emergent and in which changes in any one variable (e.g., micro or macro level) may be caused endogenously by changes in the other. Consequently, a co-evolutionary view is made up of dynamic trajectories evoked by drivers that enable and restrict change within an environment.

References

Barnett, W. P. and Burgelman, R. A. (1996) 'Evolutionary perspectives on strategy'. *Strategic Management Journal*, 17: 5-1.

Hannan, M. T. and Freeman, J. (1977) 'Population ecology of organizations'. *American Journal of Sociology*, 82: 929-964.

Jacobides, M. G. and Winter, S. G. (2005) 'The co-evolution of capabilities and transaction costs: Explaining the institutional structure of production'. *Strategic Management Journal*, 26: 395-413.

Volberda, H. W. and Lewin, A. Y. (2003) 'Guest editors' introduction - Co-evolutionary dynamics within and between firms: From evolution to co-evolution'. *Journal of Management Studies*, 40: 2111-2136.

Dynamic capability view

Dynamic capability refers to a firm's ability to integrate, build, and reconfigure internal and external competences to address rapidly changing environments. The concept of dynamic capabilities arose from a shortcoming of the resource-based view (RBV) of the firm. The RBV has been criticized for ignoring factors surrounding the creation of resources, instead assuming that they simply 'exist'. Adopting a process approach, dynamic capabilities act as a buffer between firm resources and the changing business environment. The basic assumption of the dynamic capabilities framework is that core competencies should be used to modify short-term competitive positions that can be used to build a longer-term competitive advantage. Dynamic capabilities help a firm to adjust its resource mix and thereby maintain the sustainability of the firm's competitive advantage, which otherwise might be quickly eroded. Dynamic capabilities deployment entails three processes: the capacity to (i) sense and shape opportunities and threats; (ii) seize opportunities; and (iii) maintain competitiveness through enhancing, combining, protecting, and, when necessary, reconfiguring the business enterprise's intangible and tangible assets. It can be divided into three types: (i) organizations and their employees need the capability to learn quickly and to build strategic assets; (ii) new strategic assets such as capability, technology, and customer feedback have to be integrated within the company; and (iii) existing strategic assets have to be transformed or reconfigured.

References

Eisenhardt, K. and Martin, J. (2000) 'Dynamic capabilities: what are they?' *Strategic Management Journal*, 21: 1105-1121.

Makadok, R. (2001) 'Toward a synthesis of the resource-based and dynamic-capability views of rent creation.' *Strategic Management Journal*, 22(5): 387-402

Teece, D. J., Pisano, G., and Shuen, A. (1997) 'Dynamic capabilities and strategic management'. *Strategic Management Journal*, 18: 509-533.

Game theory

The field of game theory (GT) came into being with the 1944 classic *Theory of Games and Economic Behavior* by John von Neumann and Oskar Morgenstern. GT has played and will continue to play an important role in the social sciences and is now used in many diverse academic fields. A branch of mathematical analysis, GT was developed to study decision-making in conflict situations. Such situations exist when two or more decision-makers who have different objectives act on the same system or share the same resources. GT provides a mathematical process for selecting an optimum strategy, that is, an optimum decision or a sequence of decisions in the face of an opponent who has a strategy of his or her own. Thus, GT is a theory of rational behavior for situations in which (i) two or more actors have available to them (ii) a finite number of courses of action, each leading to (iii) a well-defined outcome with gains and losses expressed in terms of numerical payoffs associated with each combination of courses of action and for each decision maker; the actors also have (iv) perfect knowledge of the rules of the game – that is, (i), (ii) and (iii) – but no knowledge about the opponents' moves and are (v) rational in the sense that they make decisions that optimize their individual gains. GT has been criticized as, for example, is neglects to account for the personalities of the players, their social ties, the communication between the players, norm-building, institutional rules, and its simplistic assumption of hyper-rationality.

References

Camerer, C. F. (1991) 'Does strategy research need game theory?' *Strategic Management Journal*, 12: 137–152.
Von Neumann, J. and Morgenstern, O. (1944) *Theory of games and economic behavior*. New Jersey: Princeton University Press.

Industrial organization

Industrial organization is a field that builds on the theory of the firm by examining the structure of firms and markets. Industrial organization adds real-world complications to the perfectly competitive model, complications such as transaction costs, limited information, and barriers to entry of new firms that may be associated with imperfect competition. The structure-conduct-performance (SCP) paradigm states that market structure would determine firm conduct which would determine performance. Market structure can be measured by the number of competitors in an industry, the heterogeneity of product and the cost of entry and exit. Conduct refers to a number of specific actions taken by a firm, which include price taking, product differentiation, tacit collusion, and exploitation of market power. The performance of the firm can be measured with productive efficiency, allocative efficiency and profitability. Drawing on the SCP model, Porter's (1980) view on industrial organization stipulates that performance heterogeneity between firms can be explained by a firm's ability to occupy a unique market position in an industry. Porter's five forces framework is a method for analyzing competition of a business and stipulates that five forces determine the competitive intensity and, therefore, the attractiveness (or lack thereof) of an industry in terms of its profitability. An 'unattractive' industry is one in which the effect of these five forces reduces overall profitability. The most unattractive industry would be one approaching 'pure competition', in which available profits for all firms are driven to normal profit levels. The five forces are: (i) threat of new entrants; (ii) threat of substitutes; (iii) bargaining power of customers; (iv) bargaining power of suppliers; and (v) competitive rivalry. Porter also introduced three (four) generic strategies: cost-leadership, differentiation, and focus. A firm may be attempting to offer a lower cost in that scope (cost focus) or differentiate itself in that scope (differentiation focus).

References

Bain, J. S. (1959) *Industrial organization: A treatise*. New York: John Wiley.
Porter, M. E. (1980) *Competitive strategy*. New York: Free Press.
Porter, M. E. (1981) 'The contributions of industrial organization to strategic management'. *Academy of Management Review*, 6(4): 609–620.
Porter, M. E. (1985) *Competitive advantage*. New York: Free Press.

Institutional theory

With an open system perspective, institutional theory (IT) states that firms are strongly influenced by their external environments. Influenced by economic factors, such as industry regulations, rival behavior, and socially constructed norms and beliefs, firms organize their boundary-spanning activities to mimic other firms. That is, firms pursue activities that increase their legitimacy and cause them to appear in agreement with the prevailing rules, requirements, and norms in their business environments (Dimaggio and Powell 1983), as these rules establish bases for production, exchange, and distribution. With this logic, IT can answer how and why firms enact specific strategic decisions. In particular, this school of thought states that firms aim for legitimacy and social approval, rather than effectiveness or efficiency. Legitimacy helps ensure that the initiative receives a certain level of acceptance; without it, the initiative is unlikely to persist. Such legitimacy can be enhanced by strategic decisions, initiatives that may improve the focal firm's reputation or congruence with prevailing norms. When social behavior becomes accepted, it turns into an institution, and institutions give industry members a clearly laid route to success and lead to a bandwagon effect (Venkatraman, Koh, and Low. 1994). Bandwagon pressures also imply a lack of clarity in the firm's cost-benefit calculations. Alternatively, this pressure might induce firms to hire managers with similar industry backgrounds and experiences, who are familiar with industry practices. Beyond bandwagon pressures, firms may engage in status-driven imitations of their peers. This view of strategic decision-making implies a process of mimetic isomorphism: firms follow established rules and norms and copy, consciously or not, their successful peers. The resulting legitimacy and reputation can open doors to other initiatives that help the firm gain access to additional critical resources.

References

DiMaggio, P. J. and Powell, W. W. (1983) 'The iron cage revisited - Institutional isomorphism and collective rationality in organizational fields'. *American Sociological Review*, 48: 147–160.

Scott, W. R. (2003) *Organizations: Rational, natural and open systems*. Upper Saddle River, NJ: Prentice Hall.

Venkatraman, N., Koh, J., and Loh, L. (1994) 'The adoption of corporate governance mechanisms: A test of competing diffusion models'. *Management Science*, 40: 496–507.

Organizational change and learning

Within the strategic management field, different theories and approaches have been presented on organizational change and learning. Critiquing a deterministic-structural design view on organizations, strategic choice theory states that dominant elites within organizations have free choice in designing and therefore modifying their organizational configurations (Child 1972). Offering an extension to population ecology change explanations, structural inertia theorists stipulate that organizational change is hindered by a structural resistance against fundamental reorganization (Hannan and Freeman 1984). Critiquing the rational assumption of economic behavior, Evolutionary economists believe the economy is dynamic, constantly changing, and chaotic. Evolutionary economists propose that economic processes evolve and emerge from actions of diverse agents with bounded rationality who may learn from experience and interactions and whose differences contribute to the change. In developing their 'evolutionary theory of economic change', Nelson and Winter (1982) view firms as a collection of heterogeneous organizations guided by routines. Firms search for innovative (or imitative) solution to improve their profits, with successful firms growing at the expense of the less successful. The process is fundamentally dynamic, as firms interact and create the relative competitive environment that each faces.

References

Child, J. (1972) 'Organization structure, environment and performance: The role of strategic choice.' *Sociology*, 6: 1-22.

Hannan, M. T., and Freeman, J. (1984) 'Structural inertia and organizational change.' *American Sociological Review*, 49: 149-164.

Nelson, R. R. and Winter, S. G. (1982) *An evolutionary theory of economic change*. Belknap Press/Harvard University Press: Cambridge.

Resource-based view

The resource-based view of the firm (RBV) has emerged as one of several important explanations of firm performance differences in the field of strategic management and its main contribution is that it developed the idea that a can maximize its value by pooling and exploiting its valuable resources. According to the resource-based view (RBV), firms attempt to find an optimal resource boundary that ensures the value of their resources is realized best, compared with other resource combinations. A competitive advantage results when the firm can implement a value-creating strategy that is not being implemented simultaneously by its (potential) competitors. The core logics that distinguish it from other strategic management theories are resource heterogeneity and resource immobility. Specifically, a competitive advantage requires the firm to possess valuable, rare, inimitable and non-substitutable resources (VRIN). The heterogeneity assumption implies that competing firms may possess different bundles of valuable and scarce resources. The immobility assumptions implies that firms' resource endowments are persistent and difficult to transfer. That is, a particular resource does not become available, though demand for that resource is high. Building on these assumptions, the main RBV proposition is that VRIN resources foster a sustainable competitive advantage (Barney, 1991). However, the RBV is not without critiques, as researchers have argued that the RBV is tautological, views value creation as endogenous, neglects to incorporate value appropriation, and is subject to measurement problems, among other issues.

References

Barney, J. B. (1991) 'Firm resources and sustained competitive advantage'. *Journal of Management*, 17: 99-120.

Priem, R. L. and Butler, J. E. (2001) 'Is the resource-based "view" a useful perspective for strategic management research?' *Academy of Management Review*, 26(1): 22-40.

Rumelt, R. P. (1984) 'Towards a strategic theory of the firm'. In Lamb, R. B. (ed.), *Competitive strategic management*. Englewood Cliffs, NJ: Prentice-Hall, (556-570).

Wernerfelt, B. (1984) 'A resource-based view of the firm'. *Strategic Management Journal*, 5(2): 171-180.

Resource dependence perspective

The resource dependence perspective (RDP) is rooted in an open system framework: firms are embedded sets of relationships, which renders them dependent on their external environment. Firms cannot generate all the resources or functions they need to maintain themselves, so they must enter into transactions and relations with external actors that can supply those required resources. A firm's ability to control external resources determines its survival and provides power over external parties. Power originates through resource scarcity, which reflects three sources. First, the importance of an external resource - or the extent to which the firm needs the resource to survive - reduces a firm's relative power. In particular, intangible resources such as patents, trademarks, market or technological know-how, and human competences tend to be pivotal, whereas tangible resources, such as commodities, can be effectively obtained through market exchanges. Second, a firm's discretion over the resource allocation and use (e.g., ownership rights, access) increases its relative power. Third, the extent to which desired resources can be substituted by alternative resources decreases the firm's relative power. With this focus on desired resources, the RDP contributes insights into why firms engage in external relations, such as mergers, acquisitions, and alliances. At the heart of the RDP rests the notion that two firms prefer to avoid becoming dependent on each other's resources. To reduce uncertainty and increase its relative power, a firm may seek to become autonomous by managing its external relationships with a two-fold strategy to acquire control over (i) critical resources to decrease dependence on other firms and (ii) resources that increase the dependence of other firms on it.

References

Aldrich, H. E. and Pfeffer, J. (1976) 'Environments of organization'. *Annual Review of Sociology*, 2: 79-105.

Pfeffer, J. and Salancik, G. R. (1978) *The external control of organizations: A resource dependence perspective*. New York: Harper and Row.

Strategic agility and renewal

To cope with growing strategic discontinuities and disruptions, scholars have suggested the creation of strategically agile companies. Strategic agility entails the creation of new business models and new customer offerings rather than rearranging old products or services. Agile organizations are able to enact business transformation and renewal, continuously develop new dynamic capabilities, create imitation abilities, adopt new ways of working characterized by organizational flexibility and ambidexterity, develop learning and knowledge transfer skills, install an adaptive corporate culture, and more. Agile organizations have the ability to enact continuous renewal that includes adapting existing competencies to an ever-changing environment and simultaneously reconfiguring themselves in order to survive and thrive for the long term.

Strategic renewal is the process of (strategic) change that has the potential to determine the long-term competitiveness of a firm. The objective of strategic renewal is to provide a strategic fit between a firm's capabilities and changes in the external environment. Incremental renewal occurs through a series of regular adaptations to changes in the commercial environment. Transformational renewal is brought about through radical shifts in strategic management and the removal or replacement of key functions and units in the firm. To survive and remain viable, it is imperative that firms become strategic ambidextrous and agile (i.e., maintain fit). Though some external shifts are cataclysmic, competence destroying changes that extinguish the inner core of the firm and do not allow it to renew its business operations.

References

Agarwal, R. and Helfat, C. E. (2009) 'Strategic renewal of organizations'. *Organization Science*, 20(2), 281-293.

Lewis, M. W., Andriopoulos, C., and Smith, W. K. (2014) 'Paradoxical leadership to enable strategic agility.' *California Management Review*, 56(3): 58-77.

Weber, Y. and Tarba, S. (2014) 'Strategic Agility: A state of the art: Introduction to the special section on strategic agility'. *California Management Review*, 56(3): 5-12.

Schmitt, A., Raisch, S., and Volberda, H. W. (2018) 'Strategic renewal: Past research, theoretical tensions and future challenges'. *International Journal of Management Reviews*, 20: 81-98.

Transaction cost economics

Transaction cost economics (TCE) theory examines the transaction cost advantages of two different governance forms: hierarchy and market exchange. Two assumptions and three exchange conditions constitute the core of TCE logic. The first assumption involves opportunism, or behavior that is self-interested and deceptive. The logic thus holds that managers are inclined to break, whether implicitly and explicitly, the rules that govern a transaction. A second assumption refers to bounded rationality. That is, despite the firm's efforts to deal with complexity and unpredictability, managers have only limited ability to plan for the future and predict various contingencies that may arise. The potential for opportunistic behavior and the constraints of bounded rationality pose severe problems for governing transactions, because they drive transaction costs higher and require firms to protect themselves against exploitation. At the core of TCE are the axioms that certain exchange characteristics give rise to transaction difficulties and that different governance mechanisms vary in their cost-minimizing properties. For instance, transactions with an uncertain outcome, that recur frequently, and that require substantial transaction investments (i.e., asset specificity) are more efficiently organized through a hierarchical governance form. Exchanges that are straightforward, non-repetitive, and that require few transaction-specific investments are more likely to be organized through market exchange. Restated, firms reduce transaction costs by selecting a governance mode that is optimal, given the transaction properties (i.e., discriminating alignment). Researchers have criticized TCE arguing that it puts too much emphasis on opportunistic behavior, neglects the role of relational governance, fails to recognize the potential value generated by transaction-specific investments, represents a static approach that ignores issues pertaining to learning and innovation, and does not take into account interdependencies between the parties in a relationship.

References

Coase, R. H. (1937) 'The nature of the firm'. *Economica*, 4(16): 385-405.

Williamson, O. E. (1975) *Markets and hierarchies: Analysis and antitrust implications*. New York, NY: Free Press.

Williamson, O. E. (1981) 'The economics of organization - The transaction cost approach'. *American Journal of Sociology*, 87(3): 548-577.

Index

Note: Page references in *italic* refer to figures, in **bold** to tables, and in ***bold-italics*** to boxes.

For Product Safety Concerns and Information please contact our EU representative GPSR@taylorandfrancis.com
Taylor & Francis Verlag GmbH, Kaufingerstraße 24, 80331 München, Germany

www.ingramcontent.com/pod-product-compliance
Lightning Source LLC
LaVergne TN
LVHW080809011026
849160LV00015B/1578